Builders of the Chinese Church

Studies in Chinese Christianity

G. Wright Doyle and Carol Lee Hamrin,

Series Editors

A Project of the Global China Center

www.globalchinacenter.org

Other volumes in the series:

Salt and Light: Lives of Faith that Shaped Modern China, Three Volumes. Edited by Carol Lee Hamrin and Stacey Bieler

After Imperialism: Christian Identity in China and the Global Evangelical Movement. Edited by Richard R. Cook and David W. Pao

Wise Man from the East: Lit-sen Chang (Zhang Lisheng): Critique of Indigenous Theology; Critique of Humanism. Edited by G. Wright Doyle. Translated by G. Wright Doyle and Samuel Ling

Liang A-Fa: China's First Preacher, 1789–1855. George Hunter McNeur. Edited by Jonathan A. Seitz

Timothy Richard's Vision: Education and Reform in China, 1880–1910. Eunice V. Johnson. Edited by Carol Lee Hamrin

Builders of the Chinese Church

Pioneer Protestant Missionaries and Chinese Church Leaders

Edited by
G. WRIGHT DOYLE

☙PICKWICK *Publications* · Eugene, Oregon

BUILDERS OF THE CHINESE CHURCH
Pioneer Protestant Missionaries and Chinese Church Leaders

Studies in Chinese Christianity Series

Copyright © 2015 Wipf and Stock Publishers. All rights reserved. Except for brief quotations in critical publications or reviews, no part of this book may be reproduced in any manner without prior written permission from the publisher. Write: Permissions, Wipf and Stock Publishers, 199 W. 8th Ave., Suite 3, Eugene, OR 97401.

Pickwick Publications
An Imprint of Wipf and Stock Publishers
199 W. 8th Ave., Suite 3
Eugene, OR 97401

www.wipfandstock.com

ISBN 13: 978-1-62564-367-4

Cataloging-in-Publication data:

    Builders of the Chinese church : pioneer Protestant missionaries and Chinese church leaders / edited by G. Wright Doyle.

    x + 246 p. ; 23 cm. —Includes bibliographical references and index(es).

    Studies in Chinese Christianity Series

    ISBN 13: 978-1-62564-367-4

    1. Christianity—China—History. 2. Protestant churches—China—History. I. Title. II. Series.

BR1288 B95 2015

Manufactured in the U.S.A.

To
Carol Lee Hamrin

Contents

Acknowledgments | ix

    Introduction | 1

1 Robert Morrison: Missionary Mediator, Surprising Saint | 30
—Christopher D. Hancock

2 Liang Fa (Liang A-fa): Leader in Chinese Indigenization | 49
—Jonathan A. Seitz

3 James Legge: Linking Chinese Evangelical Spirituality with Cross-Cultural Engagement | 65
—Lauren Pfister

4 Griffith John: Faithful Pioneer Missionary | 83
—Noel Gibbard

5 J. Hudson Taylor: Advocate for China's Inland Millions | 101
—G. Wright Doyle

6 William A. P. Martin: Pioneer of Progress in China | 122
—G. Wright Doyle

7 "Pastor Hsi"—Xi Shengmo: "Overcomer of Evil" through Prayer and Preaching | 149
—Yading Li with G. Wright Doyle

8 Timothy Richard: A Missionary Who Impacted the Late Qing Dynasty | 173
—Wenzong Wang

9 Jonathan Goforth: Tireless Evangelist and Revivalist | 191
—G. Wright Doyle

Bibliography | 213
Index of Subjects | 213
Index of Names | 213

Acknowledgments

As with all books, this one results from the efforts of a number of people. Global China Center Senior Associates Dr. Carol Lee Hamrin and Dr. Yading Li originated the concept and made many valuable suggestions along the way. Dr. Li made the initial selections from the biography of Pastor Hsi, from which my chapter on him was composed. The outstanding contributors, all of them leading authorities on the persons whose biographies they wrote, spent long hours amidst very demanding schedules to complete their assignments on time. Laura Philbrick Mason, my skilled and indefatigable editorial assistant, somehow managed to go over each chapter with minute care, culling out errors and recommending improvements, while teaching flute and art, moving to another house, and having her third child. She was ably helped by her husband Vincent Mason and by Anna Barnes. Martha Stockment, our research assistant, stepped in at the last minute to provide key information. My ever-encouraging wife Dori cheered me on, especially towards the end when my energy was flagging. The skill, diligence, and patience of the editors and staff at Pickwick Publications continue to fill us with gratitude. The very detailed Indices were compiled by Anna Barnes. To all of these, and to those who faithfully prayed for this project, I owe a profound debt of thanks.

Introduction

No one knows how many Christians there are in China today, but most agree that the number is very large. Regardless of whether one accepts a "low" estimate of thirty million, or a "high" one of more than one hundred million, no one denies the fact that the aggregate total of crowds who throng worship services on any given Sunday morning in China exceeds that of church attendees in all of Western Europe. I say "aggregate" because one must include both Protestant and Roman Catholic, official and unofficial, registered and unregistered congregations, those assembling in designated buildings and those gathering in private homes. Add to that the uncounted, and uncountable, Bible study groups and prayer meetings, the private conversations taking place all over the country, the proliferation of Christian study programs, institutes, journals, and conferences for scholars of Christianity, plus the thousands of web sites, blogs, and publications of both registered and unregistered churches, not to mention the amazing interest in, and openness towards, Christianity among both intellectuals and ordinary folk, and you have a phenomenon that not even the most sanguine supporters of Christianity would have foreseen at the turn of the twentieth century.

Indeed, despite almost one hundred fifty years of dedicated Protestant missionary labors, when the door to foreign missionaries "closed" as the communists consolidated power in 1950, those connected with Christianity of any sort amounted to no more than three million, and their number seemed to dwindle almost to zero during the "Great" Cultural Revolution (1966–1976). Outside observers opined that the Chinese church had died, as Marxist theory had dictated. Mao and his comrades had created a "new man" that did not need the opiate of religion to dull their pain or satisfy their souls. Eminent historian John K. Fairbank declared in 1974 that "the missionaries' long-continued effort, if measured in numbers of converts, had failed."[1] Now we know just how grossly mistaken these pronouncements were, for even in the darkest hours of the Cultural Revolution, stalwart believers in dank prison cells and desolate rural fields were refusing to bow the knee to "Caesar." Choosing obedience to God rather than life itself, they persevered under unimaginable trials, whence they emerged after Deng Xiaoping's Opening and Reform campaign started in 1978. Slowly, stories began to trickle out of brave Christians who had stood their ground throughout those long, lonely years. More than that, we began to hear about large-scale turnings to Protestant Christianity in rural areas where Mao's movement had once been strongest.

We cannot help but ask, Where did this huge Christian movement find its roots? What accounts for the courage and conviction of the leaders and laymen who bravely followed their Lord under immense pressure to deny him? Why was the faith they espoused not erased by decades of atheistic indoctrination? How do we explain that vast preponderance of evangelical, even fundamentalist, believers and clergy among the Protestants even today, when the major government-sponsored seminary has been under the control of theological liberals? Why have so many country folk turned away from traditional Chinese religions to worship Christ?

The study of history, even if it cannot predict the future, should be able to cast some light upon both the past and the present. We can trace a mighty river like the Yangtze to its source, tiny and insignificant though it may appear high in the mountains. Likewise, today's Chinese church takes its character and owes its durability and distinctive vitality to men and women who lived and labored more than a hundred years ago, and who laid the foundation for the church we see today.

IMPERIALISM

Called by historian Kenneth Scott Latourette the "Great Century" of Christian expansion, the years between 1807 (when Robert Morrison arrived in China) and the 1920s (when the last missionaries studied in this volume departed from the scene) witnessed immense changes in virtually all arenas of human life. Science and technology progressed; the Industrial Revolution spread from Great Britain to the rest of Europe and America; wars and revolutions of all sorts changed the political landscape; new ideas transformed literature, art, philosophy, and theology; and the nations of Europe and the United States established their dominance throughout almost the entire world.

1. Fairbank, *Missionary Enterprise*, 1.

LATE QING SCENE

Before we tell the stories of the outstanding men who helped to sow the seeds that would reap such an immense harvest, let us look briefly at the nation to which they came in the early nineteenth century.

The once-vigorous Manchus who had ruled since 1644 had become effete, their ruling dynasty decrepit and decaying, their elite classes increasingly besotted by opium.[2] Though outwardly committed to the Confucian heritage of previous generations and formally the "high priests" of a complex of Confucian rites that resembled religious worship, the Manchu emperor and his family were, behind the walls of the Forbidden City, adherents of Tibetan Buddhism. They were singularly unenlightened and totally unprepared for the onslaughts that shook the foundations of their rule throughout the century. Natural disasters, population growth, and scarce resources fed rebellions by Muslims, secret societies, and even the mid-century pseudo-Christian Taiping revolution, which devastated several provinces, took the lives of perhaps twenty million, and almost succeeded in toppling the throne.

In addition to these internal troubles, foreigners came in gunboats, blasting open the gates of the Central Kingdom in the name of free trade and equality among nations, but also bringing cargoes of opium. The Dutch had occupied Formosa (Taiwan) in 1622, but were expelled by the Ming loyalist Koxinga (*Zheng Chenggong*) in 1661. Bit by bit, the Portuguese gained what would become a permanent foothold on the island of Macao, which became a base for European trade with China. In 1636, British ships bombarded river forts guarding Canton (Guangzhou) before withdrawing. The British East India Company first traded mostly through the Portuguese in Macao, and then obtained trading rights in Xiamen (Amoy) and Ningbo, and finally concentrated their operations in the small tract of land in Guangzhou which China allotted to foreign merchants. China attempted to impose strict limits on commercial activity, both because its leaders were convinced that they did not need foreign goods and because the main import became opium. When the expense of ruling India exceeded income from tea, the British began to sell opium to the Chinese in return for silver, thus draining the coffers of the Empire, debasing the populace, and enraging an increasingly inept but invincibly proud and xenophobic government.

---

2. See Tiedemann, *Handbook*, 278–343, for a concise description of the late Qing scene. Broomhall, *Hudson Taylor*, provides accurate and gripping narratives about the historical context at each point in the story. Standard histories of modern China include Spence, *The Search for Modern China* and Fairbank, *Chinese Revolution*.

After a futile ban on the import of opium, the Chinese government finally lost patience, as did the British, who had chafed under what they considered to be unfair trade restrictions and repeated diplomatic rebuffs. The governor of the Guangzhou region burned supplies of opium; the British retaliated by bombarding and capturing Guangzhou. The cycle of war had started, to be repeated several times, always issuing in defeat for a hopelessly-outgunned China and resulting in what the Chinese call "Unequal Treaties," which granted increasing rights to foreign merchants, diplomats, and missionaries. To the Chinese, these treaties were a constant reminder of their weakness and of the steadily growing influence in, even control over, their nation by the aggressive "barbarians" from the West.[3]

In the First Opium War 1839–42, then again in 1856–60, British and French firepower overwhelmed the antiquated Qing defenses and wrested treaty rights to trade and reside in five ports (1842), then to trade more widely, travel within China, and even (according to one interpretation), purchase property. On several occasions, beginning with Robert Morrison, the first Protestant missionary to China, missionaries served as interpreters and even negotiators. Though they always sought to mitigate the harsher provisions of the terms imposed on the Chinese, their persistent efforts to see that missionaries were given increasing freedom to live and work in China forever linked the foreign religion and its agents with imperialism and opium. These treaties also "increased Chinese suspicion and fear of the West which resulted in an inward-looking, reactionary xenophobia which remained a dominating strain in the country for the rest of the century."[4]

When at first the leaders of the Taiping rebellion mouthed Christian slogans, read and taught the Bible, and smashed all idols, some missionaries believed that they should be supported by Britain and France. Their allegiance shifted when the bizarre heresies and corrupt practices of the Taiping kings exposed fundamental errors, but this early advocacy, plus the perceived "Christian" character of the insurrection, further damaged the reputation of the Christian faith and the missionaries. As the China Inland Mission (CIM) took the gospel deep into the interior of China and other mission societies followed, the churches in the coastal cities were augmented by those in inland provinces. The scholars who served as both guardians of China's literary, cultural, and ethical heritage, as well as local magistrates, correctly saw that the new religion, if consistently followed, would

---

3. Broomhall, *Hudson Taylor*, vol. 1 provides a vivid narrative of the Western incursions and their implications for early missionaries; later volumes in his series on Hudson Taylor likewise set missionary advance and Chinese resistance in this conflicted perspective.

4. Barr, *To China With Love*, 13.

undermine much of their power and prestige. We should not be surprised that they frequently fomented popular rumors and riots that endangered foreign and native Christians alike, which finally erupted into the madness of the Boxer Rebellion at the end of the century.

As they gradually came to realize, "Christian" Westerners were not only seizing territory and forcing opium down their throats, but were also heralding a message that contradicted the inherent humanism of Confucianism, the worship of popular gods, and the established social order, which included the utter subordination of women. Later, when missionaries and others promoted Western science, industry, education, and even political reforms, it seemed as if the entire fabric of China's ancient civilization was being shredded. The Christian faith was revolutionary in the deepest sense of the word, for it questioned almost every article of the Chinese worldview, even if the missionaries themselves had no intention of fomenting actual rebellion.

As a consequence, from the beginning, Roman Catholic and Protestant missionaries were subject to vilification in countless tracts and placards composed by the literati and given full credence by the general populace. The best-known of these "attributed to missionaries just about every obscene practice that a race with very long experience of men and manners could dream up, cunningly combined with them modicums of truth and fragments of common hearsay," and contained incredibly vile and baseless accusations that were nevertheless effective in stirring up violent hatred for the intruders.[5]

In particular, when Roman Catholics, who believed that baptized dying babies would be saved from eternal damnation, took in foundlings and cared for children in orphanages, wild rumors charged them with gouging out the infants' eyes and other organs or even eating them. Priests and nuns were widely supposed to indulge in illicit sexual relations. When Roman Catholics used treaty stipulations to purchase land and build on it without the permission of local officials, and especially when Roman Catholic priests and bishops demanded equal treatment with government officials of similar rank, they challenged the established order and upset local customs and conditions. Protestant and Roman Catholic missionaries who sought protection or exemption from local temple taxes for their converts disturbed the legal process and deprived communities of income needed for the maintenance of the public venues that temples provided.

After the terrible defeat by Japan in 1895, idealistic and zealous reformers, influenced by writings of W. A. P. Martin, Timothy Richard, and

---

5. Barr, *To China With Love*, 67–68.

others, and led by the brilliant scholar Kang Youwei, gained the ear not only of the Prime Minister and the tutor of the emperor, but of the young emperor himself. This crushing blow by a modernizing Japan had exposed the pervasive weaknesses of China and the ineffectual rule of the backward Manchus, and calls for drastic change sounded from all directions within the educated elite, and even within the government. In 1898, wide-ranging reforms were introduced in one imperial decree after another, all of them stunningly radical, such as: the ancient essay system of education was to be abolished; temples would also be used as schools for Western education; and young Manchus would be required to study foreign languages and travel abroad.[6] The movement was betrayed at the last minute; the emperor was imprisoned within the Forbidden City; many reformers were killed; and the Empress Dowager once again took up the reins of government. Martin, Richard, and others like them were utterly despondent at the failure of their efforts.

Meanwhile, not only did missionaries increasingly penetrate the interior of China, but foreign-controlled railroads lay down tracks in total disregard for "feng shui" (ancient concepts of which locations were most propitious), not infrequently violating cemeteries to achieve the shortest route. The enraged Chinese wondered whether the natural disasters that piled up in the last few decades of the century were the work of angry gods and ghosts. It was all too much, and long-brewing resentment and fear exploded into the Boxer Rebellion of 1900. Once again, foreign troops, this time from eight nations, defeated the Chinese. British and French had captured Beijing in 1864; this time, some of the allied troops went on an orgy of butchery, looting, and rape, and the Summer Palace was burned. A huge indemnity, the permanent presence of foreign troops in Beijing, further territorial concessions, and the humiliation of the Qing government dealt a death blow to a regime that had already been totally discredited by the shock of defeat by the Japanese.

For a variety of reasons, the violent actions of Chinese in the Boxer Rebellion actually benefitted the progress of Christianity in China and the position of its representatives. Despite the atrocities committed by some of the foreign troops, Chinese people were also shocked by the barbarity of the rebels and shamed by the virtuous actions and forgiving response of many Christians, including some of the missionaries who refused compensation for losses. Because of this, many officials completely changed their attitude. Even the Empress Dowager and her advisors saw that China must institute fundamental reforms in order simply to survive, and began to implement

---

6 Richard, *Forty-Five Years in China*, 262.

many of the changes suggested by the defeated reform movement and its missionary friends. Not only so, but the courageous way in which thousands of Chinese Christians and Western missionaries had remained faithful in the face of torture and death made a powerful impression upon their former detractors, causing mass movements towards Christ. Jonathan Goforth reaped the benefit of this new climate towards the end of his career.

REVIVAL AND MISSIONS

Throughout this tumultuous period, while Western nations were imposing their self-seeking agendas upon China, hundreds of missionaries from those same countries were pouring their lives out to bring God's love to the Chinese people. Amidst all the economic, social, and political movements, and sometimes embedded within them or carried along by them, religious revivals of equal magnitude transformed Protestantism. Charles Finney, Dwight L. Moody, and a host of other less-famous evangelists built on the foundation of the Great Awakening of the eighteenth century and were instrumental in sparking renewal in Great Britain, northern Europe, and North America.[7] Again, embedded within them, and sometimes carried along by them, but also frequently further fanning the flames, was an unprecedented upsurge of zeal for the spread of the gospel in foreign lands and cultures.[8] Missionary work in China counted for a major part of worldwide Christian outreach, and provides many examples of this symbiotic relationship between revival and missions.[9]

Griffith John and J. Hudson Taylor were profoundly affected by the "deeper" (or "higher") life teachings connected with the so-called "Keswick" movement and its kin, but Taylor also played a major role as a speaker and

---

7. See Wolffe, *Expansion of Evangelicalism*, 45–94, 166, 171–72; Bebbington, *Dominance of Evangelicalism*.

8. For surveys of the nineteenth century mission movement, see Bosch, *Transforming Mission*, 262–348; Moreau, Corwin, and McGee, *Introducing World Missions*, 114–35; Robert, *Christian Mission*, 31–79; Sunquist, *Understanding Christian Mission*, 71–131.

9. Helpful treatments of the Protestant missionary enterprise in China in the nineteenth century and early twentieth century can be found in Bays, *New History*, 41–120; Broomhall, *Hudson Taylor*; Charbonnier, *Christians in China*, 350–64; Latourette, *History of Christian Missions*; Moffett, *Christianity in Asia*, 285–308, 463–501; Tiedemann, *Handbook*; major scholarly biographies of the men studied in this book; and the general works referred to in the previous note. Perhaps the best succinct survey is Lutz, "China and Protestantism." Brief articles on hundreds of missionaries and Chinese Christians can be found in the online *Biographical Dictionary of Chinese Christianity* (www.bdcconline.net).

writer popularizing this sort of piety.[10] Taylor collaborated with Dwight Moody. The Welsh revivals of the early twentieth century inspired Jonathan Goforth and Griffith John to seek more fruit from their work in China. Missionaries were extolled as examples of a "higher" Christian experience because of their assumed greater faith and deeper dedication, while they benefitted from the support—in prayer, finances, and new recruits—of the revivals back home. Acutely conscious of all this, Hudson Taylor made the fueling of renewal flames in the sending countries a priority while seeking new workers to bring the gospel to China, fully convinced that only fully consecrated men and women would have any staying power or lasting effect in their missionary labors.

A "HOST OF WITNESSES"

The following chapters contain brief biographies of nine major figures in the first century of Protestant Christianity in China. Seven were missionaries, while two were outstanding early Chinese Christian leaders who took what they had learned from the foreigners and blazed new paths in uncharted and often hostile territory. Why are so many missionaries featured in this volume, and so few Chinese? First, because, by the nature of the case, Protestantism was brought to China by messengers from the West, and these foreigners essentially laid the foundation upon which they expected Chinese to build. Secondly, for a variety of reasons, we have far more information about missionaries than we do about their Chinese converts, helpers, and successors, partly because many early Christians came from the lower classes and could not write their own story, and partly because the missionaries wrote so much. We lament the all-too-common habit the missionaries had of mentioning their Chinese colleagues only by a surname, and that often in Romanized forms that are very hard for us to decipher.

Almost all missionaries readily acknowledged that the Chinese evangelized, taught, and shepherded their own people far better than foreigners ever could, and they rejoiced to see "native" leaders rise up and spread the gospel far and wide. By no means did they consider Chinese believers inferior to themselves as Christian workers; they simply did not give us much information about them. Two notable exceptions are Liang Fa (or Liang

---

10. The role of awakenings and revivals in spurring foreign missions is briefly treated in Sunquist, *Understanding Christian Mission*, 89, 90, 92–93. Hudson Taylor's connections with the Mildmay Conferences, Keswick, and Moody, are discussed at various points in Broomhall, *Hudson Taylor*, vols. 3–7. See also Wigram, *Bible and Mission*, 58–64, 95–97, 107; Bebbington, *Dominance of Evangelicalism*, 188–90.

A-fa) and Xi Shengmo (Pastor Hsi), who are addressed in this volume. Both could read and write, and both were memorialized by missionaries who knew and respected them greatly. Other Chinese we could have featured include Dai Wenguang and Wang Tao, indispensable helpers and translators for missionaries, and the evangelists and preachers Che Jingguang and He Jinshan, as well as the educator Rong Hong (Yung Wing), and many others. We have selected Liang and Xi because of their representative nature and their fundamental contributions to the Chinese church we see today.

The seven foreign missionaries were chosen out of a potential pool of hundreds of outstanding men and women who went to China at great personal cost in order to share the saving knowledge of Jesus Christ with people who had never heard it before. Dozens of foreign workers deserve the same kind of attention bestowed on the ones whose stories are told here. Among the pioneers are William Milne, Samuel Dyer, David Abeel, Walter H. Medhurst, Sr., Elijah C. Bridgman, and Samuel Wells Williams.[11] The incredibly full, highly controversial, ultimately tragic, but broadly influential career of Charles (Karl Friedrich August) Gutzlaff has been ably narrated by Jessie Lutz, and only his unusually intimate link with opium traders and British imperialists kept him out of this volume.[12] Dr. Peter Parker, the first medical missionary (though not the first to use medicine to heal Chinese friends), is said to have "opened China at the point of the scalpel" and later became an American ambassador to China.[13] Many more could be mentioned, such as the Stronach brothers,[14] J. Lewis Chuck, Issachar J. Roberts, and William Boone, the first bishop of the American Protestant Episcopal Church in China. For the second half of the nineteenth century, another group of outstanding names come to mind, including William Burns,[15]

---

11. The careers of these early missionaries are ably recounted in Broomhall, *Hudson Taylor*, vols. 1 and 2. Milne, vol. 1: 131-37, 143-49, 155-59, 172-73, 378-80, and elsewhere. Bridgman, Dyer and Medhurst: often in both vols. Williams, vol. 1: 137, 176, 216-17, 222, 334-35, 237, 362, 409.

12. Lutz, *Opening China*.

13. Peter Parker's effective missionary work is described in Broomhall, *Hudson Taylor*, vol. 1: 9, 137, 234-35, 237, 269, 273, 280, 362, 404; vol. 2: 19-20, 135, 162, 371, 386, 405.

14. On the Stronachs, see Cheung, *Christianity in Modern China*, 39-40, 67, 74, 129-32, 153.

15. Mostly because of his intimate association with Hudson Taylor in the early years, Burns figures prominently in Broomhall, *Hudson Taylor*. See vol. 1: 10, 286, 306-7, 340, 342, 345, 390, 393; *Over the Treaty Wall*, 53, 128, 162, 237-38, 295, 301-2, 309, 312, 319-25, 327-43, 347, 359-60, 364, 366-71, 385-86, 402; vol. 3: 23, 25, 27, 29, 34-36, 44, 53, 87, and often; vol. 4: 48, 71-73, 76, 94-95, 101-3, 113, and often. See also Cheung, *Christianity in China*, in which Burns appears frequently.

Tarleton Perry Crawford,[16] and Calvin W. Mateer.[17] John Livingston Nevius'[18] famous methods were worked out by both Timothy Richard and J. Hudson Taylor, and later took root in Korea and influenced Gilbert Reid, who strongly supported the more liberal views and strategies of Timothy Richard and W. A. P. Martin.[19]

No less notable were the wives of these men and many single women who made a huge impact on Chinese Christianity. These women include the redoubtable Mary Ann Aldersey, schoolmistress and acknowledged ruler of the foreign community in Ningbo,[20] and Lottie Moon, famous among Southern Baptists.[21] What shall we say of such saintly, longsuffering, and supremely helpful companions to their more-famous husbands as Mary Morton Morrison, Eliza Morrison, Maria Tarn Dyer, Maria Dyer Taylor, Jennie Faulding Taylor,[22] and Rosalind Goforth,[23] but that they were people "of whom the world was not worthy"?[24]

MAIN CHARACTERS

The principal subjects of these chapters now need to be introduced:

Robert Morrison (1782-1834) deserves to be called the father of Protestant missions to China, for he arrived earliest and, almost single-handedly, provided the first generation of missionaries with the essential tools for communicating the message of Christ. With help from Chinese and William Milne, he translated the entire Bible and portions of the *Book*

---

16. See Hyatt, *Our Ordered Lives Confess*, 3-41, and Flynt and Berkley, *Taking Christianity to China*.

17. A short study of Mateer can be found in Hyatt, *Our Ordered Lives Confess*, 139-237.

18. On Nevius, see Hunt, "Nevius," and Broomhall, *Hudson Taylor*, vol. 2: 144-45, 188, 273; vol. 3: 23, 29, 41-42, 46-47, 88, 100-101, 150-52, 183-84, 264-65, 361-62, 373-74, 408-9, and often.

19. On Gilbert Reid, see Tsou, "Christian Missionary as Confucian Intellectual."

20. On Mary Aldersey, see Broomhall, *Hudson Taylor*, vol. 2: 86, 96, 162, 273, 274, 347, 349-50, 361-62.

21. In addition to full-length biographies, brief and balanced sketches of Moon's career can be found in Allen, "Lottie Moon," and Hyatt, *Our Ordered Lives Confess*, 68-136.

22. Maria Dyer Taylor and Jennie Faulding Taylor receive extensive coverage in Broomhall, *Hudson Taylor*.

23. Rosalind Goforth naturally includes a great deal of information about herself in her book *Goforth of China*; see also Rosalind Goforth, *Climbing: Memories of a Missionary's Wife*.

24. Heb 11:38.

of Common Prayer; composed a grammar and a massive dictionary of the Chinese language, which was also virtually an encyclopedia of everything Chinese; and translated or composed many tracts and other books. These achievements are no less significant in the light of new research that has shown how Morrison adhered faithfully to the template of pioneer missionary work which he learned at the London Missionary Society's Gosport Academy under David Bogue.[25]

When Morrison arrived in 1807, Roman Catholicism had been proscribed by imperial edict since 1724. Foreign missionaries stayed constantly on the run, subject to arrest, torture, and death, while their Chinese coverts maintained their faith in homes and private gatherings at great danger to themselves. Portugal, the Netherlands, Britain, and America had tried to establish normal diplomatic and economic relations with China, but in vain, for the "foreign devil" was feared, despised, and increasingly hated. Thus, in the early nineteenth century, foreigners were allowed to live nowhere but Canton, and that for only the six-month trading season each year, after which many returned to Macao, a pattern Morrison followed for most of his career. Fearing subversion by clever foreigners, the government forbade the teaching of the Chinese language to foreigners under penalty of death, so Morrison and his brave helpers worked under the most adverse and trying conditions.

Over more than two decades, he set a standard of unremitting labor, profound appreciation of the Chinese people and their rich culture, and total dedication to the cause of Christ that has spurred on many of his successors. Liang Fa (1789–1855; Liang A-fa) began his career as a printer, assisting in the publication of books and tracts by Morrison and Milne, but went on to become China's first evangelist and writer of Christian materials in Chinese. He provided a pattern in other ways too, for he and his entire family suffered persecution, including physical abuse and incarceration, but persevered in their faith and in their ministry. One of his works had unforeseen effects on all of China.

James Legge (1815–97) preached, trained leaders for the indigenous church, and translated some of the Chinese classics while in China. This crucial "missionary" career has often been overlooked or underplayed because of his later contribution as a great Sinologist.[26] After returning to England, he entered into a second phase in which his lifelong interest in Chinese language, literature, and religion found expression not only in

---

25. See the excellent treatment of how Morrison and his associates put into practice the education which they received at Gosport in Daily, *Robert Morrison*.

26. Girardot, *Victorian Translation*, is the prime modern example of this unbalanced approach.

teaching at Oxford University, where he was the first professor of Chinese, but more importantly, in revising and completing the translation of virtually the entire Confucian canon into English, with notes and commentary. Not only the growing number of academic Sinologists, but missionaries themselves, prized his work as essential equipment for their understanding of the culture into which they were attempting to preach the gospel of Christ.

James Hudson Taylor (1832–1905), founder of the China Inland Mission (CIM), which soon became the largest foreign mission society working in China, exemplified the piety of the growing evangelical movement that arose in the English-speaking world in the mid-nineteenth century. On both sides of the Atlantic, and then on the Continent of Europe and in Australia, he called for a closer communion with Christ that would issue in total dedication to the evangelism of the world, including China. He traveled many thousands of miles all across China, mobilized and led a band of pioneer evangelists and resident missionaries, practiced medicine, opened schools, and emerged as a leading figure in the entire China missionary movement. Of all the missionaries who went to China, Taylor holds first place in the affections of today's Chinese Christians, and for good reasons.

Xi Shengmo (1835–96; "Overcomer of Demons"), also called Pastor Hsi, was converted through the ministry of a CIM missionary, and exercised a powerful ministry that was mostly independent of foreign supervision and certainly not under foreign control. Like many other scholars, despite his learning, he became a slave to opium, and his condition seemed hopeless until he encountered—or was encountered by—the living Christ through reading the New Testament, prayer, and a dramatic experience of the Holy Spirit. His powerful personality, brilliant intellect, knowledge of the Bible, preaching ability, organizational and leadership skills, and especially his implicit faith in a prayer-answering God all combined to create a movement that led to healing and deliverance for many opium addicts and the formation of churches that developed out of the opium refuges he founded and staffed with former addicts. Like Liang Fa, he became a paradigmatic Chinese church leader.

Timothy Richard (1845–1919) is currently a favorite of historians of missions for he exemplified all that is modern, progressive, "open-minded," and tolerant.[27] A fervent believer in the uplifting power of Western scientific education, he successfully lobbied for the creation of a university and helped to produce an amazing amount of literature promoting progressive Western concepts, including political reform. He also sought to understand, appreciate, and even promote, the "worthy" elements in Chinese civilization,

---

27. Positive treatments of Timothy Richard include Ng, "Timothy Richard."

including Buddhism, which he thought contained clear pointers to some fundamental Christian teachings.[28] A man of powerful intellect, forceful personality, and undaunted perseverance, he won admirers and friends in high places, even in the Imperial Palace itself. He aimed at nothing less than the liberation of China from ignorance through "the light of education—scientific, industrial, religious." The descending order of those terms reveals his own priorities as his controversial career developed.

Griffith John's (1831–1912) long stay in Hankou—forty-five years—earned him the epithet, "John of Hankow." Constantly preaching, he itinerated in a wide circle, always returning to the same point until he became a familiar figure: "The short, muscular body, the black springy beard, keen flashing eyes, and, above all, that impassioned and resonant voice."[29] He believed that "grace, grit and gumption" were essential qualities for a missionary, and himself seemed to possess all three.[30] Unlike Timothy Richard, John found great success in preaching from an open chapel on a busy street. In time, his "large brick Gospel meeting Hall" would be filled with more than six hundred people. Though he would not speculate on the fate of those who never heard the gospel, he fully believed that the only sure way to heaven was through faith in Jesus Christ as Savior from sin.

William Alexander Parsons (W. A. P.) Martin (1827–1916) was one of the most influential modernizing missionaries of the century. An American, he became a noted Sinologist. *A Cycle of Cathay, Or, China, South and North*, and then *The Lore of Cathay, or, The Intellect of China* were major studies in the actions and thought of the Chinese which still repay careful reading. As with Timothy Richard, his deep knowledge of Chinese culture and society; strenuous efforts to introduce Western learning; and advocacy of economic, social, and political reforms won the admiration of the new generation of intellectuals and even government officials, among whom Martin exerted enormous influence. In particular, his writings in Chinese and his translations of Western books, along with his editorship of the Peking *Magazine* and service as a teacher and administrator in several government-sponsored schools, gave him a wide audience. Having served as one of the negotiators for the American delegation that produced the Treaty of Tientsin, he later switched roles and became an advisor to the Chinese government. He shared Richard's profound disillusionment after the failure of the 100 Days' Reform Movement of 1898. He too favored a more lenient approach toward rites of veneration of ancestors, but continued to adhere

---

28. See, for example, Richard, *The New Testament of Higher Buddhism*.
29. Barr, *To China with Love*, 155.
30. Ibid.

to orthodox Christianity and identified with evangelicals, though he stood on the more liberal side. He spent most of his career not in evangelism or Christian education, but in promoting the modernization of China.

Jonathan Goforth (1859~1936), the first Canadian Presbyterian missionary to China, presents a stark contrast to W. A. P. Martin and Timothy Richard. Much like the pioneer missionaries of the China Inland Mission, he became an itinerant evangelist and revivalist, taking his long-suffering wife Rosalind with him. He firmly rejected the incipient modernism and liberalism of Timothy Richard and others, and held strongly to traditional Christian theology and evangelical distinctives. He sought transformed individuals who would impact society as salt and light, not the "salvation" of China as a nation. After hearing about the Welsh Revival, he visited Korea and witnessed an amazing work of the Holy Spirit there. Taking those reports back through Manchuria to his field in Henan, he found an enthusiastic response and was invited to return to Manchuria. The great "Manchurian Revival" which broke out while he was there impelled him into a new ministry of evangelism and revival preaching. Unusual emotional reactions among both Chinese and Western missionaries evoked controversy, but Goforth saw these reactions as manifestations of the work of the Holy Spirit. His wife's biography of him made Goforth one of the most widely known of the missionaries to China, even today.

CONNECTION WITH FOREIGN IMPERIALISM

Without a doubt, the most common charge lodged against missionaries was that they served as willing accomplices to the aggressive Western powers that imposed first the odious opium trade and then humiliating territorial and legal concessions upon China at gunpoint.[31] Robert Morrison worked for the East India Company (EIC), while his son and many other missionaries, including W. A. P. Martin, served as interpreters or even negotiators for the nations that imposed the hated "unequal treaties" upon a defeated Qing dynasty. They rode on ships carrying opium and benefitted from the treaty provisions that compelled China to allow merchants and missionaries to reside in "treaty ports," then travel about the interior and purchase property. Though they detested the forced importation of opium and usually criticized Western aggression, they did not shrink from seeing the resulting

---

31. A. J. Broomhall's *Hudson Taylor* follows this sad story in detail. For the standard Chinese criticism of the alleged alliance between missionaries and Western imperialism, see Luo, *Christianity in China*, especially 24–33.

treaties as actions of a divine providence that opened up this vast country to the gospel.

Looking back on the terrible price that generations of Chinese Christians and foreign missionaries have had to pay for the baneful consequences of their decisions, we may wish that Robert Morrison had been content to live outside of China rather than stain his work by his association with the EIC; that W. A. P. Martin and others had not so eagerly assisted foreign powers as interpreters; and that Hudson Taylor and other pioneers had not violated treaties by traveling beyond the designated treaty ports. At the same time, however, we should note the harsh condemnations made by most missionaries of the opium trade and, often, of Western aggression. Missionaries also made deliberate attempts to soften the terms of treaties and had genuine love for the Chinese people and their eternal destiny, which is what impelled these men to devote their lives to sacrificial service among a people whose total welfare they sought with all their might.

THE "TERM" QUESTION

Almost all these men were participants in controversies that tested everyone's patience and forbearance and sometimes led to open division. Beginning with Robert Morrison's questions about the proper Chinese terms to translate Hebrew and Greek words such as "spirit" and especially "God," a raging debate among missionaries of equal learning but strongly divergent opinions threatened unity for decades. Indeed, the matter still evokes disagreement, though with less intensity than before. Simply put, should one employ the name of the Supreme Being of ancient Chinese religion and late Qing imperial worship—Shang Di—to translate Elohim and Theos, or should the word of lesser deities, even sometimes ghosts and demons—Shen—be used? Sadly, differences tend to run along national and denominational lines, with Shang Di favored by the British and "mainline" denominations, and Shen favored by Americans and independent missionaries. James Legge, supported by other eminent Sinologists, including W. A. P. Martin and Timothy Richard, argued that the early Chinese knew and worshiped the one true and living God under the name "Shang Di." Others with equal learning said that Shang Di was an appellation for a particular deity, while Shen corresponded almost exactly with the original generic Hebrew and Greek words and could, as in the Bible, be filled with new meaning.[32]

---

32. My own opinion can be found in Doyle, "Problems in Translating the Bible into Chinese."

ANCESTOR RITES

Legge and Martin were at the epicenter of another related argument about whether missionaries should encourage Chinese Christians to participate in ceremonies involving incense, prayers, and bowing to tablets of ancestors. Centuries before, Matteo Ricci and the Jesuits provoked a firestorm of criticism when they decided that the official rites of reverence to Confucius expressed merely respect and honor, and were civil, not religious in nature. The Franciscans and Dominicans countered that the common people always associated these ceremonies with worship of departed spirits and were thus idolatrous. Legge agreed with the Jesuits, and was in varying degrees joined by W.A. P. Martin and Timothy Richard, while Hudson Taylor and other more conservative missionaries, who constituted the vast majority, vigorously insisted that the common people would inevitably read religious meaning into these rites, which were, in their view, always connected with a sense of fear.[33]

CLAIMING TREATY RIGHTS FOR MISSIONARIES AND NATIONAL BELIEVERS

Equally vexing, and of particular interest today, was the question whether, and when, missionaries should invoke the stipulations in various treaties wrested from the Qing government at the point of the bayonet. The legal and ethical questions were quite complex, but basically, the missionaries had to decide whether to seek consular, and perhaps military, support and protection for themselves, their property, and their Chinese converts. At first, Pastor Hsi demanded that his church members be protected and recompensed for damages in accordance with treaties, but later reversed that policy and taught his people to be willing to submit to persecution rather than try to assert their rights. Early in Hudson Taylor's missionary career, after an episode when he was highly, and wrongly, criticized for appearing to call in British gunboats after a riot in Yangzhou led to the destruction of CIM property and considerable personal injury, he resolved never to go to his consul for help and told his workers to rely entirely on God, although he did believe in seeking protection from the local magistrate in certain cases. Members and leaders of other missions, on the other hand, frequently called upon their consuls to intervene in cases when either they or their converts suffered loss of injury at the hands of anti-Christian mobs or were embroiled

---

33. Broomhall provides an excellent analysis of this controversy in Broomhall, *Hudson Taylor*, vol. 6: 283–88; vol. 7: 139–43, 522–23, 632–33.

in personal disputes with Chinese neighbors. These "religious" cases, which ran into the hundreds, aroused great antipathy among the people and their magistrates.[34]

EVANGELISM OR EDUCATION?

For the first fifty years or so, most foreign missionaries agreed on their priorities for reaching Chinese with the gospel. Beginning with the translation of the Bible and other Christian literature into Chinese, along with distribution by paid colporteurs, they relied on street preaching, then chapel and church meetings, to disseminate the Word as widely and deeply as possible. Interested persons would be invited to meetings for regular instruction in the Christian faith. When they seemed to understand, repent, and believe, they were baptized and formed into small congregations, which very gradually grew in size and number.

In addition to evangelism and edification of believers, missionaries very frequently provided medical care and primary education, viewing these as simple demonstrations of the love of God as well as opportunities to share the gospel verbally. How could they neglect the crying needs of the suffering masses around them? Missionaries gained medical skills because they wanted to spread the truth by both word and deed. Schools were opened to teach converts how to read the Bible, and to prepare young men for church ministry and girls to serve as their wives and helpers. When famines struck, especially during the great and horrible disasters of 1876–1881, missionaries dropped everything else and plunged into relief work. All the mission agencies joined hands to raise funds and distribute food and other necessities.

As the years passed, however, a sharp debate arose: Should education replace evangelism as the primary means of advancing God's kingdom in China? Timothy Richard emerged from the harrowing experiences of the famine with one word etched upon his mind: "Education!" He had seen first-hand how ignorance had exacerbated the effects of natural disasters and hindered the efforts of officials to respond effectively. From then on, he devoted his energies to the education of China's elite classes, in the hopes that they would institute lasting reforms that would not only reduce the frequency and severity of famine but also promote the general welfare of the entire nation. He went so far as to claim that direct evangelism was largely futile and fruitless, based on his own personal experience. Less strident in their rejection of traditional missionary methods, but joining with Richard

34. See Luo, *Christianity in China*, 24–33.

in the campaign to bring modern Western learning to China's leaders, were W. A. P. Martin and Gilbert Reid.

Other missionaries, however, including Griffith John, Hudson Taylor, and Jonathan Goforth, believed that the causes of China's troubles went deeper than the mind. The root problem, they argued, was the heart, which only God could change as the Holy Spirit worked repentance, faith, and transformation of life in the lives of individuals and then in communities of Christians through the verbal proclamation of the biblical message. The ignorance that they primarily sought to combat was the lack of the knowledge of God. Placing little faith in what they saw as superficial remedies to the fundamental source of corruption, self-seeking, superstition, and official incompetence, they focused on what they considered to be the wellspring of all these, the cause of the "disease" rather than the symptoms. They found biblical support for this emphasis in the words of the Great Commission, which mandated preaching that led to faith in Christ and commitment to him (baptism), and ethical instruction that would lead to obedience to all that Christ had commanded in Scripture.

Debates about the proper medium of education (Chinese or English) and the content of the curriculum also raged intensely during our period. Should English be used, in order to please the growing number of educated, elite families in mainline, urban churches who wanted their children to have the best possible Western education in order to get prestigious jobs in the modern professions that were opening up to them? Or should the schools use only Chinese, to discourage students and parents with such motives and to attract people who wanted an explicitly Christian education in order to be equipped for service in the church or, for girls, for marriage to Christian preachers. Should the Chinese classics be taught, or should the curriculum confine itself to scientific and practical subjects? How many courses on the Christian faith should students be required to take? Increasingly, the more liberal colleges decided to conduct most, or all, teaching in English. Chinese literature and culture were either de-emphasized or neglected entirely, and biblical and theological courses reduced in number. Finally, the Nationalist Government in the late 1920s required that attendance at chapel be made totally voluntary, and courses on Christianity turned into electives.[35]

In time, this divergence became not just personal but also institutional, as colleges were founded by the more liberal mission organizations while the more conservative ones continued to concentrate upon evangelism and biblical teaching, augmented by medical work and pre-college education.

---

35. For the debates about curriculum and English as a medium of instruction, especially in the twentieth century, see Bays, *China's Christian Colleges*, 80–82, and elsewhere throughout the volume.

Especially in the early years of the twentieth century, the educational effort consumed vast sums of money, but its goal was nothing less than the creation of a Christianized—which often meant "modern" and "Westernized"—society, in which democratic and scientific reforms would benefit the bodies and minds of millions. Evangelism and edification, on the other hand, pursued the dream of a nation in which the souls of millions would be saved from eternal punishment through faith in Christ and their lives so transformed by Christ that they could experience joy and peace and, incorporated into church communities of faith and love, express God's grace and truth to those around them, amidst the inevitable trials of this life. In time, these people and the churches they formed would, it was believed, have a "salt and light" effect on the entire civilization.

FROM "BELOW" OR FROM "ABOVE"?

Depending on their evaluation of the strategic and religious value of Western education, missionaries split also on whether they should aim their evangelism at the masses or whether they should strive to impact that small group of men who wielded enormous influence in Chinese society: the educated elite. One way followed the example of Christ teaching the common people, who gladly heard him while their leaders despised and rejected him as a threat to their culture, their customs, and their own social standing and power. This approach could also appeal to the example of Jesus, Paul, and Peter, who proclaimed a message focused on personal reconciliation to God requiring repentance from sin and faith in Christ, who had died on the Cross for our salvation, and leading to the formation of churches. Indeed, Paul explicitly rejected any attempt to appeal to the "wise" and educated elite of his time, determined to "preach Christ crucified," and to "not to know anything . . . except Jesus Christ and Him crucified."[36] The other took its cue from Paul's debating with the intellectuals on Mars Hill in Athens and Christ's conversation with Nicodemus, a ruler and teacher among the Jews. Again, Taylor, John, and Goforth exemplify the focus on those who lived "downstairs," while Martin and Richard sought favor with those who lived "upstairs."[37]

---

36. 1 Cor 1:23; 2:1–2.

37. Richard found Scriptural support for his approach in Matt 10:11, where Jesus told his disciples to seek out one who was "worthy" in a town and reside with him. He seems, however, to have ignored the context of this instruction, which was training men to engage in widespread, public evangelistic preaching.

To be fair, we should note that from his earliest days Hudson Taylor and other missionaries like him constantly tried to bring his message to scholars and magistrates, while the women in the CIM frequently conversed with their wives. Throughout his career, Taylor and his coworkers in the CIM had found many high officials and their wives to be quite friendly and open to the gospel, and eager to hear of the saving work of Christ upon the Cross.[38] W. A. P. Martin and Timothy Richard hobnobbed with the rich and powerful, but did so with the aim of relieving the sufferings of the poor and downtrodden. No one would question the immense value of a truly converted elite—"Pastor Hsi" was the CIM's "poster boy." It was only a question of how best to reach these men. Nor did any doubt the necessity of taking Chinese culture and history seriously, as the rigorous language study course of the CIM made clear. The questions arose only about the proportion of time one spent mastering Chinese literature, and then in what way to seek points of contact with the educated class.

More traditional missionaries like Taylor, Burns, and Goforth, would agree with Richard that raising up a large number of Chinese evangelists and pastors was a high priority, for they could almost always be more effective in speaking to their own people. The debate between them dealt with whether more missionaries should be recruited, as Taylor and others thought, or whether most efforts should be directed towards the conversion and mobilization of the educated elite, as Richard proposed.

THE KINGDOM OF GOD

Underlying the split over education and evangelism that widened into a chasm lay differing conceptions of the kingdom of God. Hudson Taylor and other evangelicals looked for a future kingdom, to be brought by the return of Christ, who would establish a realm of perfect justice, peace, and well-being on earth. Until then, they believed, our task was to make disciples by bringing them first to faith in Christ and then to maturity in Christ as members of churches. Conservative Christians thought that regenerated individuals would influence society through their own individual lives and also through the church, as we have seen. As Griffith John famously put it at the Shanghai Protestant missionary conference in 1877, "We are not here to develop the resources of the country, not for the advancement of commerce, not for the mass promotion of civilization, but to do battle with the

---

38. See, for example, Taylor, *Hudson Taylor*, vol. 2: 119; Broomhall, *Hudson Taylor*, vol. 4: 377.

powers of darkness, to save men from sin and conquer Chinese for Christ."[39] Especially towards the end of the century, many conservative missionaries held to a pre-millennial eschatology.[40]

Another vision, however, impelled Timothy Richard and thousands who came after him in the early twentieth century: the establishment of the kingdom of God on earth through the transformation of society. As Richard put it, he sought for nothing less than "the national conversion of China."[41] For Richard and others, present ills seemed to be more pressing than the threat of future punishment in hell. Clearly, in their eyes, the crying needs of China's millions were for food, health, just social relations, and better government, and these could be brought to a significant degree by education, better agriculture and industry, and political reforms, undergirded, to be sure, by a worldview shaped by Christian convictions.[42] By these means, God's righteous rule would manifest itself in a more just and prosperous society.[43] The chief means by which they sought this transformation was education, especially through the colleges they founded. As John K. Fairbank wrote, "these institutions did a solid job of teaching modern subjects, and under the influence of the liberal trend within the Christian community, they increasingly stressed God's kingdom on earth and dedicated service as the ideal of life."[44] The advocates of education and reform also thought that by focusing on such tangible things they would win the confidence of China's ruling class, who would then relax their firm opposition to the spread of the gospel.[45] Most of these proponents of social services, reform, and education believed in a post-millennial eschatology.[46]

---

39. Quoted in Barr, *To China With Love*, 156.

40. That is, the belief that Christ will return soon to establish an earthly kingdom which will last for one thousand years, following which a new heaven and earth will be established, in which believers in Christ will live forever in resurrected and glorified bodies, and others will suffer eternal punishment in hell.

41. Ng, *Chinese Christianity*, 122.

42. For a brief explanation of Richard's later vision for the kingdom of God, see Walls, *Cross-Cultural Process*, 256–57.

43. See Bays, *China's Christian Colleges*, and Lodwick, "Good Works," in Tiedemann, *Handbook*, 431–34.

44. Fairbank, *Missionary Enterprise*, 13.

45. For a conciliatory, even sanguine, comparison of these two approaches, see Pfister, "Rethinking Missions in China."

46. Post-millennialism held out the hope that the world would be so influenced by the spread of the gospel that all sectors of all nations would be substantially transformed into the kingdom of God on earth. Many also thought that Christians should work in anticipation of that kingdom through reforms in education, society, and government.

FUNDAMENTALIST-MODERNIST CONTROVERSY

The general evangelical consensus shared by missionaries for most of the nineteenth century began to show strains in the final decades. While W. A. P. Martin was considered by most to be orthodox, and thus could sustain warm friendships with men like Griffith John and Hudson Taylor, some doubted the soundness of Timothy Richard's theological developments.[47] Richard never denied the central tenets of traditional Christianity, though he employed "expressions and statements . . . that no traditionally minded Christian of that day would dream of using."[48] By the turn of the twentieth century, however, the theological cleavage became clear, as what has been called the "fundamentalist-modernist" controversy spread from the West to the mission field, and then back again, when the more conservative missionaries complained that new arrivals were not sound in doctrine. Even at the end of the century, Hudson Taylor was aware of the growing influence of German higher criticism, but could simply ignore it. Only a few years later, however, Griffith John and Jonathan Goforth felt compelled to speak out against what they considered unorthodox beliefs of new workers arriving in China.

In other words, what had earlier only seemed to be different emphases—education rather than evangelism, reform rather than regeneration of individuals, accommodation to Chinese beliefs rather than clear distinctions, aiming to influence the educated elite rather than preaching to the masses, material rather than spiritual help, secular rather than religious education—now became hallmarks of two quite divergent approaches reflecting sharply disparate theological orientations. After the Centenary Missionary Conference of 1907, when essential unity of faith and practice was asserted, "the Protestant mission consensus in China began to face a serious challenge."[49] Under the impact of German higher criticism, the Social gospel, evolutionary theory, and liberal theology, "the progressive thinking of such missionary pioneers as Timothy Richard and W. A. P. Martin was developed into full-blown liberalism."[50] The huge shift in missionary personnel and

---

47. Martin, John, and Taylor posed together for a famous photograph in 1905, but Taylor and Richard became permanently estranged as a result of their deep disagreements over missionary methods and even theology. A number of Richard's fellow Baptist missionaries also thought his views too radical, and separated from him.

48. Walls, *Cross-Cultural Process*, 241. For example, he wrote that "in *The Essence of the Lotus Scripture*, as interpreted by Chinese and Japanese 'initiated' Buddhists . . . , we find the same teaching as in the Gospel of St. John in regard to Life, Light and Love." Richard, *The New Testament of Higher Buddhism*, 2.

49. Yao, *Fundamentalist Movement*, 36.

50. Ibid., 39.

financial investment from evangelism and church growth to higher education and modern medical work mirrored an increased concerned for the body rather than the soul.[51] One observer said of the new arrivals, especially after the First World War, "the missionary became difficult to distinguish from the social worker."[52] Eventually, when most of the denominational missions had united to form the National Christian Council in 1922, most conservative mission agencies would either not join the organization or, like the CIM, would pull out in 1926 after its liberal theological stance became clear.

The more conservative missionaries formed the Bible Union in 1920 as a response to their growing apprehension about the liberal theology which was becoming more and more characteristic of what Daniel Bays has called the "Sino-Foreign Protestant Establishment" (SFPE), that is the extensive network of "mainline" denominational missionary societies and the institutions which they created and administered, along with the growing corps of Chinese Christians who had been educated abroad or in one of the Christian colleges.[53] The YMCA, a major player in the SPFE, had also become dominated by young people who had imbibed the new theology that reigned in many universities, churches, and theological seminaries in North America and elsewhere.[54] The Bible Union stressed the fundamental doctrines of Christianity: the saving work of Christ on the Cross and at the Resurrection; the necessity of individual repentance, faith, and regeneration; and thus the priority of preaching over all other forms of service.[55] At the first organizational meeting, Jonathan Goforth was elected as one of two vice-presidents.

MISSIONARY METHODS: AN EVALUATION

A hundred years later, we are in a position to assess these debates and their different outcomes with a little bit more perspective, as we see how they played out in the twentieth century and up to the present.

On the one hand, there is no doubt that Christian colleges and publications exerted enormous influence on China, as increasing numbers of graduates went on to establish careers in education, medicine, publishing,

---

51. Ibid.

52. Valentin Rabe, quoted in Yao, *Fundamentalist Movement*, 41.

53. Bays, *A New History*, 92–120.

54. On the liberal theological turn of the YMCA, see Yao, *Fundamentalist Movement*, 37–38.

55. See especially Yao, *Fundamentalist Movement*, 57–99.

science, and politics. Girls were educated and their feet ceased to be bound; concubinage was outlawed. Modern methods of hygiene, agriculture, and healing improved the lot of millions. "Science" and "Democracy" became watchwords, even idols, in the early part of the century, leading to major changes in all sectors of society. Both the Nationalists and the Communists rejected many traditions that missionary-initiated higher education had shown to be deleterious to the welfare of the populace. Educated Protestants profoundly influenced the government of the Republic of China, particularly during the Nanjing Decade (1927–37) and then later on Taiwan.[56] Even the communist government pursued policies that sounded very much like the program of reforms advanced by missionaries.[57] Overall, there is no doubt about the benefits of Western education, which has led to longer life expectancy, better health, technical and scientific advances, and the elimination of much that hindered Chinese from enjoying the basic benefits of modern life. Missionary-founded institutions of higher learning definitely played a key role in the modernization of China.

Furthermore, the contributions of foreign missionaries, and later Chinese Christians, in building a better society did deflect, and even disarm, some of the hostility that the literati and rulers of China had felt towards Christianity, for they saw both the good will of some of its representatives and the beneficial effects of many of their efforts to ameliorate deplorable conditions, particularly in light of their own ineffectual efforts. They also valued Christianity as a means of strengthening China against its external enemies, who were on the verge of slicing up their nation. Even today, government officials as well as many intellectuals credit Richard and others with helping to bring China into the modern world, and thus see Christianity in a more favorable light than in official communist propaganda. They are seen as having "played a very significant role in the introduction of Western ideas, institutions, and values into China."[58]

On the other hand, considering that the goal of these institutions was "to Christianize the national life of China,"[59] we should note that reforms resulting from Western education have not touched the systemic weaknesses of Chinese culture that render any changes in the political structure ineffectual and that vitiate many of the policies designed to improve the lot of the people. Elite graduates of Christian colleges usually did not accept the faith

---

56. See especially Barwick, "The Protestant Quest."
57. See Fairbank, *Missionary Enterprise*, 2, for an impressive list of such programs.
58. Shen and Zhu, "Western Missionary Influence," 155.
59. Dunch, "Science Religion, and the Classics," 76.

of their zealous and well-meaning teachers.[60] As Fairbank expressed it, "'I taught him English to bring him to salvation,' says the missionary; 'I learned English so I could help save China,' says the convert."[61] Those that did profess faith in Christ tended to assume leadership in the increasingly liberal denominations that ran the schools, and to imbibe the liberal theology that was already gaining ground in the last decades of the nineteenth century.[62] Their legacy can be found in the top echelons of the official Three-Self Patriotic Movement and among some of the "culture Christians" in academic circles. This is not surprising, since, as the curricula of missionary-founded schools became more and more secular, the education they provided looked increasingly like that of government-sponsored schools.[63]

Social reforms did alleviate the sufferings of women, whose feet had been broken and bound and who were treated as being of less value than men in marriage, family, and education. Even today, however, infant girls are still abandoned or killed in the womb; men often take a number of modern-day concubines, sex trafficking is rampant, and physical abuse of wives is endemic. It is a similar story in the political arena. Something like democracy was tried for a while, and has finally succeeded in taking root in Taiwan (at least partially), but mainland China has been under autocratic rule for decades, sometimes causing far more cruelty and oppression than the rule of the emperors, despite the technological, economic, and social advances that were initiated by missionaries and carried forward by their intellectual heirs in the past one hundred years.

Both Timothy Richard and W. A. P. Martin thought that if educated Chinese could be shown the superiority of Western civilization and its roots in Christianity, they would then abandon their resistance to the Christian message and its missionaries. In the event, however, as Peter Ng, in an otherwise laudatory chapter on Richard, wrote, "it turned out that even though Chinese people were willing to accept Western civilization, it did not necessarily imply that they would take Christianity accordingly. Worse still, Chinese intellectuals even turned against Christianity using Western weapons of Science and Communism."[64]

60. See Lodwick, "Good Works," 433.

61. Fairbank, *Missionary Enterprise*, 2.

62. See Fairbank, *Missionary Enterprise*, 13, and Hutchison, "Modernism and Missions," 110–24.

63. This was the case even before the Republic of China forbade required chapel services and religious instruction after the Anti-Christian Movement in the late 1920s. See Bays, *China's Christian Colleges*, 77–79.

64. Ng, *Chinese Christianity*, 130.

We can see that the pietism of the more conservative missionaries and their Chinese converts often failed to teach Christians how to apply the fundamental principles of the Bible to all domains of society. They left this to the liberals, with their more optimistic, and thus ultimately disappointed, confidence in the goodness of human nature and the extent to which the visible rule of God would be manifested on the earth in this age. If these missionaries had brought more of a Reformed perspective to their work, they might have equipped Chinese Christians to make a more significant impact on society and culture, as Lit-sen Chang (Zhang Lisheng), a prominent Chinese theologian, argued in many of his works in the latter half of the twentieth century.[65]

At the same time, the focus on evangelism, church planting, and leadership training by Hudson Taylor, Griffith John, Jonathan Goforth, other missionaries like them, and thousands of faithful Chinese evangelists and pastors, led to the creation of a "Chinese church that would not die,"[66] despite all the ravages of war and persecution.[67] Many have claimed that the methods of their representative, Hudson Taylor, failed.[68] That judgment must surely be placed against the fact that by the end of his life, "the annual total of baptisms recorded by the CIM had risen from hundreds to thousands, . . . 2,500 in 1905" (the year he died).[69] Only a few years later, while Timothy Richard was still advising high government officials in hopes of promoting political and social reform, and engaging in friendly dialogue with leaders of the great Chinese religions, Griffith John and Jonathan Goforth were preaching the "old fashioned," "confrontational" gospel and seeing thousands either converted or significantly revived in their faith. Contrary to what Richard believed about the best way to reach the literati, "many of the gentry," "officials," "leading men of the town," and "prominent men" in various places asked Jonathan Goforth to explain the gospel to them.[70]

Furthermore, Chinese Christians have now begun to permeate all sectors of society, bringing both the gospel and a Christian world view to more and more people. Transformed lives are beginning to penetrate a rotten

---

65. See Chang, *Strategy of Missions*; *Critique of Indigenous Theology*.

66. A reference to a book by Wang and England, *The Chinese Church*.

67. McGavran, *Understanding Church Growth* showed long ago that a focus on institutions will not build a healthy Christian movement; evangelism, training of believers, and planting of indigenous congregations will.

68. See, for example, Ng, *Chinese Christianity*, 130.

69. For a most helpful comparison and contrast between Taylor and Richard, see Broomhall, *Hudson Taylor*, vol. 7: 524-29.

70. Goforth, *Goforth of China*, 245.

society with healing "salt and light,"[71] and thousands of educated believers are beginning to propose meaningful reforms and to demonstrate their care for the poor and oppressed in a variety of ways, such as education for the children of migrant laborers, care for the elderly, and relief for victims of natural disasters.

In other words, while W. A. P. Martin, Timothy Richard and other advocates of Western education and reform movements are to be counted among the builders of the liberal wing of Chinese Christianity, Liang Fa, Pastor Xi, Griffith John, Hudson Taylor, and Jonathan Goforth are recognized as among those who laid the foundation for the evangelical (and even charismatic) churches that account for at least ninety-five percent of today's Chinese believers. (Robert Morrison and James Legge may justly be claimed by both types of Chinese churches.) Beyond that dichotomy, however, today's Chinese Christians are also returning to caring for the crying needs of the larger society, which most nineteenth century missionaries would have approved. Leaders of the new urban unregistered congregations, as well as Christians in the academy, are also re-opening discussions of the proper ways in which the Christian faith should be fully indigenized, fulfilling the dream of the late Lit-sen Chang (Zhang Lisheng) for a comprehensive Christianity that would make its mark in every corner of Chinese civilization.[72] When we consider that the leaders of these urban congregations are mostly conservative and evangelical in their theology, perhaps the title of the two-volume re-publication of A. J. Broomhall's biography of J. Hudson Taylor may be on the mark. Taylor and those like him indeed played a crucial role in *The Shaping of Modern China*.[73]

THE NATURE AND PURPOSE OF THIS STUDY

Partly under the influence of the "great man" theory of history, and partly reflecting the flowery and laudatory style of Victorian biography, especially Christian biographies, previous accounts of the lives of outstanding missionaries frequently focused on strengths and victories, not weakness and defeats. In the twentieth century, especially in the aftermath of World War I and the ongoing revelations of the moral and spiritual failings of political

---

71. Matt 6:16; title of three volumes in the series Studies in Chinese Christianity, edited by Hamrin and Bieler, published by Pickwick Publications.

72. See Chang, *Strategy of Missions to the Orient*, and *Critique of Indigenous Theology*.

73. Broomhall, *The Shaping of Modern China* a republication of the original seven-volume work, *Hudson Taylor and China's Open Century*.

and even religious leaders, historians have tended to dismiss these accounts as mere "hagiography."

Nor have missionaries been spared. Far from the altruistic saints of nineteenth-century lore, they are now seen as men and women with clay feet, portrayed as willing accomplices of brutal Western imperialism, despisers of the Chinese and their ancient civilization, and intent upon foisting both a foreign religion and a foreign culture on these poor "heathen" folk who were deemed to be sunk in darkness and devoid of redeeming qualities. Worst of all, the charge now goes, they meant to subjugate the Chinese church under their own benevolent dictatorship, and China itself under a social and political system of their devising, using the pretext that the benefits of modern Western science and democracy could replace a decrepit and dying society.

There is enough truth in these accusations to make them seem plausible to those who do not take the time to study the missionaries more carefully and broadly. Even some scholars who do read the sources bring such a biased perspective that they cannot accurately assess or describe reality, especially if they do not share the religious convictions of the more evangelical missionaries. Pat Barr's portrayals of Protestant missions in the last half of the nineteenth century is one example of this genre. Alvyn Austin's acerbic treatments of Hudson Taylor, Pastor Xi, Henry Frost, and others furnish other instances of seeing everything through a jaundiced eye and thus failing to perceive the very real competence, faith, hope, and love that the missionaries and their most eminent converts were almost universally said to have possessed to an unusual degree.[74]

In the chapters that follow, we hope to present a fair and balanced picture. The contributors were asked to be both appreciative and critical. After all, Christian teaching holds that "there is none righteous, no, not one," for "all have sinned and fall short of the glory of God."[75] At the same time, however, we have tried to show why these men exercised such great influence over others and have received such honor, not only in their own time but in ours as well.

As for previous "hagiographic" biographies being virtually worthless as historical sources, in at least a few cases this is not true, for two reasons. First, they typically contain quotes from letters and statements by contemporary

---

74. Barr, *To China With Love*; Austin, *China's Millions*. For a review of Austin, see G. Wright Doyle, "China's Millions: The China Inland Mission and Late Qing Society 1835–1905," http://www.globalchinacenter.org/analysis/christianity-in-china/chinas-millions.php. Girardot, *Victorian Translation*, furnishes another example of a supercilious attitude towards missionaries.

75. Rom 3:10, 23.

eyewitnesses. For example, the biography of Hudson Taylor by his son and daughter-in-law, while composed in a style we would certainly not employ today, does make convincing reading largely because of the generous use of descriptive comments about Taylor and others made by those who knew them well.[76] Likewise, Geraldine Taylor could call upon Dixon E. Hoste, who worked closely with Pastor Xi for ten years, as well as other missionaries, to give a rounded portrait of a complex man. In addition, these books do not entirely hide the flaws of their subjects. In the case of Xi, shortcomings are explicitly and frequently mentioned. Taylor's son and daughter-in-law do not criticize him, but they do tell of his inner struggles with faith, hope, and love. Rosalind Goforth's anguished reactions to her husband's radical demands come through loud and clear.[77] These earlier works deserve our continued attention and, because they were penned by people who shared the deepest convictions of their "heroes," may provide us with a more accurate assessment than hypercritical treatments by cynical modern debunkers who cannot seem to imagine that anyone could be that good.

We believe that these were truly great men, whose piety, passion, and perseverance, not to mention their labors, love, and suffering, merit our admiration and even emulation. In an age sorely needing real heroes, perhaps these men can give us some hope.

---

76. Taylor, *Hudson Taylor*.
77. Goforth, *Goforth of China*.

1

Robert Morrison
Missionary Mediator, Surprising Saint

Christopher D. Hancock

ROBERT MORRISON'S ARDUOUS LIFE and catalytic work as a Bible translator and educator set him apart from the many other great missionary figures in China. A poor Geordie lad with a fine mind and strong will, Morrison was the first Protestant missionary to operate in mainland China. Born on January 5, 1782, he grew up in an austere Scots Presbyterian home in the aftermath of the eighteenth-century Evangelical Revival. Morrison was converted as a teenager; an event he described later as "a change of life, and I trust, a change of heart too."[1] Thereafter, like many of his peers, he sought to honor God and began to hunger for adventure in the pursuit of a missionary vocation. After a simple diet of Christian education and basic language learning (Latin and Greek) in his native Newcastle-upon-Tyne and at the new evangelical colleges in Hoxton, London, and Gosport, Hampshire (under the inspirational figure David Bogue), Morrison landed in Macao on September 4, 1807.[2] Thereafter, except for a prolonged sabbatical back in the UK,[3] Morrison divided his time between various residences in Macao

---

1. See Morrison, *Memoirs*, vol. 1, 5.

2. For a full description of Morrison's education under Bogue, and how this set the pattern for his entire missionary career, see Daily, *Robert Morrison*.

3. He was away from China from December 1823 to September 1826.

and (for six months of the year) his bridge-head labors at the international "factories" of the Free Trade port of Canton eighty miles further up the Pearl River. Circumventing East India Company and imperial censure of missionary activities, Morrison fulfilled the dual role of "official interpreter" for the East India Company (EIC) and the London Missionary Society's (LMS) first Chinese Bible translator.

Tough, single-minded, and controversial in life and death, Morrison was a pioneer in Chinese translation work. As he learned the Chinese language, he systematized it for those who followed and then applied his skills to the translation of the Bible (New Testament, 1814; the whole Bible in 23 vols., 1823), preparation of a multi-volume Chinese-English Dictionary (1815–23), and publication of a range of other texts for use in China or for the purpose of interpreting China to the West.[4] This work earned him a Doctor of Divinity degree from Aberdeen University (1817), a prestigious Fellowship of the Royal Society (1825), an audience with King George IV, and international acclaim for his bravery, scholarship, endurance, and unique achievement. Unlike so many early missionaries, Morrison survived twenty-seven long years of service at his missionary "post;" like many of his colleagues, he was predeceased by his first wife (Mary, d.1821) and first son (John, d.1810). Morrison's life is full of ambiguity, pain, disappointment, and failure; it is also alive with a compelling zeal to advance the Christian cause in China that brooked no opposition, reconciled conflicting agendas, and overcame extraordinary odds. As the LMS's "Register of Missionaries" records, "Few missionaries have encountered the difficulties with which he had to contend, or have needed the self-denial by which he overcame all obstacles. He saw little direct result in the conversion of the Chinese, but he prepared the path for others."[5] In this chapter, we study Morrison as a mediator and a saint. These are profiles that are often neglected in contemporary studies of Morrison, although we glimpse something of them in the great missionary historian Latourette's classic summary of the man: "He possessed unusual breadth of vision, integrity, singleness of purpose, devotion, scholarship and sound judgement."[6]

---

4. On China, its language and culture, see esp. Morrison's, *Grammar of the Chinese Language*; *Dialogues and Detached Sentences*; *A View of China*; *China: A Dialogue*; *Chinese Miscellany*.

5. London Missionary Society, "Register of Missionaries," entry 106.

6. See Latourette, *A History of Christian Missions*, 215. For further details on Morrison's life and work see Hancock, *Robert Morrison* and its bibliography for primary sources and secondary studies.

MORRISON THE MEDIATOR

Morrison's mediatorial role developed as his long residence in China unfolded. Linking the evolution of this vocation to the events of his life, we will look at Morrison's political, social, ecclesiastical, cultural and vocational identities. In these different spheres, Morrison reveals an attractive—and progressive—proclivity to reconcile divergent perspectives and to seek to accommodate sharp differences of opinion. Though traditionally (and plausibly) read as an awkward firebrand, insensitively single-minded in pursuit of his high calling as scholar, missionary, and servant of the Chinese people, Morrison is also an adept politician and skilful intermediary, who adapted rigorous spiritual principles to the demands of necessity and opted for a "both-and" strategy when many of his evangelical peers embraced an "either-or" simplicity. Dubbed by some to this day a choleric compromiser and hard-edged dogmatist, there is another story to be told about a man who is still respected by secular sinologists and feared by China's elites. Why? Because, as we will see, he embraced a nuanced attitude towards East-West cultural relations that impresses skeptics of missions and threatens the exceptionalism that claims that outsiders can never understand Chinese culture—a claim that Morrison's life and work self-evidently disprove. John K. Fairbank's incisive remark is still true and fits Morrison, "In China's nineteenth-century relations with the West, Protestant missionaries are still the least studied but most significant actors in the scene."[7]

We begin with Morrison's political profile. "Political" refers to his official role as interpreter for the EIC and to his informal style as a man inhabiting an alien culture and a colleague belonging to various social groups. Morrison's decision, on his wedding day in 1809 (February 20), to accept a position and salary from the EIC as "Chinese translator to the English Factory at Canton,"[8] has provoked comment, especially from missionary agencies and critical Chinese sources. Eliza Morrison, his second wife and biographer, explains and justifies the decision, "Upon this incident the great usefulness of Morrison's life turned; and by this it is hoped the immortal interests of millions were decided."[9] Morrison reasoned in his diary, with St Paul's tent-making in mind, "If secular employment were lawful in him I know not why a missionary may not attend to secular affairs for his own support."[10] Despite the tacit (pragmatic) support of the LMS, Morrison's

---

7. See Barnett and Fairbank, eds., *Christianity in China*, 2.
8. Morrison, *Memoirs*, vol. 1, 269.
9. Ibid., 245–46.
10. Broomhall, *Robert Morrison*, 60.

new role stirred the charge from fellow Christians of receiving funds tainted by trade, mammon, and prejudice,[11] while to hostile Chinese he was now self-evidently a stooge of British imperialism and enemy of the people he sought disingenuously (and misguidedly) to "proselytize." But Morrison's public-private roles as mercantile agent and pioneer missionary troubled others more than Morrison himself. He consistently defended his tough decision and new position on the hard-headed grounds of finance and law; with inadequate funding from the LMS and an illegal status as a missionary operating in EIC territories and mainland China, how else could he remain in Canton once his missionary cover was blown?[12] In Morrison's decision we glimpse a capacity for astute political behavior that many of his later colleagues lacked.

Morrison's role as official interpreter involved him during the trading season in long hours of detailed translation (oral and written) of complex trade and diplomatic negotiations. While to Eliza, exercising his new responsibilities providentially provided "so many lessons in Chinese,"[13] William Milne's *Retrospect* (which Morrison heavily edited) is more realistic: "The duties of that situation were at first extremely oppressive, through his still imperfect knowledge of the language."[14] To the end, this was a role that drained Morrison physically and emotionally. His scholarly nature was better attuned to long hours of isolation than the rough and tumble of tricky trade talks. It is a cause of wonder that he found time and energy to compile his multi-volume *Chinese-English Dictionary* and to translate the majority of the Old and New Testaments. Morrison's letters and diaries, as captured in the *Memoirs*, shed some light on Morrison's political activity for the EIC. We find him struggling to accept the EIC's aggressive (if not immoral) approach to the lucrative opium trade and to the British government's arrogant attitude towards Anglo-Chinese diplomacy. He castigates the opium trade in an 1822 letter to his diplomatic patron during early years in Canton, Sir George Staunton, as "a traffic which is far from being reputable either to the English flag, or to the character of Christendom."[15] Reflecting on the diplomatic row over the trial and execution in 1821 of the American seaman, Terranova,

---

11. See his colleague William Milne's comment, "It was rumoured that he had deserted the cause for which he had left home and country . . . as this idea was founded in mistake; it did not gain general belief." in Milne, *A Retrospect of the First Ten Years*, 79.

12. See Morrison, *Memoirs*, vol. 1: 256, where Morrison links the new position to his need for a solid base on which to develop his publishing program.

13. Ibid., 256.

14. See Milne, *A Retrospect of the First Ten Years*, 78.

15. Morrison, *Memoirs*, vol. 2: 175.

who was condemned by the Chinese authorities for (accidentally?) killing a passerby with a large pot dropped from his ship, Morrison maintains:

> Sufficient pains have not been taken to cope with the intellect of the Chinese, such as it is: and it must be confessed, that many of the officers of government are by no means despicable either in respect of natural sagacity, or in knowledge of human nature... if all that is recommended here were adopted, homicides would occasion considerable trouble; still, it is not likely they would lead to such distressing dilemmas, nor to such dishonorable compromises, as have heretofore occurred.[16]

At the end of his life, when Lord Napier's mission to negotiate a new trade agreement was rebuffed for ignoring Chinese protocols, Morrison was caught in what he saw as a diplomatic row of Britain's making. He wrote ruefully on July 22, 1834, ten days before his death, "He [Napier] will not negociate [sic] with Hong Merchants, but with Government Officers; this will make my presence always necessary when any interview takes place ... I am sorry to have to travel to Canton in this hot weather; for I am by no means strong."[17] It is tempting to dismiss these remarks as the shallow irritability of a tired public servant or the muffled manner of a long-term resident in a hostile environment. In reality, they are indicative of Morrison's patience and predisposition to advocate accommodation and seek hard-won common ground more than easy conflict. We should not doubt Morrison's accumulative weariness and acute sickness at this stage of his life; nor should we question his persistent readiness to commend mediation as always, like charity, "the more excellent way."

He wrote memorably of the missionary's vocation:

> A Christian missionary from England is not sent to India or any other part of the world to introduce English customs, but Christ's gospel. He should not be shocked or irritated by the innocent usages of other nations, which happen to differ from his own... A notion which some people possess, that there is nothing good or comfortable out of England, that all God's works, everywhere, are inferior and to be despised, in comparison with what He hath done for England, may be called patriotism; but

---

16. See his frank advice to the British authorities published at the time, Morrison, *Remarks on Homicides Committed by Europeans on the Persons of Natives at Canton* appended to his *A Narrative of the Affair of the English Frigate Topaze 1821-22*; Morrison, *Memoirs*, vol. 2, 145.

17. Morrison, *Memoirs*, vol. 2: 526ff.

it is a notion that is unjust, and of an impious tendency, and is unworthy of a Christian Missionary.[18]

In his interpersonal relations Morrison is no less generous. Though he is represented often as brusque, single-minded, and insensitive, the evidence of private correspondence suggests rather a man who was, yes, toughened by the trials of his long years in China, and incorrigibly self-disciplined, but also self-aware, self-critical, generous, and humane. In his social relations, his habits of life are courteous and kind, thoughtful and caring. He was as much a politician at home, or away from work, as he was on duty for the EIC. This aspect of Morrison's character is too often overlooked, in part, perhaps, because social accommodation was to his more hard-line evangelical contemporaries (and successors) indicative of a weak spirit or a wobbly gospel. To some, the faithful must always offend; not so, Morrison. Reading the *Memoirs*, and especially the private papers, we find a man who could cultivate and keep friends, love and be loved by his nearest and dearest, adjust socially, and reserve public judgment pending private discussion. Yes, he could be direct; he could also be quite extraordinarily patient, indulgent, forgiving, and caring. Hence, we find a warmth and intimacy—and subsequently deep sense of pain and loss—in his letters to his family and close missionary friends William Milne and Thomas Wilson.[19] He was Dada to his children and wrote almost daily to Eliza when separated from her during his final years in China.[20] Though he was initially reserved in what he said about his first wife Mary's state of mind and health in correspondence with the directors of the LMS, he was less guarded in letters to friends and family. To a friend, he explains in December 1809, "Mary has no mother, or sister, or friend within thousands and thousands of miles; but I trust the Lord will ere long lift the light of his countenance upon her, and give her peace."[21] Likewise, he writes to his friend, William Shrubsole, of "my beloved and afflicted Mary"[22] and to another of "My poor afflicted Mary . . . [who] 'walks in darkness and has no light.'"[23] A year later, from his "solitary exile," he reports to another friend, "Though well myself, I have

18. See Morrison, *A Parting Memorial*, 386.

19. On Morrison's friendship and correspondence with Milne, see Hancock, *Robert Morrison*, 133ff. Morrison's moving reaction to Milne's death on June 2, 1822 is extensively reported in Morrison, *Memoirs*, vol. 2: 159–64.

20. See Hancock, *Robert Morrison*, 228ff. I am grateful to the Hobson family for showing me family letters in which the warmth of Morrison's character is all too evident.

21. Morrison, *Memoirs*, vol. 1: 286.

22. Ibid., 284.

23. Ibid., 286.

often wept over my wife."[24] Writing to his father on the death of his first child, he painfully records, "My grief is great, dear father, great. I sorrow for the sufferings of my poor helpless Mary."[25] This is the Morrison too few have honored, whose mind did not always rule his heart, and whose emotions were as strong as they were pure. As son, husband, father, relative, and friend, Morrison was a rounded personality and attentive individual. We do not need to project impassibility onto a human subject. Outside of the inner circle of family and friends, he was impressively tactful, gracious, and positive; and this despite Eliza's cryptic admission that faced by multiple, petty requests for information, cultural artifacts and botanical rarities from overseas correspondents, Morrison "had no great *tact* in such matters, but did the best he could."[26] Morrison's capacity for single-minded concentration and prolonged study is more impressive still when balanced by honest recognition that his time was often not his own, his priorities were adjusted by others, and his absorption of pettiness and disruption matches the most impressively tolerant and abundantly patient. But as missionaries, Robert and Mary Morrison felt marginalized at times by the EIC community and itinerant traders. In visitors like the Hobsons (Mary's parents) and residents like Sir William Staunton, and later the American merchant D. W. C. Olyphant, Morrison found rare kindred spirits and irregular tangible support. The affection directed towards Morrison by the expatriate community on the death of Morrison's first wife and child, and the outpouring of grief associated with his own death, bear ample testimony to the professional and personal regard in which he was ultimately held by the expatriate communities in China. Was Morrison a social mediator, with a warm heart and capacity for love, friendship, and strong relationships? Absolutely.

One of the more surprising arenas in which we find Morrison's mediatorial spirit at work is in relation to theology and, especially, church politics. By background and reputation, Morrison is a hard-line Calvinistic Presbyterian with an exclusive Protestant theology and an equally strict view of Christian spirituality, liturgy, church polity, and the sacraments. His Nonconformist[27] hackles are raised when his offer to provide chaplaincy cover in the Canton factory in 1832 is rebuffed by Sir William Fraser, president of the EIC's local Select Committee. Morrison writes, "It is a lamentable state of religious or irreligious feeling, that in the true spirit of popery, un-

---

24. Ibid., 301.

25. Ibid., 295. On Morrison's heart-rending account of Mary's death in child-birth on June 10, 1821, see ibid., vol. 2: 99–101.

26. Ibid., vol. 2: 366.

27. That is, non-Anglican. [Ed.]

der no circumstances (except reading prayers over the dead) will they have communion with any who will not bow down to absolute authority, and yield an implicit uniformity. If such persons '*believe*,' they don't act upon the article in the Creed, 'Communion of saints.'"[28]

Closer study does not contradict Morrison's confident Protestantism: it does reveal, however, a remarkable readiness to embrace difference, commend theological provisionality, and critique venerated evangelical shibboleths. Missionary hagiography has struggled to admit this aspect of Morrison's public profile; or, worse, it has damned with faint praise his liturgical and spiritual eclecticism, his respect for his catholic scholarship and courage, and his mature grasp of a holistic approach to Christian ministry and mission. There is much to support this larger view of Morrison, and little to justify the less generous attitudes and actions of later China missionaries (we even find Morrison bemoaning the strictures of Scottish Calvinists in Macao!). Hence, by the end of 1817, Morrison and Milne had prepared for publication *Morning and Evening Prayer* (adapted "because excellent and suitable" from the 1662 *Book of Common Prayer*, with the prayers for rulers changed[29]), a thirty-day version of the *Psalter* (for "social worship" and individual devotions[30]), and in 1818, *Hymns in Chinese*. Eclecticism was not uncommon in Dissenting[31] spirituality at the time, but it was less obviously a feature of front-line missionary activity. Morrison's report to the LMS in September 1817 expresses his position well:

> The Church of Scotland supplied me with a catechism—the congregational churches afforded us a form for a Christian assembly—and the Church of England has supplied us with a Manual of Devotion as a help to those who are not sufficiently instructed to conduct social worship without such aid. We are of no party. We recognise but two divisions of our fellow-creatures—the righteous and the wicked—those who fear God, and those who do not. Grace be with all them that love our Lord Jesus Christ in sincerity.[32]

Similarly, though Morrison's strict Sabbatarianism was offended by Portuguese Catholics in Canton who "do business on the Lord's Day, as on any other,"[33] his attitude towards the historic Catholic mission to China and

---

28. Morrison, *Memoirs*, vol. 2: 375.
29. Ibid., vol. 1: 477.
30. Ibid., 477.
31. That is, non-Anglican. [Ed.]
32. Morrison, *Memoirs*, vol. 1: 478.
33. Ibid., 165.

local Catholic priests and laity, is strikingly generous. To the secretary of the LMS, Morrison commends his Chinese Catholic assistants, who are, he observes, "much more ready to communicate what they do know, than any of the heathen that I have seen."[34] Though strongly opposed to Catholic theology and its "idolatrous rituals,"[35] Morrison did not crow over Catholic persecution. We find him studying a Roman Catholic prayer book,[36] approving of Catholic ideas respecting the Chinese language,[37] anxiously monitoring the fortunes of Roman Catholic missionaries, having "occasional intercourse with a native Roman Catholic" who was "sometimes dissuaded by the Romish clergy from visiting the 'heretical missionary,'"[38] meeting with the French Catholic priest, Richenet,[39] and reporting the prohibition against Chinese attending Portuguese churches in January 1809[40] and the burning of a Portuguese church.[41] Most memorably, Morrison's *Chinese Miscellany* (1825) contains the following comment, "The earliest Catholic Missionaries, Ricci, Schaal, Verbiest, possessed the most ample means of acquiring a thorough knowledge of all that concerned China: and they were able men who availed themselves of the opportunities within their reach."[42] In his famous exchange with the evangelical missionary bishop of Calcutta, Daniel Wilson (1778-1858), Morrison's objection is not to episcopacy *per se* but to what he calls "the exclusive pretensions of episcopacy" and the necessity of Episcopal ordination; especially when such views were articulated by a bishop who was sympathetic to, if not expressive of, evangelical missionary endeavor. As his Journal for July 15, 1834 records, "I have finished a long essay on the use and abuse of the word Church: trying, I fear in vain, to break down the *exclusive* system."[43]

Morrison's long years of mission service taught him much: they softened him and shaped him spiritually, theologically, and pragmatically. A classic instance of his intellectual development is associated with his experience of the great fire of Canton in 1820.[44] Horrified by the lack of compas-

---

34. Ibid., 167-68.
35. Ibid., 225.
36. Ibid., 235.
37. Ibid., 339.
38. Milne, *Retrospect*, 80.
39. Morrison, *Memoirs*, vol. 1: 205, 210, 214, 216.
40. Ibid., 247.
41. Ibid., 247.
42. Morrison, *Chinese Miscellany*, 51.
43. Morrison, *Memoirs*, vol. 2: 522.
44. For Morrison's reflections on the fire see his *Narrative of the Fire at Canton* in

sion shown by the Chinese to suffering neighbors, Morrison grasped the central, and distinctive, place practical Christian love ("benevolence," as he called it[45]) must have in effective Christian mission. Consciously embracing the word-act theology of his friend and evangelical comrade William Wilberforce, he stressed that printed evangelistic and educational material must be supplemented by holistic benevolence by Christian people.[46] This was of a piece with Morrison's evangelical sense that humanity, in all its cultural, physical, and racial diversity, was made "in the image of God," and was to be respected, loved, and served as such. This was radical in Morrison's day; it expresses his conscious distancing from a condescending evangelical Christianity that rubbished alien cultures and effectively denied God's universal love of the world—however much that world still needed to hear and to accept the good news of Jesus Christ's saving death for sin. Morrison's *A Parting Memorial* contains a selection of essays and sermons in which he sought to articulate his theology of mission on the eve of his return to China. A sermon on Acts 17:26, "*God hath made of one blood all nations of men,*" expresses well Morrison's mature humanitarianism: "Too long have false notions of individual superiority, of family greatness, and of the right of some nations to dominate the rest; and notions of a mistaken patriotism led men to despise and disregard, if not to hate and injure their fellows, for all of whom we this day claim the rights of consanguinity and of brotherhood."[47] Morrison is less easily categorized theologically than some would like; in this lay his pioneering power and missionary authority.

Morrison's role as a cultural mediator is far better known and more widely esteemed. In addition to becoming one of the few English-speakers who knew Chinese and one of the pioneers of Western sinology, Morrison possessed a cast of mind and sense of purpose that consistently commended cross-cultural understanding as an essential prerequisite of effective missionary activity.[48] Painstaking language-learning and the production of practical aids to support successors in their engagement with China and

---

Morrison, *Memoirs*, vol. 2, Appendix, 33ff.

45. As he declares on one occasion, "Universal benevolence . . . is a scriptural idea, and to cherish such a sentiment a Christian duty" in Morrison, *Memoirs*, vol. 2: 276.

46. See an example of this in his *Proposal for Bettering the Morals and Conditions of Sailors in China* dated September 25, 1822 in Morrison, *Memoirs*, vol. 2, Appendix, 43–45.

47. See Morrison, *A Parting Memorial*, 171. On Morrison's sabbatical sermons, see Hancock, "A Parting Memorial," 45–72.

48. On the importance of literature and language learning, see Morrison's "Review of the First Fifteen Years" in Morrison, *Memoirs*, vol. 2: 180ff.

Chinese culture served this higher purpose.[49] He was critical of those whose laziness or presumption sought to circumvent the toil or the tool the Chinese language represented; as he wrote to his friend from Hoxton days, John Clunie, "How preposterous it is, that a *living language*, one of the *oldest* in the world, and known by one-third of our species, should be entirely neglected in England and Scotland; and that amongst all sets and parties, both religionists and scholars! Cannot a few persons be spared to study Chinese, which is the language of *five* nations, and contains thousands of volumes of original literature?"[50]

At a critical juncture in his life, Morrison surrendered his passion for linguistic excellence to the pragmatic needs of simple expression and sufficient understanding; as he wrote to a friend on October 19, 1824:

> If I go on learning the polite literature of China, I may go on learning to my dying hour; but I can write intelligibly in Chinese, therefore I think I had better desist from learning pagan lore and teach Christianity, in the simple Chinese phrase. Pagan Chinese reading is, to my taste, as offensive (but not more so) as the profligate poets, &c. of Greece and Rome, and modern Europe. Horace, the most elegant, and most read, is full of abominable stuff, much worse than mi lord Biron.[51]

We should, though, understand Morrison's skill and desire to embrace Chinese language and culture as reflective as much of his humble origins and habitual critique of British culture as of native wit or a well-developed missionary strategy. His predisposition towards cultural mediation lay in his unprepossessing background (from which a missionary vocation enabled escape) and his strident internationalism, which an iconoclastic evangelicalism sucked from elitist bigotry and cultural barbarism in the English abroad. That said, Morrison's cultural legacy is immensely impressive: advisor to the nascent American Board of Commissioners for Foreign Missions, counselor to countless EIC and British government officials, mentor in Chinese and missionary work of the earliest generation who joined him in Canton, Macao, and at his pioneering educational establishments in Singapore, Malacca, and London, and respected unofficial ambassador of all things Chinese in Britain, the United States, and the continent. Morrison stands head and shoulders above those who later glided along the cultural

---

49. This principle was enshrined in Morrison's abortive attempt to begin a language institution in London to equip missionaries linguistically when on furlough in the UK; see Hancock, *Robert Morrison*, 188ff.

50. Morrison, *Memoirs*, vol. 2: 518.

51. Ibid., 381.

and linguistic paths he had cut and who churlishly vilified the shortcomings of his work. Morrison never claimed his work was finished or good; sufficiency was all he craved. As he wrote memorably to the Rev A. Brandram on December 22, 1827, after his Chinese version of the Bible had come under attack from a few cynical academics:

> The Quarterly of June, which hypocritically admits the good principle of the Bible Society, whilst it blames all that it has done, has, I perceive, condescended to reproach the humble Dr. Morrison . . . He claimed not to be a perfect Chinese scholar, nor to be a perfect translator; and therefore he should not have translated for the press. Admirable logic! As if any version—even the English, were perfect—or the Vulgate perfect. If none but faultless, perfect versions are to be sent forth, the principle will as completely interdict the Bible in vulgar tongues, as any papal bull that was ever promulgated. I wish the *perfectionists* all success; not in vituperation, but in making perfect translations whenever they may condescend to undertake the work.[52]

We might say more of Morrison, the cultural mediator; it is a central feature of his enduring legacy.

Lastly, Morrison was also a vocational mediator. He embodied a missionary vocation for skeptics, and promoted a collaborative attitude towards missionary strategy. In both areas, his patience and foresight are inspiring. Post-colonial commentators have been harsh in their critique of missionary motivation. Diligent servants of Jesus Christ and of a host nation have been dubbed imperialistic oppressors or cultural bandits. Self-sacrifice has been re-named a "neurosis." Willful penury is called avarice or "taking commercial advantage." It is hard to land any of these skeptical punches on Morrison's robust biography, however. The embodiment of selflessness, Morrison inspired generations of others to risk their lives for a higher cause than human greed or a finite reward. Morrison exemplifies the transparent integrity and rugged spirituality of a seasoned Christian soldier, guarding the Christian standard against overwhelming odds.[53]

If Morrison wins begrudging respect from those who admire the pioneer and explorer, he embarrasses the unrepentant or un-reflective who claim that their strategy, mission society, or historic legacy are the best, or only way to work. Morrison's crushing humility sits ill with the spiritually proud and psychologically strident. Morrison was a team player. He hated

---

52. See Ibid., 395.

53. Broomhall, *Hudson Taylor and China's Open Century*, vol. 1: 170; see also Morrison, *A Parting Memorial*, 306ff.

the divisions and decisions that sundered Christ's witness to the world. When the LMS refused to sanction his children's return with him to China in 1826, he contemplated challenging their "unmerited disapprobation," but accepted their decision lest his protest "compromise . . . his missionary character."[54] As he stated movingly to friends gathered at Hoxton Academy to hear his final sermon before returning to China:

> Who are we, that we should go to the kings of heathen nations, and attempt to deliver the people from heathen bondage? We have no authority from princes, or from kings; we are not eloquent; we have no diplomatic finesse or chicanery; we are not men of address, and if we had all these things we should renounce all dependence upon them. But we rely upon the presence of God . . . Let us ever be silent as to our afflictions. Let us call to mind the suffering which Christ endured and then our trials will appear light![55]

While we may not understand, or even admire Morrison's message or methods, we cannot fail to be impressed by the gracious manner in which he lived and the courage with which he died "at his post" in 1834.

MORRISON THE SAINT

Should Morrison be thought of as a "saint," a hero of the faith? What acts or qualities of character, mind, and life justify the ascription "saint" to one who some quietly suggest fathered a child out of wedlock, abused his nearest and dearest, and initiated a missionary campaign in China that laid the groundwork for the ghastly brutality and disastrous political legacy of the two Opium Wars in the 1840s? These are difficult questions that require careful attention. At stake is not whether Morrison's name should be added to ecumenical lists of feast days, nor whether a shrine should be established in his honor at which prayers should be offered and answers expected. The questions challenge claims and assumptions about Morrison's status in the history of the Protestant China mission and the quality of his legacy.

Let me address first, and briefly, the dark veils mysteriously hung at times over Morrison's private life. Some scholarship suggests that the short courtship (while on sabbatical) and lack of a date[56] and marriage certificate for Morrison's wedding to his second wife, Eliza Armstrong (1795–1874),

---

54. Morrison, *Memoirs*, vol. 2: 328.
55. Ibid., 337, 340.
56. Cf. Douglas, "Morrison, Robert," dates the marriage 1824.

hide the fact that his third child, Robert, was conceived out of wedlock. We have no material evidence to support this claim; nor should its denial, therefore, be required. If true, Morrison's legacy is neither lost, nor irredeemably besmirched; as Morrison's Lord cautioned accusers of an adulterer, "Let him who is without sin cast the first stone." The potentially ambiguous evidence may be plausibly explained by the fact that Morrison had good reason to marry promptly due to his short residence in the UK during his sabbatical and desire to have a wife who could return with him to China. Morrison had earlier acquaintance with Eliza through missionary circles, and her age (she was 30) and decisive character (note her management of the publication of Morrison's *Memoirs*) would have made procrastination unlikely once a proposal of marriage had been made. Thus, it is likely that they married well before their child was born. Suggestions produced by a later smear campaign by rivals are as unworthy as they are unlikely.

The more perplexing issue is whether the degree to which Morrison's own missionary vocation and single-minded pursuit of it exposed his immediate family to excessive physical risk and long-term psychological damage. To some extent these questions can be leveled against every married missionary, particularly during the nineteenth and early twentieth centuries when tropical medicines were primitive, travel was consistently dangerous and mortality rates (especially of children and mothers) were high. But was Morrison somehow more guilty than others? Could his family relationships be termed "abusive"? We have alluded above to the warmth and intimacy of his family relationships, but he was still aware that he had a capacity for "stern severity," As he reflected towards the end of his life:

> There is in my character a mixture of the softest affection, and of stern severity when duty calls. In the day of battle, I cannot be the coward that would stay at home. Heaven help me, and do you encourage me to behave valiantly in the good cause we have espoused; to do so will, I am convinced, my love, soothe your mind in suffering and in health. Much happiness will arise from the interchange of thought, and the reciprocity of tender affection and love, whatever our external trials may be.[57]

It is conceivable that this material is misleading; words may hide as well as disclose meaning and there is evidence to suggest that though his son, John Robert, willingly followed in his father's footsteps as a missionary and translator of the Bible in China, his daughter Mary Rebecca remained distant both from her stepmother and, initially, from her father's legacy.[58]

---

57. Morrison, *Memoirs*, vol. 2: 333–34.
58. See Hancock, *Robert Morrison*, 247.

The proposition that missionary families are free of vocational conflict and personality clashes is spurious. Given the duration and demands of Morrison's missionary service, his prolonged separation from parts of his family, his willing self-sacrifice of companionship and comfort, and the inspiration he gave to his son, John, to replace him, and to his wife, Eliza, to memorialize him, we should not rush to pronounce Morrison an unsuccessful family man, however severe the demands placed on his nearest and dearest. He expresses well the ambivalence he felt about his vocation in something he wrote on December 7, 1826, his first day at sea on his final voyage to China: "I have some misgivings or apprehensions that I may not live to return and be buried in China; but, all circumstances and probably events considered, I hope that this voyage will be for my own good—for your good (Mary and John), and for the good of the heathen. Oh may the Lord grant it for Jesus' sake!"[59]

On what basis, though, might we articulate a more positive spiritual portrait of Morrison? For there is much about Morrison's life that does not conform to classic models of sanctity or unusual spiritual significance. He was not an emaciated ascetic caring for the dying: indeed, portraits of him have to nuance his ample girth and high color. Nor was he a prophetic firebrand lighting up a generation, who died in the ensuing conflagration. His style and achievements were (and still are) mostly appreciated, like a Ming vase, by the spiritual and sinological *cognoscenti* more than the general public. His solitary existence for months at a time in Canton has a hermetic ring to it, and his unselfish discipline an inspirational appeal, but Morrison's day-to-day existence was little more than that of a bookish scholar and a middle-ranking bureaucrat. This is not the usual stuff of hagiography. Early biographies by Wylie (1867), Townsend (1888), Dixon (1902), Williams (1908), Walker (1920), Broomhall (1924), Hayes (1925), Millicent and Margaret Thomas (1936), and Ride (1957) strain to make inspiring, let alone interesting, Morrison's monotonous plod through language-learning, dictionary compilation, and Bible translation.

That said, faithfulness, vision, acceptance of obscurity, and imperviousness to earthly plaudits, are the stuff of saints' lives, and Morrison reflects these values in spades. In a rare, unguarded moment we find him poking fun at Wilberforce as too vain and self-seeking, writing to Eliza at the time of the reformer's death: "By the way, I see from American papers that Wilberforce is dead! He *directed* his burial to be simple. Now that is a topic which in life I would rather let alone. A pompous funeral, however, I have no reason to fear, and therefore I may be the more indifferent about it.

59. Morrison, *Memoirs*, vol. 2: 237.

But why not leave such matters to survivors . . . I suppose if Mr. Wilberforce had a pompous funeral bestowed upon him, no body would blame or praise him for it."[60]

There is more than jealousy or pique in this remark: Morrison genuinely aspired to a quality of sanctity that penetrated through any and every human standard of excellence in honor of the God he served selflessly to his dying breath. In line with this, Morrison "the saint" most notably demonstrates three qualities.

Firstly, he exhibited pioneering faith in the biblical promises of God. There is an almost Abrahamic quality in Morrison's readiness to wait more than twenty years before he saw any notable return on his linguistic and evangelistic efforts, and even then the number of converts was paltry. He trusted his divine call, put faith in God's written word, and lived into and out of the truths he discovered there. He was self-consciously a pioneer, writing in terms that illuminate those aspects of his inner life that his contemporaries disregarded, "The pioneer is forgotten. Missionaries who *first* enter pagan lands, are only pioneers . . . I fear the patience of British Christians will be tried, if not exhausted, before the fruits of the Chinese Mission exhibit any striking appearance."[61] Though he found support from the LMS erratic and the attentiveness of friends and family unreliable, he appears not to have wavered in his sense of duty or commission. Given the level of frustration, betrayal, disappointment and weariness through which he persevered, the epithet, "He trusted in God" is surely as applicable to Robert Morrison as to Abraham and John Wesley.

With this trust came an extraordinarily calm strength and a palpable readiness to attempt the humanly impossible. His dual charge to master Chinese and then to translate the Bible into Chinese was dismissed by many great men as a mad aspiration rather than a feasible goal. As Charles Grant (1746–1823), director of the EIC, declared, "the undertaking was a *practical* impossibility . . . for the nature of the language would not allow any translations whatever to be made of it."[62] That Morrison ever attempted these seemingly unassailable heights is testimony to a quality of character very rarely seen, even on the early mission field. He was, like every truly holy person, set apart from the rest for God's service regardless of hindrance, delay, failure, and weakness.

---

60. Ibid., 512.

61. Morrison, *A Parting Memorial*, 111.

62. See Moseley, *The Origin of the First Protestant Mission*, 20; see also Moseley, *A Memoir*.

Secondly, Morrison's life was marked by exceptional physical courage in ever-changing, life-threatening situations. Be it the heat and sickness of Macao and Canton, the threat of Chinese violence, the risk of early exposure by the EIC, the brigands who hunted on the Pearl River, or the multiple risks attending long sea voyages to and from China, Morrison's physical safety was daily on the line. That said, we find little if any sense of fear or foreboding in his letters and diaries. Far from fleeing risk, from before he set out for China, Morrison embraced a sense of military commissioning and a martyr's calling. His desire to return to China to die there after his sabbatical in England is clear. In one of his final sermons before returning to China, he proclaimed, "Let us ever be silent as to our afflictions. Let us call to mind the suffering which Christ endured and then our trials will appear light! . . . Let us look to Christ—to Christ in all his love, and mercy, and mediatorial work. Let this ever dwell in our hearts. So shall we be cheered in every bereavement, and find ourselves at home in every clime! Farewell!"[63]

Some will read this as characteristic of a certain kind of dated, muscular missionary Christianity that scorned pain and embraced bravado, or more troublingly, interpret it as an unhealthy kind of spiritual masochism that relished penury and trial as the necessary accessories of a true disciple's loyalty. That Morrison reflects an otherworldly Christian culture is clear; that he suppressed all thought of his own earthly safety and security less so. His readiness to protest his desperate need of funding and support in his early years belies any suggestion of self-mutilating asceticism or stifled sensibility. It seems rather—and herein, surely, lies his saintly character—Morrison self-consciously calculated the daily risks he faced and chose not to avoid or evade them. Like the Christian soldier he aspired to be, he saw his work as a daily fight against the world, the devil, and the flesh, and diligently sought to overcome all odds with all of his strength and all of his will. Likening the missionary's vocation to that of a soldier, Morrison writes tellingly of his struggles, particularly with those who he looked to for support:

> But this soldier-like feeling and resolution, to fight till death, striving to dispossess spiritual enemies, does not make him insensible of the neglect of fellow-Christians; nor are the Churches, who constitute the Commissariat Department at home, justified in gratuitously adding, by their parsimony or neglect, to the sufferings of the soldier in the field. Still, if they do carelessly add to his sufferings, the good Missionary will, nevertheless, remain

---

63. Morrison, *Memoirs*, vol. 2: 337, 340–41.

at his post, as long as ever the banner of the cross continues to be unfurled.[64]

Morrison's dull daily biography acquires more radiant hues when seen as the consistent exercise of a remarkable will committed to the Christian cause. Very few have matched Morrison's achievements, for very few can match his diligence, fortitude, courage, and linguistic gifts. He is, like every true saint, unique in calling and accomplishment. In his physical rigors and willing risk-taking, he is more a Stephen or Polycarp than a Luther or Calvin. To his peers, he raised the bar on missionary service and inspired a quiet generation to follow in his invisible train.

Lastly, if Christian love and Christ-like holiness are cousins, Morrison's exemplary charity towards friend and foe should earn him plaudits as a holy man. Though Morrison's daily companions were parchment and pen, his habitual interest and life-long preoccupation were with those whose language he sought to master and spiritual needs he sought to serve. It is possible to overstate Morrison's single-mindedness to the point that he appears never to learn and never to change: this is far from the case. His decision to join the payroll of the EIC signaled a significant change in direction and profile, and was one, as we saw earlier, that cost him dearly whilst paying bills. As we saw earlier, the great fire of Canton represents another watershed in Morrison's career. In espousing the necessary convergence of word and deed in the China mission, Morrison forged a path others were later to follow. The prominence of education, healthcare, and ministries to orphans, widows, single mothers, prisoners, and social outcasts in later Protestant mission in China has its roots in Morrison's prophetic decision to adjust his work to render the divine word and Christian love in fleshly, practical forms. In his final years, when his strength was failing and health weak, Morrison's willing encouragement of potential successors and deliberate concern for needy co-residents in Macao and Canton are striking. Though Morrison was not unique in compassion or concern, his articulate presentation of a holistic gospel and willing integration of hands-on service into his heady scholarship constitute a notable feature of his legacy. In both, he risked the respect of his evangelical and missionary peers while challenging an impractical, bifurcated, pietistic evangelicalism more concerned with souls than with bodies. In threatening stereotypes and critiquing shibboleths, Morrison let love shape his thought and action more than principle. This is in every sense the rasping independence of a saintly nonconformist.

---

64. Broomhall, 170; see also Morrison, *A Parting Memorial*, 306ff.

CONCLUSION

There is much about Morrison's life that remains a mystery. More often than not, lacking hard evidence, we project assumptions onto the vast gaps that remain in our knowledge of his daily life in Canton or Macao. There is, I believe, sufficient evidence, as we have seen, to represent Morrison as both a many-sided mediator and, in his own way, a "saint." He deserves more attention than he has hitherto received. By opening up China to the West and the West to China, he became one of the truly world-changing figures of the nineteenth century. Those who will not trouble to study him risk missing a pioneer interpreter of the modern world and an exemplary advocate of global harmony.

2

Liang Fa (Liang A-fa)
Leader in Chinese Indigenization

Jonathan A. Seitz

> The demand for an "indigenous" church turns attention to what makes it "indigenous." And when one looks on the spreading branches of this tree, the flowers and fruit of which are increasingly beautifying and enriching the new life of this old land, the question as to the seed from which it grew takes us back to this pioneer Chinese evangelist who, through lonely, long, and fiery testing, evidenced the strength and sincerity of his faith.[1]
>
> —George H. McNeur, 1934

Liang Fa embodies the indigenization of Chinese Christianity—a process that proceeded with bursts and stops, periods of foreign patronage and internal persecution, and struggles over what it meant to be Christian and Chinese. In his early life, Liang grew up in a village where he participated in local religious life. As a young adult in the employ of the recently arrived London Missionary Society, Liang experienced a strong conversion that soon led to the baptism of family members and work as the first ordained evangelist. By midlife, he was participating in most of the institutions of the early Protestant missionary movement (the missionary press, proto-church-

---

1. McNeur, *China's First Preacher*, 5.

es, schools, a hospital, etc.). In late life, he remained steadfast to his faith, although perhaps troubled by the apparently slow spread of Christianity and problems in his own family. Liang showed a tendency towards iconoclasm, and embraced a form of Christianity that was strident in rejecting idolatry. His family life became more complicated as he aged, but showed several layers of conflicts that marked becoming Christian: the real risk in professing faith in Christ, the challenge of participating in religious or ritual life, and tensions over the next generation. As McNeur writes above, Liang Fa is often described as the first fruit or the seed of the indigenous Chinese Church, and his story is fascinating.

Before we begin his story, however, it is important to briefly say something about the challenges in telling it. Writing about Liang nearly two hundred years after his baptism, Liang's would-be biographers face some difficulties. On the one hand, we have more from Liang than almost any of his Chinese Christian contemporaries. He left behind an evangelistic journal, written in his own hand, and he published a number of tracts, most notably the famous *Good News to Admonish the Ages*, from which comes one of the accounts we have of his conversion.[2] Almost all of the missionaries of the London Mission Society (LMS), for which Liang worked, wrote affectionately about his ministry. There also are a few short biographies.[3] The most substantive of these was written by George Hunter McNeur more than seventy-five years ago and is being republished in this same series.[4] This is all to say that in describing him, any biographer must rely on fragments or snippets, and creating a whole from these pieces is not easy.

LIANG'S EARLY YEARS

Liang Fa was born in Samchow (Sanzhou) in 1789, in the village of Lohtsun (Gulao Cun). This was the fifty-third year of the reign of Emperor Qianlong, the last of three emperors who ruled during the middle period of the Qing. McNeur describes the village as situated on a plain in a flood bank, where dykes helped control flooding but where disaster was always a possibility. Liang would have played under the leaves of banyan trees; he may have helped his family with farming, caring for smaller animals like ducks or

---

2. Liang, *Good News to Admonish the Ages*.

3. The most recent scholar to write regularly about Liang is P. Richard Bohr, who has written a number of articles: "Liang Fa's Quest for Moral Power," "Jesus, Christianity and Rebellion in China," and "The Theologian as Revolutionary." There is also a short simple biography: Sng, *I Must Sow the Seed*.

4. McNeur, *China's First Preacher*.

pigs, or herding buffaloes or cattle. His family property sat in the west ward of the village. A family ancestral temple would have held the tablets for the family and a watchtower provided guard for times of community conflict (for instance, between Han and Hakka, or during periods of religious or political tumult). After his original family house was washed away in an 1833 flood, Liang built another one, which was later located by McNeur. When he was eleven, Liang began his schooling. Though his family was probably relatively poor, they made the effort to help him begin the classical process of studying and writing. Liang and his biographers write some about his early religious beliefs, which would have included the cult of the dead (veneration of ancestors), and also would have involved devotion to the Buddhist deity Guanyin.[5]

As a young adult, Liang left for the big city, in this case Canton (now Guangzhou), seeking work or perhaps enough money to pay for a bride price. McNeur places this in the year 1804, just a few years before the English London Missionary Society missionary Robert Morrison would arrive in Canton, illegally and via the United States, to begin his mission work. Liang's first job in Canton appears to have been as a pen maker, but he soon became apprenticed as a printer and worked under a master for four years. The work of a printer entailed carving wooden blocks that could be used to print books.[6]

The missionary William Milne would note that Liang can "read a plain book with ease, but has had only a common education; is of a steady character and frugal habits."[7] Liang's work in many ways paralleled that of the evangelical missionaries with whom he worked. The generation of missionaries that included William Carey and Robert Morrison typically came from crafting trades and were known for their industry and piety. The Nonconformists were denied access to the establishment universities and created their own institutions for the training of missionaries. The schools Morrison attended, Hoxton and Gosport, became models for the types of institutions the missionaries would develop, notably in Malacca.[8]

For Liang, the effort to find a trade and a new life in the city had its own costs. Life in the city must have involved a great transition, and the death of Liang's mother in 1810 would have been an even bigger trauma.[9] A

5. Ibid., 7–11.
6. Ibid., 14–15.
7. Milne, *A Retrospect*, 178.
8. For the missionary strategy which emphasized translation and publishing, see Daily, *Robert Morrison*.
9. McNeur, *China's First Preacher*, 18.

new vocation, the death of his mother, and physical distance from his father and hometown may have given Liang greater freedom in choosing his own religious path.

WORK WITH THE MISSIONARIES

Liang's first contact with the LMS mission was through another Chinese assistant, Tsae Low-heen, who helped supervise the printing of the New Testament under the direction of Morrison. Although Morrison already had a number of assistants, over the coming years Liang proved himself to be the most faithful.

The bigger influence on Liang, however, was not Morrison but his younger colleague William Milne. Morrison is often depicted as the dourer of the pioneer missionaries, where the younger Milne comes across as an enthusiast; together the pair formed an early duo that accomplished several of the major works of the mission, including the translation of the Bible, the start of the Malacca schools, and the publication of English and Chinese journals. Milne had arrived in Macao July 4, 1813. He was aided in language study by Liang, and Liang eventually accompanied him to the start of the Malacca mission in April 1815.[10] Liang was not the first convert. This was Tsae A-ko, one of three Tsae brothers engaged in the mission. However, Tsae's legacy was more ambivalent—he left only a short conversion account translated into English, was often criticized by the missionaries for his behavior, and died apart from the mission, perhaps having left the faith. By contrast, Liang comes across as a mirror to Morrison—pious and reliable—and the adjective McNeur applies to Liang more than a dozen times is "faithful." The word denotes Liang's craftsmanship, his service to the ministry, and his faith.

Liang's baptism is forms an exceptional story recounted not only by the missionaries, but by Liang himself. There are two main accounts, one by Milne which was written at the time of the baptism, and another fifteen years later by Liang that was included in his work *Good News*. Taken together, the narratives provide a three-dimensional description of what becoming Christian meant for Liang and Milne.

In April 1815, Liang had travelled with Milne to Malacca, where he worked on the publication of Milne's *Treatise of the Life of Christ*. Milne records a first person account by Liang of his conversion, which was circulated widely. In it, Liang describes his religious upbringing. He says he

---

10. Ibid., 20. For a good account of the LMS Anglo-Chinese College in Malacca, see Daily, *Morrison*, 159–190.

"seldom went to the temples" and "sometimes prayed towards heaven, but lived in careless indifference."[11] He drank occasionally and mentions unnamed vices, adding, "before I came hither, I knew not God; now I desire to serve him." Milne writes that "a more than usual attention to the truth was observed in a Chinese employed as a printer to the Mission."[12] Milne adds that he instructed Liang carefully and prayed with him often. In time, Liang came to accept the faith as his own and requested baptism. Milne described the baptism in a brief narrative that would be reproduced many times in missionary publications:

> *Nov. 3—Sabbath.*—At twelve o'clock this day I baptized, in the name of the adorable Trinity, Leang-kung-fah, whose name has already been mentioned. The service was performed privately, in a room of the mission house. Care had been taken, by private conversation, instruction, and prayer, to prepare him for this sacred ordinance: this had been continued for a considerable time. Finding him full stedfast in his wish to become a Christian, I baptized him. The change produced in his sentiments and conduct is, I hope, the effect of Christian truth, and of that alone,—yet, who of mortals can know the heart?[13]

During the baptismal ceremony, Milne asked Liang five questions, beginning with whether he had "truly turned from idols, to worship and serve the living and true God, the creator of heaven and earth, and all things?" The second question was to determine whether he understood he could not save himself. The third question was whether Liang trusted in Christ for salvation. The fourth question asked whether Liang expected any material benefit from conversion. The final question asked whether he would maintain this duty for the rest of his life.[14] A key aspect of Milne's account is the missionary's fear of reproach over the speed of the baptism. Other LMS missions had watched an explosion of conversions followed by an equally rapid collapse, so Milne was understandably wary. He wrote that, however, although "some superstitious attachments may, for a considerable time, hang about the first converts from paganism, and that it *is in the church, and under the ordinances thereof*, that these attachments are to be entirely destroyed, I did not think it adviseable to delay administering the initiatory ordinance."[15]

11. Milne, *A Retrospect*, 178.
12. Ibid., 177.
13. Ibid.
14. Ibid., 179.
15. Ibid., 178.

Liang's own account is described in a thirty-page section of *Good News*. What is fascinating is how much it differs from Milne's account. In this version, Liang notes that he used to worship or *baibai* on the first and fifteenth of each month, and that sometimes chanted the Heart Sutra.[16] Liang, in Milne's language, was "never much given to idolatry and seldom went to the temples." Nonetheless, Liang, writing after his conversion, struggled with "lust and evil thoughts" and a "mouth of falsehoods and evil words."[17] Despite his effort to be a better person and to refrain from evil thoughts, he found himself continuously struggling. With the arrival of the LMS missionaries, he found a new way. At the baptism, he read from the scriptures and was examined by Milne. Liang writes: "[Milne] sprinkled water on my head, and I received the ceremony of baptism with thanksgiving to God in Heaven. I again asked Mr. Milne, 'When people believe in Jesus, what sign is there?' Mr. Milne replied, 'with your whole heart follow goodness: this is the sign that you have faith in Jesus.'"[18] The baptism provided new energy and hope to Liang:

> This time I thanked Mr. Milne and departed, and returned to my small building alone and sat secretly and securely. I trusted that I had obtained the remission of sins and that Heavenly God on High had purified my great sins. Then I took a name for myself, called, "Student of the Good," [*Xueshanzhe*] and from then on, my heart turned from evil and I studied the good.[19]

Initially, Liang writes that he was cautious in sharing about his faith, but in time he became more and more bold. P. Richard Bohr writes that after Liang's baptism, "Both Morrison and Milne noted a remarkable personality change in their convert."[20] Liang's story of baptism anchored his conversion and remade him as the Student of the Good, a penname he would use in subsequent years.

FAMILY AND EARLY MINISTRY

The years after baptism were one of the most productive periods of the ministry, beginning with the baptism of his wife and son. The 1810s through mid-1820s saw the conversion of Liang's wife and the birth of a son, Liang's

16. Lai, "The First Chinese Christian Gospel," 83.
17. Ibid., 84.
18. Liang, *Good News to Admonish the Ages*, 302.
19. Ibid., 302–3.
20. Bohr, "Liang Fa's Quest for Moral Power," 40.

ordination as a preacher, and major transitions in the LMS mission. Liang was present for the establishment of the Anglo-Chinese College in 1818, an institution that was moved to Hong Kong by William Legge many years later (although Liang was around then also).

One of the most fascinating characters in Liang's life is his wife. Liang's relocation to Canton and then Malacca may have been for the purpose of finding a larger salary so that he could afford a bride price. Liang baptized his own wife and records the account of her baptism in *Good News*. We know her surname was Lai. As near as we can tell, neither Morrison nor Milne met her. Liang recorded the baptism of his wife with simplicity. Kwok writes, "The ceremony took place in a shabby cottage in a village about fifty miles southwest of Guangzhou. Having no baptismal font, the couple used a Chinese rice bowl instead."[21] The missionaries noted her baptism, saying only that Liang had conducted the ceremony. The image of the young Liang baptizing his wife with a rice bowl is powerful, and it may also have challenged the missionary theology of the times. Baptism was tightly regulated by Reformed churches, but the missionaries probably accepted that given Lai's geographic distance, this approach was necessary. (Alternately, Liang may have simply performed the baptism without being fully aware of church teachings.)[22] His daughter, A-chim, was born in 1829.[23] The times in which Liang lived were dangerous ones, since the threat of fatal illnesses made everyone's life precarious. Milne, for instance, lost a son in 1816, a daughter in 1817, and his wife in 1819. Morrison's wife died in 1821 and Milne died in 1822. Liang's first wife died in 1849.[24]

The family member of Liang's about whom we know the most is Liang Jinde (Liang Chin-Teh), Liang's son and the first child baptized in the mission. Jinde's name means "entering virtue." In mission literature, he was usually referred to in a colloquial form "A-teh," (Ade). Jinde, unlike his mother, was baptized by a missionary—in this case Robert Morrison. After the ceremony on November 20, 1823, Morrison wrote, "Oh that this small Christian family may be the means of spreading the truth around them in this pagan

---

21. Liang's account does not even mention a bowl. McNeur says a rice bowl, and the 1955 Chinese translation of McNeur is cited in Kwok, *Chinese Women and Christianity*, 1.In any case, rice bowls would have been the most useful for such a purpose. Notice that effusion—pouring- is the mode used by Liang, probably following the example of the missionaries, who were not Baptists.

22. Actually, all branches of Christianity allow for the administration of baptism by any baptized believer in cases where an ordained minister is not available. [Ed.]

23. McNeur, *China's First Preacher*, 58.

24. Ibid., 109.

land."[25] In 1831, when he was eleven, Jinde was placed in the care of Elijah Bridgman, who instructed two other boys as well.[26] Bridgman saw caring for them as a duty, but wrote that he believed it would help his own language development, something which he described as a "delicate experiment."[27] In an 1832 letter, Bridgman mentioned a conversation with Jinde in which the latter stated that his first duty was "to worship and obey God" and the second was "to honor and obey [his] parents."[28] Bridgman asked him what "ought next to engage" his attention, to which Jinde replied (echoing the Great Commission requirement), "Learning, so that I can teach all men."[29] When asked about the possibility of persecution, Jinde replied, "God will protect me, and I shall not suffer."[30] Bridgman concluded the letter with the hope that Jinde would become "an able advocate and promulgator of the Gospel to this nation."[31] Liang Jinde's later life is spiritually complicated; McNeur describes him essentially leaving the church, but Bridgman's wife includes a mention of Jinde receiving the Lord's Supper in 1856, and Jinde wrote a letter in English mourning the death of Bridgman.[32] Jinde is one of the only second-generation members of the mission. The closest parallel is probably Morrison's son, John Robert Morrison, who also worked in translation and was involved as interpreter in the diplomatic wrangling between England and China.

There is a fair amount of information on Liang's evangelistic work. Liang's own conversion came about through the efforts of Milne and Morrison, and he seems to have absorbed their individualistic and focused approach to evangelism. His travel diary, for instance, devotes a lot of space to dialogues he had with others, most notably with a Mr. Lam (Lin). Lam was also a printer, so much of his work would have been printing tracts, sutras, or other materials for Buddhists and popular religionists. For Lam, to become Christian would certainly have threatened his livelihood, and so much of the conversation is comprised of Liang's criticism of Chinese

---

25. Morrison, *Memoirs of the Life and Labours of Robert Morrison*, 225.

26. Elijah Coleman Bridgman (April 22, 1801–November 2, 1861) was the first American Protestant Christian missionary appointed to China. He served with the American Board of Commissioners for Foreign Missions.

27. Bridgman, *The Pioneer of American Missions in China*, 58.

28. Ibid., 75.

29. Ibid.

30. Ibid.

31. Ibid.

32. Ibid., 215, says that the younger Liang was not admitted to the Lord's Supper until 1856. On p. 243, Bridgman mentions Liang's son as pupil, and on p. 69 Jinde writes a letter in English mourning Bridgman's passing.

religions. In this context, Liang quoted Matthew 10:37, "Whoever loves father or mother more than me is not worthy of me; and whoever loves son or daughter more than me is not worthy of me" (NRSV). As the first Chinese pastor, Liang inevitably faced frequent rejection.

Despite Liang's early struggles, McNeur describes the years 1831–35 as Liang's "most fruitful" in Canton.[33] This period saw his baptism of Lam and several others, including Li San, who would become an assistant preacher. The small community of Christians rose to around ten, a modest number given the years of Liang's service, but also the kernel of what would grow in the years ahead. In one year, Liang printed seventy-thousand tracts. Many of these were distributed to the tens of thousands of candidates who participated in the exams which allowed for entry into government service. Little is known of Liang's work with other Chinese colleagues. There is reference to some sort of long-standing conflict with another preacher in the mission, Kew A-Gong, which was eventually resolved.[34]

During this time, Liang published his most famous book, *Good News to Admonish the Ages* (*Quan Shi Liang Yan*). *Good News* is widely known for its influence on the Taiping (see below), but it also possesses interest as a work in its own right. There are several small studies of the volume, but most are simply outlines, and scholars have tended to gloss over the book, either describing it as "tract," or placing it in the context of a question like scripture translation. *Good News* is actually a five hundred page tome, divided into nine chapters, although, for publication, individual chapters seem to have circulated separately and it apparently often circulated in four volumes. The work fits within the English tract tradition, which sought to be comprehensive or to promote a singular vision (different from the modern variation, where a tract often consists of just one or two pages). It also fits within the Buddhist "morality book" or "good book" (*shanshu*) tradition, and the Morrison collection at the London University School of Oriental and African Studies actually contains two other popular (non-Christian) religious books that begin with the words "Admonishing the ages." At the same time, the word for tract used later by Chinese Christians was an "admonishing the world text" (*quanshiwen*), perhaps reflecting Liang's influence.[35]

Good News included earlier tracts Liang had written, and was notable for two unique sections: a criticism of Chinese religions and the story of his

---

33. McNeur, *China's First Preacher*, 67.

34. Ibid., 99.

35. Mathews, Wang, and Chao, *Mathews' Chinese-English Dictionary*, 235. This dictionary is often described as a "missionary dictionary" and was associated with the China Inland Mission.

conversion.[36] It is hard to know how Liang himself understood the work. Was it to be his *magnum opus*—an effort to communicate Christianity in an idiom slightly different from that of the missionaries? Or was it more like many of the other missionary publications of the generation—a first-draft effort to explain Christianity? I have not been able to determine its circulation, and the few remaining copies do not help in explaining how it was used. Regardless of how Liang understood it, it stands as a hallmark of Chinese Christian literature. Liang showed genuine creativity in his efforts to expound the basic tenets of Christianity, including the use of novel names for God.

In August 1834, Robert Morrison died as he was helping Lord Napier in his failed diplomatic visit which antagonized the Qing court.[37] The loss of Morrison made Liang's position more precarious. Just a few weeks later, and several days into a period of distributing tracts to provincial exam candidates, the police came for Liang and those who accompanied him. An assistant and materials were seized. Liang fled, but soldiers searching for him seized several family members in Samchow. Eventually, Liang made his way to Macao. With the help of John Morrison (Robert Morrison's son), Liang received ransom money for his family members. Liang's troubles were likely the result of the English diplomatic mission under Napier, which had produced materials in Chinese arguing for the British position. As a printer who worked with foreigners, Liang was particularly vulnerable in this type of international conflict. That it was still illegal to teach Chinese to foreigners or to print foreign materials only exacerbated the situation.

Liang's place stands against a backdrop of colonialism, warfare, and unequal treaties. Missionaries provided a nearly continuous criticism of the colonial enterprise from the Opium Wars until the 1949 Revolution, but in practice inequalities were glaring and intractable. Missionaries continued to run core institutions, such as schools and hospitals, up until the 1949 Revolution.[38] The Qing court lost control of basic functions of government, had property controlled or taken from it by force, and was ransacked during times of instability. Missionaries were typically the most culturally adept foreigners, and played a role as interpreters and even negotiators in these

---

36. The conversion section has been partially translated by Whalen Lai Lai ("The First Chinese Christian Gospel," 83–105), and I treat the complete conversion account elsewhere.

37. Lord Napier was Britain's Chief Superintendent of Trade at Canton (now Guangzhou). In 1834, frustrated by failure to negotiate a trade agreement with the Viceroy of Guangzhou, he ordered two frigates to bombard the city. Illness forced him to retire to Macau, where he died shortly afterwards.

conflicts.[39] This background influenced both the broader context and the local context in which Liang worked. During the period of rising tension before the opium wars, Liang alternated between work in Canton, Malacca, and Singapore. In Canton he faced imprisonment and physical punishment, but had total freedom in other regions. After the Opium Wars (1839–42 and 1856–60), the Qing government faced gradual weakening, as it dealt with internal rebellions and new impositions by the foreign powers.

LIANG AND THE TAIPING[40]

A major part of Liang's work was the distribution of tracts, and candidates for the imperial exams were a major target, since the events brought together thousands of aspiring intellectuals or literati. Liang's presence at one set of exams appears to have led to one of the most historically interesting syntheses of Christianity and Chinese religions. According to McNeur, it was during the few days before he fled Canton in 1834 that Liang handed a set of his tracts to Hong Xiuquan (Hung Hsiu-Ch'uan), the leader of the Taiping Rebellion. The details are a little hard to figure out, but by 1855 sources already connected Liang's tracts to the founder of the Taiping.[41] Some authors, however, place the evangelism of Hong in 1833. There is no clear record of the transmission (by Liang or Hong), so we should at least consider other alternatives. It is plausible that it was someone from another mission who passed Liang's materials to Hong, and it may also be that rather than *Good News* it was a different work from Liang's writings or the LMS corpus. Nonetheless, most historians see Liang's *Good News* as the book Hong received during the exams and which inspired his vision in later years. Writing during the years of the Taiping Rebellion, the missionary Theodore Hamberg (Gutzlaff's successor at the Chinese Union) wrote an account called *The Chinese Rebel Chief* in which he writes that Hong received a complete set of *Good News* at the 1836 exams, when he was twenty-three years old.[42]

39. There is a fascinating analysis by Lydia Liu, who, for instance, tracks the evolution in how missionaries like Robert Morrison understood the word translated "barbarian," which even found its way into treaty prohibitions. See Liu, *The Clash of Empires*.

40. The Taiping Rebellion, led by Hong Xiuquan, broke out in southern China in 1850 and lasted until 1864, leaving much of China devastated and exhausted from years of battle, plunder, and slaughter, with a loss of perhaps twenty million lives.

41. Hamberg, *The Chinese Rebel Chief*.

42. Ibid., 14–15. Hamberg's work is also interesting in that it provides what may be the first study of *Good News to Admonish the Ages*, offering an outline of the work, 27–30, and noting that "The nine volumes have often been bound up as four," 27. McNeur

It is certainly possible that, regardless of the exact year, Liang and Hong were present at the location of the same exams sometime in the early- or mid-1830s. Hong would have been on his way to an examination failure at the same time that Liang distributed his illicit tracts. Out of this small encounter the largest revolution of the era—indeed, in that era, of the world— was born. Hong and Liang shared much in common. Both were born in what are now adjoining districts of Guangdong. Liang began schooling late, and Hong's studies were sometimes interrupted to help with farming or other needs of a family that was relatively poor but sought social mobility. Like Liang, Hong wished for baptism from a missionary, but where Liang had been a steady worker and a model inquirer, Hong's request for baptism was denied by the American Southern Baptist missionary Issachar J. Roberts because his beliefs or commitment seemed lacking. So Hong found his own way. When Hong and his cousin baptized each other, they may have used Liang's conversion account as their model.[43] Liang's baptism took place in the heavily regulated world of missionary culture, but it certainly could look sectarian in the Chinese telling, where a single missionary baptized a single convert away from public scrutiny.

The bridge from Liang to the Taiping is significant for several reasons, particularly in highlighting the revolutionary milieu in which Liang lived and the ways in which Christianity might be flexed or twisted to include new teachings. Liang grew up in the shadow of the White Lotus rebellions and his Christian faith could certainly have taken on an entirely different form. Instead, Liang's evangelism took place primarily under the aegis of missionary activity, and his connection to the London Missionary Society seems to have cemented his commitment to a classical Christianity.

LIANG'S LEGACY

Joseph Lee has used the division of "preaching, worshipping, and believing" to describe the activities of early Chinese Christians, and this characterization certainly fits Liang's experience. The strength of Lee's approach is that it uses the language of participants to express a path on which many Christians in South China travelled. For Liang also, the goal was a mode of discipleship which would lead other Christians along the same path he had walked. This was a journey on which Liang was frequently frustrated, since few he encountered became Christian, fewer still stayed within the church, and of those only one or two in his generation became a leader of similar

---

also mentions Meadows' 1856 book, *The Chinese and their Rebellion.*

43. Michael, *The Taiping Rebellion*, 25.

stature. Nonetheless, Liang's influence follows several important lines: his contribution to the work of missionaries like Peter Parker, Samuel Dyer, and Benjamin Hobson his efforts toward the nurture of a small Christian community, and the legacy he left through writing (and perhaps family).

During the mid- to late-1830s, Liang worked in Malacca and Singapore with many of the major missionaries of the day. In 1835, Peter Parker, an American medical missionary, opened a hospital focused on ophthalmology in Canton; evangelism had to be muzzled since it was still illegal in the country. When Parker spoke before the US Congress in 1841 he reportedly quoted Liang in saying, "When I meet men in the streets and villages and tell them the folly of worshipping idols they laugh at me. Their hearts are very hard. But when men are sick and are healed their hearts are very soft."[44] In 1845 (after the First Opium War), Liang went to serve as the chaplain for Parker's hospital. His duties included leading worship regularly and visiting patients. According to Parker's accounts, Liang often shared his own story of conversion and taught from the scriptures.[45]

Liang also worked closely with Samuel Dyer, an influential printer in the mission. In the late 1830s, Liang and a co-worker, Kew A-Gong, contributed to a spike in baptisms in Malacca—at one point, more than thirty in just a few months.[46] However, the conversions proved to be fleeting, and led to an argument between the missionaries over the meaning and standards for baptism. Eventually the Malacca mission would be shut down, but it had served as the main incubator for LMS work on missions to the Chinese. According to Alexander Wylie, this is also when Liang published two tracts in conjunction with the American Board missionary, Ira Tracy: "Incentives to Abandon Opium" (*Yapian su gai wen*) (1835) and "Address of the Singapore Agricultural and Horticultural Society to the Chinese Agriculturists" (*Xinjiapo zaizhonghui gaosu zhongguo zuochan zhi ren*) (1837).[47]

The other missionary with whom Liang formed a close partnership was Benjamin Hobson, who had married Robert Morrison's oldest daughter. Liang helped him locate housing and space to establish a small medical center. Hobson's dispensary could treat more than two hundred people a day, and Liang moved his evangelistic work from Parker's hospital to Hobson's. Liang gathered ten people, four men and six women, in the new chapel. When public worship was offered, more than two hundred people

---

44. McNeur, *China's First Preacher*, 89.

45. Ibid., 102.

46. Ibid., 84.

47. Wylie, *Memorials of Protestant Missionaries*, 79–80. Both of these works are held in Harvard's collection of Chinese Protestant works.

sometimes gathered to watch the event. The hospital served as an ideal site for Liang, providing a steady stream of people to consult him about his faith.

One important aspect of Liang's ministry was his collaboration with missionaries and locals, which influenced institutional work and ministry. McNeur tells the story of a Mr. Chau, a friend of Liang's with literary aspirations.[48] He was willing to help Hobson with illustrations for his translation of a physiology text. In time, Chau became a Christian. He eventually served as a pastor, succeeding Liang at Hobson's hospital after Liang's death and eventually serving for approximately forty-five years. In this setting, Liang acted as friend and recruiter, as well as mentor and model.

Liang's wife is one of the many figures in Liang's life about whom we wish we knew more. She died in 1849. Hobson called her "a quiet good woman in feeble health."[49] Since she did not have Liang's proximity to the mission, she may have suffered more than he, but also showed herself an able evangelist. According to McNeur, in time "her old mother and widowed sister" became Christians. McNeur says that Liang's daughter-in-law was also a church member and a member of the household. Intergenerational living would have been quite common, but Liang's family life is difficult to reconstruct.

McNeur records some information cannot be located elsewhere. Apparently, Liang remarried after the death of his wife (McNeur offers the reason that his relatives were "anxious that the old man should have proper care"). This second wife left him, however, and married another man. McNeur adds that, "Another wife was then arranged for, who survived him."[50] Apparently neither of these weddings were "church ceremonies." It is unclear if this is because they came at the encouragement of a non-Christian family, if Liang himself was unaware that he was transgressing Christian norms, or for another reason.[51] While there was clearly a Christian community at this point, it is also worth asking whether there were any precedents for Christian remarriage or what they would have looked like.

Liang died on April 12, 1855, a Tuesday. He had preached the two days prior, speaking Sunday on Matthew 10:28 ("Be not afraid of them which kill the body, but are not able to kill the soul; but rather fear him which is able to destroy both soul and body in hell." KJV), and returning to the hospital on Monday to preach. In his final days, according to Hobson, he is said to have

48. McNeur, *China's First Preacher*, 107–8.

49. Ibid., 187.

50. Ibid.

51. A friend in a Singaporean church once told me that pregnant brides are not allowed to marry in the church worship room, and clearly some churches reserve weddings in the sanctuary only for sanctioned marriages between Christians.

spoken with his son, Jinde. Liang hoped his son would honor the Sabbath, and leave the government position which prevented him from doing so. After Liang's son notified him of his father's death, Hobson gathered three Chinese Christians and two recently-arrived Wesleyan missionaries (W. R. Beech and J. Cox). They returned to Liang's house and read scripture and offered prayer. According to McNeur, Liang's granddaughter, 'Autumn Gold,' related this story to Congregational missionary J.C. Thomson some sixty or so years later. Although she was married to a non-Christian husband later on, McNeur writes, "she could never escape the memory of that Christian deathbed, and sixty years afterwards she came to a Wesleyan church in Wuchow seeking membership."[52] A theme in the telling of Liang's life is how the apparently meager results he saw in his own life would become a larger harvest in subsequent generations. Hobson wrote a letter to the LMS at the time of Liang's death, a short passage of which gives an idea of Liang's importance in the mission: "His place will not soon be filled, and it may be long before we see his like again. He kept up, while alive, an interesting link with our noble predecessors, the one who baptized him [Milne] and the one who set him apart to the work of an evangelist [Morrison]. Now he is gone, and we have no one left in this wide field of that generation."[53]

McNeur tells the fascinating story of Liang's descendants. After Liang's death, his son Jinde remained involved in the Chinese Maritime Customs, where his knowledge of English was an asset, but he ceased attending worship. Most of Jinde's eight children died without survivors. However, his daughter returned to the Christian faith late in life, and sponsored three of her nieces (a brother's daughters) to attend a Christian school, where they also became Christians. Finally, the brother—Liang's last remaining grandson—met with a preacher on his deathbed and was baptized at age sixty-three. The narrative illustrates the fragility and unpredictably of Christian history, for Christian genealogy can seem to skip generations or fade, only to return after many years.[54]

EVALUATION

Liang's family history and ministry challenges highlight his humanity and the dilemma that Chinese Christians often faced. While his minority status was exceptional compared to today—it is hard to know if he would have found any candidates for marriage in the tiny Christian community of his

52. McNeur, *China's First Preacher*, 114.
53. Ibid., 115.
54. Ibid., 118–19.

day—the general difficulties he faced are often typical of Chinese Christians. Many of Liang's deepest struggles continue to vex first generation Christians: how should Christians witness in a pluralistic community, choose and support leaders, find spouses and rear children, and create an identity that is distinct from the missionary religion while sustainable and clearly Chinese? How can one be Christian in a society which suppresses or resists Christian witness? What does it mean for Christianity to be indigenous?

Liang remains exceptional for a number of reasons, most related to the status he gained as the first fruit of mission. He was baptized, ordained, and served admirably. Liang ministered in the context of a "first draft" Chinese Protestantism—one which required great flexibility and diligence. Other accomplishments bore witness to his own personal traits: his persistence, his creativity, and his ability to cooperate with foreigners. Almost every milestone attributed to the missionaries—the translation of the Bible, the creation of grammars and dictionaries, the start of churches, schools, and hospitals—occurred with the help of "Chinese assistants." Liang and his Chinese colleagues were largely responsible for these tasks. They negotiated, translated, corrected, taught, printed, prayed, preached, and facilitated most of the work of the early generations of missionaries.

Liang has also left a mark on some of the broader encounters of the day. He was swept up in the aftershocks of the Lord Napier event. More remarkably, he seems to have provided the tinder that served as the initial fuel for the Taiping Rebellion. In this respect, it is easy to see how Liang's project could have moved in other directions: extinction, or absorption into an indigenous religious or social movement. While it is tempting to focus on Liang's role in the Taiping uprising, it is also notable that he helped steer the early Christian movement towards an interpretation that was faithful to what he had received but also was clearly articulated in a local voice.

As the bicentennial of Liang's conversion approaches, it is worth remembering his efforts towards the translation and indigenization of a faith that must have at first sounded so incoherent and foreign. Liang's story of call, conversion and ministry echoes others throughout Christian history, even as it was accented and inflected in new ways. Liang was a key source of guidance and aid during this process. In a period of turmoil, Liang provided a source of continuity for two generations of mission and indigenization.

3

James Legge
Linking Chinese Evangelical Spirituality with Cross-Cultural Engagement

LAUREN PFISTER

DURING THE LAST FEW years, there has been a strong indication of sustained scholarly interest in the life and work of James Legge (1815–97) in both contemporary China and Scotland. At the end of 2010, the republication of James Legge's five-volume set of *The Chinese Classics* by a university press in Shanghai[1] stimulated further intellectual waves of interest across the wide ocean of Chinese mindscapes, the volumes being accompanied by extensive critical introductory essays in Chinese for a Chinese readership.[2] It was claimed that the six hundred sets published at that time were all sold within two years after its official publication date. At nearly the same time, in Legge's small hometown of Huntly, Scotland, major cross-cultural artistic events involving Chinese artists and scholars as well as American and British specialists in Chinese studies took place in 2009 and 2010.[3]

---

1. Legge, *The Chinese Classics*, 2010.

2. This author was told that the 600 sets of this Chinese edition of Legge's *Chinese Classics* published in Shanghai were all sold within two years after it had been published.

3. Associated with Deveron Arts; see the major town event in 2009 recorded with images at http://www.deveron-arts.com/utopia-group.

Furthermore, in the summer of 2013, Chinese television crews from the documentary channel in the Chinese Central Television (CCTV) organization began exploring Legge's life and works by means of extensive interviews, intent on creating a program that would serve as the fourth in a series of nine programs dealing with "overseas sinology."[4] In addition, because Legge spent twenty-one years as the first professor of Chinese Language and Literature at Corpus Christi College in Oxford (1876–97) after serving as a professional missionary representing the London Missionary Society (LMS) in Hong Kong (1842–73), there is a major multi-volume collection of Chinese renderings of Leggian texts, lectures, and sermons which is being planned for publication by Chinese scholars to celebrate the bicentennial of his birth in 2015.[5] Even now, three international conferences in Hong Kong, Beijing, and Edinburgh are being planned to celebrate the bicentennial of the birth of this "Great Scot" from various angles of interpretation.

Yet, while Legge's sinological scholarship has recently been widely reconfirmed, especially within mainland Chinese academic circles, far less has been understood regarding his work of evangelism and his involvement in building up communities of Chinese and other Protestants living in southeastern China during his missionary years (1843–73). Even from the angle of the contemporary Chinese Protestant Church in Hong Kong and other parts of mainland China, the vast majority of Chinese Christians, as well as their pastoral leaders, are almost completely unaware of Legge's historic contributions to the nineteenth-century Chinese Protestant churches. This is understandable in the light of the fact that most of Legge's activities with Chinese Christians occurred in Hong Kong, which was at that time a British colony, and even though he published Protestant Christian tracts in Chinese media,[6] his efforts in these realms remained unknown by the vast majority of Qing dynasty citizens during his missionary career. Even though Legge expended remarkable and monumental efforts to become thoroughly engaged with the dominant cultural ideology of Qing dynasty China—the classical scholarly texts of the Ruist or "Confucian" traditions[7]—how these

---

4. A team from CCTV channel 9, its documentary channel, interviewed this author in Beijing in July 2013, and subsequently also in Hong Kong in November 2013, along with many others. The program dealing with James Legge is the fourth in a nine-part series on "overseas sinologists" and is scheduled to be aired to Chinese audiences sometime in mid-2014.

5. Being worked on in coordination with colleagues from the China Institute of Overseas Sinology at Beijing Foreign Studies University along with other colleagues in Beijing, Fujian, Hong Kong, and elsewhere.

6. Such as Legge, *Shenghui zhunshen, Wang Jinshan yaojue, Yabolaihan jilüe, Yesu mentu xinjing,* and *Yueshe jilüe.*

7. This involves Legge's extensive English translations found in *The Chinese Classics*

related to his own preferred missionary methods and their relationship to the development of Chinese Protestant communities within the Qing dynasty is a question that is still largely neglected among Chinese Christians themselves. In this light, then, this chapter will seek to reveal more about Legge's contribution to the development of fledgling Chinese Protestant churches in southeastern China.

UNUSUAL PREPARATIONS AND VISION FOR CHINESE MISSIONARY WORK

Legge was one of the few early missionaries who entered the Chinese missionary field with extensive scholarly preparation.[8] He was part of the second generation, following Robert Morrison (1782–1834) and William Milne (1785–1822); like Legge, both of them were members of the LMS, and Milne had come from the same Scottish church in Huntly. Legge earned a master's degree from what was then King's College in Aberdeen,[9] graduating with high honors in 1835, and in 1838 he also obtained a Master of Divinity with an emphasis in missions from Highbury College, a Congregational seminary in England.[10] He was now competent in handling classical Latin, Greek, and Hebrew languages. Unlike the vast majority of his predecessors and contemporary missionary colleagues, he also received a year's initial training in Chinese language at the University of London before he left for Malacca in 1839.[11] These classes were given by Samuel Kidd (1804–43), an experienced missionary-scholar who had worked with Chinese people in Malacca.[12]

Unlike others who would come during the third generation of foreign missionaries to the Qing dynasty, Legge did not follow the trends adopted by James Hudson Taylor (1836–1904) and others, who lived within Chinese villages, wore Chinese clothes, ate Chinese food, and so adopted a form of

---

and *The Sacred Books of China*, including fourteen different volumes in their first editions.

8. Documented in detail in Pfister, *Striving*, vol. 1, 63–89.

9. This institution later became part of the larger University of Aberdeen in the 1860s.

10. Documented in Pfister, *Striving*, vol. 1, 99–106.

11. Documented in Barrett, *Singular Listlessness*, and Pfister, *Striving*, vol. 1, 114–17.

12. It can be added here that Legge also earned two honorary doctorates: one in the early 1840s from an American university in New York and another in 1884 from the University of Edinburgh.

Christian life which could be identified as "thoroughly Chinese."[13] He did, however, learn to live and work in Chinese languages, having started briefly with Fujianese, then shifting to Cantonese, and later to what we now would call Mandarin.[14] He preached and published religious and other pamphlets in Chinese, both in the more literary style, or *wenli*, as well as in Cantonese demotic (popular language), teaching Chinese students in the Anglo-Chinese College.[15] This set the cross-cultural stage for his most important engagement with Chinese intellectual life: the creation of English renderings and Protestant Christian interpretations of the Ruist ("Confucian") Scriptures—the Four Books and the Five Classics.[16] He initiated this work with the publication of the Four Books[17] in 1861 and continued it following his 1868 retirement as a missionary for the LMS, while serving as the English pastor of Union Church from 1870–73, and subsequently as Oxford's first professor of Chinese language and literature at Corpus Christi College (1876–97). He completed the largest and last volume of the Five Classics, the *Record of the Rites* (*Liji*), in 1885.[18] How this all related to his approach to establishing and nurturing Chinese Protestant churches in Hong Kong and the Qing empire is a matter we will consider in greater detail below.

---

13. Consult Pfister, "Attitudes towards Chinese Cultures."

14. Proof of his work in the first two languages came from an early phrase book he published. See Legge, *Lexilogus*, 1841. Later, in the 1850s he also published several Chinese Christian tracts in Cantonese. Only when he began working with Wang Tao (1828–97) in 1863 did he determine that he needed to learn the official's language to converse with his scholarly collaborator.

15. The Anglo-Chinese College (referred to in Chinese as the *Ying Hua shuyuan*) had been initially established by Robert Morrison and William Milne in Malacca in 1818. It was taken over by Legge in 1840 and subsequently moved to Hong Kong in 1843 soon after the colony of Hong Kong was established. Though Legge himself disbanded the school in 1856 for reasons concerning that it was not fulfilling its Christian mission (Legge, "The Colony of Hong Kong"), it was later re-established in Hong Kong in the 1920s and continues to exist there in the twenty-first century. See one account of Legge's role in that institution in Malacca in Harrison, *Waiting for China*, and an alternative in Pfister, *Striving*, vol. 1: 128–51.

16. As embodied in Legge's *The Chinese Classics* and *The Sacred Books of China*.

17. Consisting of the *Analects*, the *Great Learning*, the *Doctrine of the Mean* (or his preferred title: *The State of Equilibrium and Harmony*) in the first volume of *The Chinese Classics* (in that order), and followed in the same year with the publication of the *Mencius* in the second volume.

18. This goal was fulfilled by means of the full eight tomes in five volumes of Legge's *Chinese Classics* (1861–72) and the first four volumes of his contributions to *The Sacred Books of China* (1879–85).

UNUSUAL ROOTS IN SCOTLAND AND GREAT BRITAIN

As we know from Legge's extensive preface to a volume honoring his eldest brother George after his death,[19] he came from a family of Protestant Dissenters[20] in Huntly, Scotland, who were profoundly influenced by Congregational piety and Christian progressiveness.[21] This involved a Scottish form of Sabbath culture that highlighted biblical exegesis within worship and a post-millennial eschatology which motivated James' understanding of his mission. George (1801–61) became a noted pastor-scholar, and later the principal leader of the Congregationalist movement in Great Britain, and so was one whom James, as the youngest of four sons, sincerely revered.[22]

James Legge's own rise as a scholar was already manifest in 1835, at the time he graduated with highest honors from King's College, Aberdeen. He had excelled in classical Greek and Latin training as well as in the study of Scottish Realism, or the Scottish Commonsense philosophical tradition. This Christian intellectual tradition he learned primarily through the reading of Dugald Stewart's (1753–1828) writings. After he had served as a teacher in Blackpool for a few years, Legge's Christian convictions became self-conscious, and his commitments to mission work emerged as the goal of his life, so that when he started seminary training in the fall of 1837 at the Congregational school, Highbury College, he declared himself to be a "missions student."[23] There he learned biblical Hebrew and sharpened his classical Greek by practicing exegesis in New Testament Greek. Within a year, he had also initiated his study of Chinese language at University College in London.[24] Lessons were based on directions gained from Robert Morrison's dictionary and the initial renderings of *The Four Books* by David Collie,[25] another missionary educator who had worked in Malacca. As

---

19. A preface of over 110 pages in length, providing numerous details about his childhood, found at the beginning of Legge, *Lectures on Theology, Science and Revelation*.

20. That is, non-Anglican.

21. See a summary of this background in Girardot, *Victorian Translation*, 17–31, and an alternative account in Pfister, *Striving*, vol. 1: 18–34, 43–61.

22. This Scottish form of filial piety, enacted in Legge's own effort to edit a volume in his elder brother's honor after his death (Legge, *Lectures on Theology, Science and Revelation*), gave the missionary great sympathy with Chinese forms of filial piety. Consult Pfister, *Striving*, vol. 2: 138–40.

23. Pfister, *Striving*, vol. 1: 99–100.

24. See an account of Kidd's role in the emergence of British Sinology in Barrett, *Singular Listlessness*.

25. A work published in Malacca in 1828.

others have clarified, this was a meager, but still promising, way to begin Chinese studies.[26]

Before travelling to Asia, Legge married the daughter of the Reverend John Morison (1791–1859), who was one of the directors of the LMS and pastor of Trevor Chapel, where Legge served as a young minister.[27] Imbued with missionary zeal like her husband, Mary Isabella Morison (1815–53) was a mainstay as both a missionary educator of girls and familial supporter of the missionary-scholar, having also learned Chinese in her own right.[28] Five years after Mary's death in childbirth in Hong Kong, Legge married the widow of a Congregational minister, Hannah Mary Willetts (*née* Johnston, 1822–81). Hannah accompanied him to Hong Kong during the period when Legge began to publish *The Chinese Classics*, but she found the climate too difficult to endure and so returned to Britain in 1865, awaiting the eventual return of her husband two years later.[29] Such were the sacrifices of foreign missionaries in Hong Kong and China.

Still, one might say that it was John Morison that left the deepest impression, along with George Legge, on James Legge's distinctive theology. They both advocated a form of eschatology referred to technically as postmillennialism, a distinct theological commitment of many British evangelical Protestants in the mid-nineteenth century. It argued that Christ's presence would not be made known at the end of history through the resurrected Jesus' personal return, but by means of the overflowing of the Holy Spirit throughout the world.[30] This prompted hope that the Qing empire would join the family of "Christian nations" due to the impact of foreign missionaries, a vision that was expressed in some of Morison's and James Legge's works as well as in George Legge's lectures.[31]

UNUSUAL HABITS AND CHARACTER

How can one briefly characterize this unusual missionary and portray something about the qualities of his life as well as the vigor that allowed him to be such a productive force within both Chinese Protestant traditions

---

26. Elaborated in Pfister, *Striving*, vol. 1: 111–12.

27. Morison's own prolific authorship and influence on Legge is undeniable. See Pfister, *Striving*, vol. 1: 106–11, 242–47.

28. Pfister, *Striving*, vol. 1: 112–17; vol. 2: 6–7, 26–28.

29. Pfister, *Striving*, vol. 2: 86, 145–46, 165–68.

30. Pfister, *Striving*, vol. 1: 106–8, 242–45.

31. See in particular Legge's "Land of Sinim" and *Lectures on Theology, Science and Revelation*.

and Anglophone Sinological worlds? Being a fairly portly figure by the time he finished his missionary career in 1868, Legge as a young man sported a head of wavy reddish hair and was hampered so much by being tone deaf that those who did not know the Chinese languages he spoke could still discern his Scottish accent when he spoke in Chinese. Nevertheless, his tone-deafness did not make him unwilling to prepare poetry for hymns and hymnals, which became a vital part of the Protestant form of life he helped to nurture among Chinese converts. More significantly, he learned early in life to get up early in order to read and study,[32] and so in Hong Kong he continued to use the early morning hours for scholarship, while he devoted normal daylight hours to missionary and pastoral work. All of this supererogatory effort was accompanied by a remarkable ability to memorize at length, a strength which became particularly notable in his biblical meditations and his preparation of *The Chinese Classics*.[33] Undoubtedly, as a Christian missionary, Legge was a master of the Bible, leaving for posterity more than four hundred sermon notebooks handwritten in English during the nearly thirty years of his missionary career. These reveal much about his theological orientation, spiritual values, and worldview, as well as missionary reflections about his Chinese context.[34]

UNUSUAL CONTRIBUTIONS TO THE CHINESE PROTESTANT CHURCH

Because Legge served as a Protestant missionary during the period when Protestant missionary societies had their first sustained encounter with the Qing empire, and because his own work was set in the context of a British colonial setting (distinct from those working within the Qing empire itself), his efforts at consolidating a small Protestant community took on the force of pioneer precedents. We see this in his discussion of the nature of church life, his promotion of weekly rhythms in which Christian worship had a major part, and the basic cross-cultural effort that it took for Legge and

32. Stimulated by a very serious accident that forced him to spend most of his time in bed for nearly three months. See Pfister, *Striving*, vol. 1: 48–53.

33. While on a boat to China in 1847, Legge memorized the whole book of Hebrews in the New Testament. He was also known to have access by memory to many passages of the Ruist canonical texts which he had rendered and interpreted for Anglophone readers, demonstrating this on numerous occasions. This certainly was an immensely important skill in China, where memorization of the Ruist canon was the basis of traditional education for young men.

34. These are currently held in the Archive of World Christian Missions at the Library of the School of Oriental and African Studies in London.

his Chinese compatriot (and later co-pastor), Ho Tsun-sheen (He Jinshan 1817–71),[35] to explain and assert alternative forms of calendars. With regard to Sunday worship, he not only asserted his role as a minister offering sermons, but he also created Chinese Christian pamphlets and produced Chinese hymnals, all reflecting Protestant values within a self-consciously chosen Chinese intellectual context.

Soon after arriving in the Hong Kong colony and being granted land to establish the LMS base, Legge joined a few others in 1844 in founding a new kind of Protestant church, an ecumenical community named Union Church. This was a bilingual Cantonese-English Protestant congregation, established with the Christian gospel as its main focus, without presenting any distinctive denominational label.[36] Though innovative in its own right, this effort was quickly challenged by the presence of Anglican, Baptist, and Roman Catholic institutions, so that it later developed into something more like the Congregational church orientation that Legge had experienced in Scotland. Nevertheless, it never did assume a specific denominational label. In the 1870s (after Legge departed Hong Kong for the last time) it split into two independent communities along linguistic lines, which remain to this day.[37]

Rather than following the more elaborate and traditional forms of worship found in Roman Catholic and High-Church Anglican traditions, Legge supported a form of worship based upon biblical preaching and teaching,[38] accompanied by contemporary Protestant hymns that were being translated, written, and promoted as aspects of worship within Congregational settings. Fang-lan Hsieh has documented how Legge, following a precedent established by his predecessors in the LMS, created a Chinese hymnal in 1842, which included twenty-seven new hymns under the title *Sacred Odes to Nourish the Heart-Mind* (*Yang xin Shen Shi*).[39] It can be assumed that

35. Also known as Ho Fuk-tong in Hong Kong history, this person from the Nanhai District of Guangdong province worked with Legge as a student, colleague, and, finally, co-pastor of the bilingual Union Church from the period of 1840 until his death in 1871. See Pfister, "A Transmitter but not a Creator."

36. As described in Pfister, *Striving*, vol. 1: 167–68.

37. The English language congregation maintained the name "Union Church" in English and now has two congregations on the Hong Kong island and Kowloon peninsula. The Cantonese language congregation became known as the Hop Yat Church and also has several communities still surviving under this name on the island and in Kowloon within the Chinese Christian churches in Hong Kong.

38. As documented in the Chinese leaflet Legge prepared before he retired from his missionary position; see Legge, *Shenghui zhunsheng*.

39. Hsieh, *Chinese Christian Hymnody*, 14–15. Notably, this was the year before he travelled with a small group of other like-minded persons, including his Chinese

he involved his Chinese co-workers, Liang Fa and Ho Tsun-sheen, if not others, in the translation and production process of this hymnal.[40] Every ten years he revised and lengthened it, so that by 1852, it had seventy-nine Chinese hymns and seven doxologies, and in 1862, when Legge himself had become something of a local hero,[41] he produced a another hymnal under a new name with eighty-five Chinese hymns and seven doxologies.[42] These precedents influenced and inspired the creation of other hymnals by foreign missionaries in both Hong Kong and elsewhere in China.[43] The original hymns were often sung without any instrumental accompaniment in Scotland, unlike the choirs led by elegant organ music as found in other Christian traditions of his day in European settings.

Yet, having affirmed this distinctive kind of worship as biblically sound, Legge asserted (along with other missionaries, Protestant and Roman Catholic alike) that an even more basic element in the Christian life was the rhythm of congregational worship on the seventh day of every weekly cycle. This temporal and cultural condition was necessary for establishing congregational worship as a "form of life," the setting aside of one day within a seven-day week when the normal patterns of work-life were suspended, and worship and activities which promoted Christian worship took precedence. Linking it to the fourth commandment in the Mosaic Decalogue, Legge also supported this form of life because it sustained and extended the influences of the fledgling Chinese Christian community within the larger society. We have previously described this as "Sabbath culture" (*anxiri wenhua*).[44]

While Legge was manifestly intent on transferring his British experiences of Sabbath culture to the complicated Chinese-Malay context in Malacca, and later to the primarily Cantonese context of Hong Kong and southeastern China, this "transplanting" involved fundamental shifts in the nature of cultural timing that challenged prevailing imperial precedents that still influenced Chinese people who immigrated into the British colony of Hong Kong during the first two decades of the colony's existence. Legge's awareness of this basic problem is found in his early attempt in the

---

colleagues, to the newly established colony of Hong Kong.

40. This is not mentioned by Hsieh, but can be concluded from the style of work he maintained in both Malacca and Hong Kong. See Pfister, *Striving*.

41. Described in Pfister, *Striving*, vol. 2: 67–220. Illustrated in Legge, *Journal of a Missionary Tour*.

42. Documented in Hsieh, *Chinese Christian Hymnody*, 15, 28.

43. Those hymnals produced by William C. Burns (1815–88), Rudolph Lechler (1824–1908), and John Chalmers (1825–99), as documented in Hsieh, *Chinese Christian Hymnody*, 35, 49–50.

44. In Pfister, *Striving*, vol. 1: 30–34, 110–11, 140–43, 159–60; vol. 2: 224–28.

mid-1840s to offer an alternative form of life and calendrical time to the imperial calendar published every year and promoted throughout the Qing empire. He did this in collaboration with Ho Tsun-sheen in a set of articles attached to the imperially authorized calendar for the year 1844.[45]

Legge and Ho's determination to "set the times" right through this almanac was complicated and counter-culturally bold. First of all, the Qing imperial calendar was based on a lunar cycle, so it did not fully overlap with the solar year of the nineteenth-century Christian calendar. In general, therefore, the "normal" solar week generally did not overlap with the lunar week, making it very confusing for any Chinese person unaware of what a "Sunday" was to make sense of those Christian claims. So, though there was a seven-day week employed in Chinese calendrical thinking, nevertheless each lunar month consisted of four seven-day weeks, with special days serving as auspicious and inauspicious days determined by other standards than Christian holidays such as Easter and Christmas. For foreign Christians to assert the value of their own holidays while de-emphasizing the imperially sponsored "auspicious and inauspicious days" could be seen (if taken in the most controversial light) as an attempt at trumping the imperial order of time.

Most significantly, Chinese persons were not at all accustomed to setting aside a day for religious worship on a weekly basis. As a consequence, this had to be justified thoroughly, not only in the light of European standards of the "Sabbath" or "Sunday" worship cycles, but also within Chinese canonical texts.[46] On the contrary, due to the rude materialistic and sensate attitudes of many British and Scottish merchants who took up residence in Hong Kong during the 1840s and 1850s, those Chinese workers that they hired were easily influenced to take up a similarly materialistic and self-oriented form of life. Due to this, Legge presented three sermons addressing the nature of the "Christian Sabbath," preaching these first from the pulpit of Union Church and then later publishing them for public consumption within the colony among Anglophone readers.[47] Especially in the third sermon, Legge minced no words in criticizing the greedy and selfish attitudes of nominally Christian persons who lived in ways that opposed Christian values and who promoted "workaholic" extremism, sensual profligacy, and gross materialistic selfishness that he considered to be nothing less than

45. See Pfister, "Resetting 'Our' Time-pieces" and Pfister, *Striving*, vol. 1: 173–77.

46. Legge himself became aware of one such attempt produced in a "morality book" authored most likely by an older Ruist scholar he had met in 1843, a person named Luo Zhongfan (d. c. 1850). Some account of Legge's interaction with Luo is found in Pfister, "Discovering Monotheistic Metaphysics."

47. Legge, *The Ordinance of the Sabbath*.

shameful among Chinese workers. Here we see Legge's own efforts to promote Sabbath culture not only among Chinese residents of the colony of Hong Kong, but also among British, Scottish, and other foreign residents living within the colony.

In relationship to the very small Chinese Protestant circles of those times, there is no doubt that these commitments promoted by Legge directly influenced the lives of Ho Tsun-sheen, along with the Chinese manager of the Anglo-Chinese press, Wong Shing (Huang Sheng, 1827–1902), and others within the Chinese community of Union Church. Notably, Legge and Ho's ministry and form of Sabbath culture had an unusual influence on the writings of one of the most notable leaders among the Taiping reformers, Hong Rengan (1822–64), who served as an evangelist apprentice with Legge and Ho in the LMS from 1854–58.[48] Another less prominent as well as less consistent Christian, but nevertheless an important educational reformer in the Qing empire, Wang Tao (1828–97) was also directly influenced by Legge's life in this regard.[49]

UNUSUAL CHALLENGES

Among the explicit goals of many nineteenth-century missionaries to China was the hope of creating an indigenous Chinese Protestant church with its own leadership and an intergenerational form of life that could endure through all the transformations that its members' lives would have as a consequence of their becoming Christians within the Qing empire. But serious debates took place about which methods should be employed, some including the famous missionary Carl Gutzlaff (or Karl Gützlaff 1803–51), who believed that it would be easier to spread the gospel by means of Chinese colporteurs, without any need of foreign missionaries joining them. Legge and others opposed this approach because it could be easily abused, and they demonstrated that Gutzlaff's efforts were ultimately defeated by colporteurs who had cheated him, making false reports, and not achieving most of the goals that Gutzlaff had set out for them to do.[50]

---

48. This unusual influence on Hong Rengan has been elaborated in Pfister, *Striving*, vol. 2: 30–33, 40–44, 48–60.

49. As documented in part in Pfister, "The Response of Wang Tao," as well as Pfister, *Striving*, vol. 2: 146–52, 233–35.

50. The discovery of the deception and cheating involved among Gutzlaff's members of the "Chinese Christian Union" was one of the burdens Legge took upon himself in 1849. See Pfister, *Striving*, vol. 2: 11–13.

Nevertheless, Legge encountered surprises, including the development of a genuinely voluntary Chinese Christian local movement in a small town named Poklo. It involved an unusual figure who had been the keeper of the Temple to Master Kong in that town, a person named Chëa Kam Kwong (Che Jinguang, c. 1800–1861).[51] As it turned out, Chëa became a voluntary evangelist who, independent of missionary guidance, began to gather together new Chinese Christian converts in that area. He began to interact with Legge and Ho Tsun-sheen early on in order to verify his Christian experience and to lead those who had followed his evangelistic efforts into a more stable form of communal Christian life. This unexpected challenge opened the door to a number of new and risky steps in missionary work in the Qing empire in which Legge personally took part.[52]

Legge himself sought to create an indigenous Protestant church in Hong Kong. He hoped to establish church communities that did not reflect the cultural and political differences that many Protestant denominations necessarily involved. Along with Ho Tsun-sheen, Legge supported the establishment of Union Church as a bilingual community, led by several foreign pastors and one Chinese pastor and based strictly upon biblical principles that reflected Legge's own Congregational background. In addition, mission outreaches within the nearby Qing dynasty were accomplished by well-trained and articulate Chinese Christian representatives. So, even though the experiences in the town of Poklo were unusual, it is notable that Pastor Ho Tsun-sheen led a group of Chinese members from Union Church to help establish a missionary station of their own during the late 1860s within the larger eastern Cantonese town of Foshan or "Buddha Mountain."[53] In all such cases, as we will see, these efforts were taken because of the freedoms made possible by "unequal" treaties, so they regularly provoked resentment on the part of Chinese people who were antagonistic toward what they perceived to be a foreign religious presence in their own home towns.

Another major challenge that faced foreign missionaries in the 1850s was related to these questions about the means of indigenization. A group of theistic Chinese militants began to follow a person they referred to as the Taiping King, and some wondered if this kind of indigenous Christian uprising could ultimately benefit foreign Christian missionary work. The military successes of the disciplined Taiping armies were eventually undone by the corruption of its king and leadership, and they were ultimately

---

51. Story recreated in Pfister, "The Proto-Martyr of Chinese Protestants."

52. Described in Legge, *Journal of a Missionary Tour*. See also Pfister, *Striving*, vol. 2: 121–24.

53. Described in Pfister, *Striving*, vol. 2: 198–99, 207–8.

destroyed by Qing and foreign forces in 1864. Yet throughout the decade in which they overran nearly half of the Qing empire, the Taiping became a major challenge to foreign missionaries, including Legge, who sought to discern the actual spiritual character and level of political stability of this unusual indigenous religious rebellion.

One sign that Legge was not simply transplanting Scottish Congregationalism into the Hong Kong environment, but facing new Chinese cultural and Hong Kong colonial situations with a sensitivity to concrete needs, is manifest in his involvement with public education. Having been the principal of the Anglo-Chinese College in Malacca early in his career, Legge shut it down when he was in Hong Kong and began promoting a government-sponsored progressive approach to Chinese Christian education. In both cases, he had sincerely hoped this form of education would lead to a viable Chinese Protestant lifestyle among his students, but having seen that the Anglo-Chinese College had generally not achieved this purpose with its relatively small number of students, he chose to shift his focus to public education instead.[54] In this regard, Legge stood against his own Congregational denominational tradition in Scotland and England. There, Congregationalists preferred not to have any government involvement in education and promoted strong alternatives in the form of Sunday schools. Living in the British colonial context within Hong Kong, Legge reconsidered the feasibility of such a counter-cultural expression of education in what was essentially a southeastern Chinese cultural context, and he chose to support a government-funded educational system which could still have strong elements of Christian teaching.[55] The progressive nature of this colonial education system included a strong commitment to childhood education, including both male and female students in separate schools, as well as support for theological training for all prospective Chinese pastoral candidates. The Christian influences in the Hong Kong education system have remained a major factor in Hong Kong public education ever since that time in the early 1860s.

Perhaps the most significant cross-cultural challenge addressed by Legge was the question of the relationship between Protestant Christianity and the intellectual and spiritual traditions of Ruism or "Confucianism." Having come to his convictions with the regular and immense interpretive

---

54. Legge had established a seminary as part of the Anglo-Chinese College with the hope of nurturing a generation of Chinese Protestant pastors, but the vast majority of the Chinese students did not take up this role for their lives. Nevertheless, his part in establishing the public education sector in Hong Kong was profound and pioneering. See Wang Man Kong, "Chinese Culture."

55. Dealt with briefly in Pfister, *Striving*, vol. 2: 96.

support of Ho Tsun-sheen in the late 1840s, Legge remained a strong advocate for the transformative alignments between various elements of Christianity and Ruism, and he essentially supported what could be referred to as a Ruified form of a Chinese Protestant sub-culture. He justified this and practiced it selectively by several means and at different cultural levels.

First of all, this Ruified Protestant culture showed itself through his choices for rendering theological terms in Chinese in all his works, particularly in his translations of biblical passages,[56] and through his understanding of the religious nature of Ruism.[57] Legge firmly supported a style of translating key theological terms in the Chinese Bible with terminology that was either borrowed from or resonated well with Ruist canonical literature.[58] In this light, then, he argued for the use of "*Shangdi*" as the equivalent for "God" (that is, *Elohim* with singular verbs and *ho theos* in the main biblical languages) and "*shenling*" as opposed to "*Shen*" and *shingling* for the "Holy Spirit." Notably, he also preferred "*xili*" (the ritual of "washing") to" *jinli*" (the ritual of "immersion") to render the term "baptism" in the New Testament, following the practices of Scottish Congregationalists of his day.[59] In addition to this basic orientation that affected the preaching, hymn renderings, and the way of worship that he and others promoted within Union Church, Legge and others also employed the teachings of Mencius to justify the Christian lifestyle.[60] In other words, there were moral values in the Protestant Christian lifestyle that completely agreed with certain ethical values promoted in this major work of canonical Ruist traditions. Finally, Legge honored the ancient Ruist teachings that supported the worship and reverence of *Shangdi*, which he and some other missionary-scholars took to be the equivalent of the basic concept of God in the Bible. All of these factors were subsequently realized in the two Chinese commentaries of the first two books of the New Testament produced by the Reverend Ho Tsun-sheen in the 1850s, a creative effort exemplifying a nineteenth-century Ruified form of Protestant traditions, which had Legge's full support and which continued to be influential for at least three decades within Hong Kong and the Qing empire.[61]

56. Pfister, "Bible Translations" and Pfister, *Striving*, vol. 1, "Interlude," 187–96, 279–86.

57. Legge, *Religions of China* and Pfister, "Nineteenth Century Ruist Metaphysical Terminology."

58. Consult Legge, *An Argument for Shang-Te* and *The Notions of the Chinese concerning God and Spirits*.

59. General details about the debates can be found in Zetzsche, *The Bible in China*.

60. Elaborated in Pfister, "Mengizian Matrix."

61. Pfister, *Striving*, vol. 2: 34–42.

Finally, Legge confronted one of the most difficult challenges of his career in opposing British and other foreign forms of militarism as well as British mercantile involvement with selling opium within the Qing empire. He addressed both of these issues publicly and consistently throughout his careers as a missionary in Hong Kong and professor at Oxford.[62] In 1861, within the first volume of his *Chinese Classics,* Legge made explicit in his introductory essays, with a literary subtlety that might be overlooked by some, that he preferred the humane form of Ruist government to British militarism.[63] This was also fulfilled in his willingness to die rather than have gunboats punish angry Chinese mobs when he travelled up the East River in Guangdong Province in 1861,[64] indicating the sincerity of his convictions, which stood in antagonism to militaristic attitudes even under the "unequal" treaty conditions that he could have upheld. The unusual level of these challenges entailed even his own preconceived death at the hands of a mob, but he was willing to lay down his life, just as Chinese Christians he had known had done.

UNUSUAL CONFLICTS AND FAILURES

While we have already indicated the conflicts that arose due to different approaches to mass evangelization and means of indigenizing the Protestant way of life in China, particularly in Legge's contrast to the methods of Gutzlaff, Legge's most poignantly felt conflicts came with the sufferings and deaths of Chinese Christians whom he worked with and knew personally. These included the murder of Chëa Kam Kwong in October 1861,[65] and the mob violence endured by his co-pastor, Ho Tsun-sheen, which ultimately led to his early death in 1871. Ho had been greatly traumatized during the public inauguration of a new Protestant chapel in the town of Foshan in 1870 when a mob surrounded the building and set it afire while the worshippers, including Ho, were still in the building.[66]

Perhaps the most painful conflict which stood in opposition to Legge's advocacy of a Ruified form of Christianity, his accommodationist form of

62. Legge's earliest public statements in England against opium and British militarism came in 1859, Legge, "The Land of Sinim." Later, in his ethical reflections comparing Christianity and Ruism, he continued to return to the problem of opium. See Legge, *Christianity and Confucianism Compared* and Legge, "Confucianism in Relation to Christianity."

63. Legge, *The Chinese Classics,* vol. 1 (1893), *Prolegomena,* 105.

64. Pfister, *Striving,* vol. 2: 122.

65. For other details see Pfister, *Striving,* vol. 2: 88–91, 113–18, 121–24.

66. Documented in Pfister, *Striving,* vol. 2: 207.

missionary apologetics, and his scholarship related to Ruist spirituality, came in the charge that he was actually promoting a heresy.[67] His opponents were fellow missionaries in China, yet these charges were taken up in Shanghai in 1877 and 1878 after he had already left China. These charges did not cause Legge to waver in his convictions, as was repeatedly testified in later writings.[68] One might recognize a parallel set of critiques of a different order from Marxist, Orientalist, and post-colonial perspectives as having a similar sharpness, but even here Legge's arguments and way of life largely stand up to scrutiny.[69]

When we consider Legge's contributions and involvements in the life of nineteenth-century Chinese Protestant churches, we must not overlook his own sense of failure at some key junctures of his own missionary and pastoral careers. First of all, his dream of providing theological education for an indigenous Protestant clergy through the seminary associated with the Anglo-Chinese College failed; he closed its doors in 1856, which he spoke and wrote about it publicly in Hong Kong.[70] Secondly, the denominational structures of Protestant Christianity tended to overwhelm his own vision of a "united church." Even though both the English and Chinese congregations of Union Church exist even today in twenty-first-century Hong Kong, they are now part of the normal Protestant denominational matrix and are not the alternative ecumenical form of spirituality that he had hoped to foster in Hong Kong and China. Related to his pastoral concerns were the immense troubles caused by the extreme sufferings of Chinese missionary efforts pursued by Chëa Kam Kwong and Ho Tsun-sheen. Though in later decades Protestant communities did re-emerge in both Poklo and Foshan, and Legge could rejoice in these realities, the initial defeats profoundly disturbed him and others. Furthermore, though Legge and Ho Tsun-sheen argued for a form of Chinese theological discourse that would allow for Ruist-inspired terminology to be infused into Chinese versions of the Bible and Protestant worship, their justifications were only partially successful. The problems of the "interminable term question" would continue to pester missionary debates for decades after Legge passed away. Later in life, Legge accepted that he may have been too forceful in his assertions, and accepted the compromises adopted in Chinese biblical translations in a rather stoical fashion.

---

67. Elaborated in Girardot, *Victorian Translation*, 192–234.

68. Seen in Legge's *Religions of China*, in the first, third, and fourth volumes of *The Sacred Books of China*, and in his essay, "Christianity and Confucianism compared."

69. Pfister, "In the Eye of a Tornado."

70. Legge, "The Colony of Hong Kong."

More personally difficult for Legge to handle were criticisms that came from the hierarchy of the London Missionary Society in the 1860s that questioned the value and the use of time involved in his producing *The Chinese Classics*. This disturbed him significantly, but the criticisms were later overcome in his favor by the majority of the directors of the LMS. So, while these criticisms did not deter him from continuing his efforts, they probably did hasten his retirement from missionary service.[71]

Finally, major political events highlighted some of Legge's deeper frustrations and points where his post-millennial hopes were severely tested. With regard to British and missionary questions related to the early stages of the Taiping movement, Legge had advocated a principled neutrality, hoping this might lead to a more balanced and transformative influence of Protestant Christian leaders on the Taiping leadership. But hotter heads prevailed, including the involvement of his younger evangelist apprentice, Hong Rengan, who later was executed as one of the key leaders in the later stages of the Taiping Rebellion. Legge's dismay and great disappointment at the outcome of these matters was palpable in everything he wrote about it. As a consequence, he was particularly enraged at the perfidy of the British Foreign Secretary in 1863, Frederick Wright-Bruce (1814–67), who spoke publicly of the "problem" that foreign missionaries were in the Qing empire. Legge produced a scathing and brilliant critique of the British leader's judgments, publishing it in both London and Hong Kong.[72] But this battle would continue to be a source of painful struggle for British missionaries in subsequent decades as well. Ironically, their culturally transformative influence among Chinese Protestants was being negated by the capitalist and militant attitudes of the British government, right at a time when cross-cultural understanding and symbiotic forms of Chinese Protestant life promised far more balanced and fruitful possibilities, even though still minuscule in numbers and size.

UNUSUAL ACHIEVEMENTS FOR THE CHINESE CHURCH

Serving as a missionary, educator, pastor, and scholar, Legge's impact on the fledgling communities of Chinese Protestant churches is one of the key factors in their stability and growth in the mid-nineteenth century. His promotion of a distinct form of Sabbath culture has become a cultural standard of Chinese Protestant communities, though they have certainly been

---

71. Pfister, *Striving*, vol. 2: 137, 144.
72. Discussed in Pfister, *Striving*, vol. 2: 140–42.

transformed through the two revolutions that occurred in 1911 and 1949, after Legge's death in 1897. Having nurtured a form of Ruified Christianity in his missionary, pastoral, and scholarly roles, Legge could point to the work of the indigenous Chinese Protestant Ho Tsun-sheen and the efforts of the indigenous Chinese Protestant missionary efforts in Poklo and Foshan as manifestations of this unusual form of Chinese Christian indigenization. In later decades following Legge's departure from Hong Kong, the bilingual Union Chapel evolved into a number of different church communities based on either English or Cantonese languages. This evolution indicated the continuing need for indigenization even in Hong Kong. While this went beyond Legge's concern for a form of ecumenical Protestant life, these communities have continued to participate in the far more significant Christian influences within Hong Kong in the last two centuries.

Whatever else one might say about Legge's missionary-scholar career, his effort to provide a way forward in addressing Ruist-Christian ethical and cultural questions increased the creative possibilities for Chinese Protestants to express their Christian worldview and values in a form of life that could be indigenized in justified ways within the Qing empire.

4

Griffith John
Faithful Pioneer Missionary

Noel Gibbard

GRIFFITH JOHN WAS A missionary in China with the London Missionary Society. During his stay of over fifty years, he made substantial contributions as a pioneering evangelist and able organizer, establishing churches, schools, and hospitals. He also authored numerous books and articles, and committed himself to Bible translation.

BACKGROUND

Griffith John was born in Swansea, Wales, on December 14, 1831. The town had prospered by this time because of the growth of industry, particularly copper.[1] John's father, Griffith John, Sr., was a copper man and became a foreman in the Vivian and Sons works, which meant that he earned a better wage than most of the workers. However, his parents were not "moderately wealthy," as some authors have claimed.[2] The family of six lived in a small, terraced house. In a cholera outbreak in 1832, John's mother died, leaving his father with four children. John lost his father to cholera in 1849, the very

---

1. Jones, "Industrial Community," 119–20.
2. Tiedemann, *Handbook of Christianity*, 183; Greegan, *Great Missionaries*, 76.

year in which he was preparing for college.[3] In his application to college, he wrote that he was unable to pay tuition.[4]

Swansea was staunchly Nonconformist[5] in religion. Griffith John's father had been a deacon at Ebenezer Independent Church, where he and his wife had enjoyed the ministry of David Davies in their youth. Davies was an outstanding, missionary-minded evangelical preacher, who zealously supported the London Missionary Society. This interest in mission was maintained by Davies' successors at Ebenezer, Thomas Davies and Elijah Jacob. John was received into membership when he was eight years old, having experienced deep religious impressions. He also started preaching at a young age, and by the time he was sixteen years old, he was known as the "boy preacher."[6] Elijah Jacob prepared the young man to enter Brecon Independent College, and John commenced his studies there in 1850.[7] During this time, he began to desire to work overseas. Two factors confirmed that desire: the reading of Isaiah 6 and the visit of David Griffiths, a former missionary to Madagascar.[8] John received further training at Bedford Academy in England, before being accepted by the London Missionary Society. Initially, he thought of going to Madagascar, but agreed with the directors to go to China.

In 1855, Griffith John sailed to China with his wife, Margaret, the daughter of David Griffiths. The journey took four months, but John did not waste his time. He settled down to a regular course of study that added to his preparation for work in China. His studies included the biblical languages, mathematics, natural philosophy (science), animal and vegetable physiology, and chemistry. In a letter to his minister in Swansea, John mentioned specific works, including, "Barnes on Revelation, Gilbert on the Atonement, and Dr. Payne on Original Sin."[9] His reading was wide-ranging and developed his convictions concerning God, creation, and salvation. Griffith John was ready to begin the work of a lifetime. Little did he know that he would spend the whole of his life in China.

---

3. Gibbard, *Griffith John*, 15, 27, and the chapter as a whole.
4. "Questionnaire," box 27, no. 246, Council for World Mission.
5. That is, non-Anglican. [Ed.]
6. Thompson, *Fifty Years*, 9.
7. Ibid., 13–15.
8. Gibbard, *Griffith John*, 27.
9. John, "Journal," Griffith John Papers, June 1855, 6, 9.

SHANGHAI

When Griffith John arrived in Shanghai, he could not have wished for a better reception. Some of the outstanding London Missionary Society missionaries were stationed in the city. Referring to them later in life, John wrote of Dr. Medhurst, "with forty years of magnificent service"; William Muirhead, "one of the greatest evangelists the Christian Church has ever given to China"; Dr. William Lockhart, whose "reputation as a physician stood very high"; Joseph Edkins, "the great sinalogue and a friend"; and Alexander Wylie of the British and Foreign Bible Society, "the most remarkable man I have ever met."[10] The city, however, was not so welcoming. It had been opened to foreign trade in 1842, resulting in a greater concentration of people, greater volume of noise, and more dirt in the streets, making it difficult for the newcomer to settle in.

Three main challenges faced John. First, he had to tackle the language, which was absolutely necessary for mission work. It was a "colossus,"[11] but by the end of nine months, he was making good progress.[12] Once he had grasped the essentials of the language, John was ready to face his second challenge: taking the gospel into the interior. He visited a number of places, traveling as far as the Grand Canal with William Muirhead, but not without experiencing strong opposition.[13] The third challenge was to visit the Taiping rebels in order to find out what they really believed, share the Christian gospel with them, and discuss religious liberty. They were a dissenting religious group, influenced by aspects of Christian teaching, mainly through Issachar Roberts. The religious and social implication of their teaching was doing away with idolatry, and the political aim was to get rid of the Manchu dynasty. Their patriotism was expressed in a hostile attitude toward foreigners.[14]

Griffith John visited the rebels on two occasions, first in April 1860, and later in November of the same year. In spite of the devastation of the country as a result of the clash between the rebels and the imperial troops, John originally had sympathy for the rebels, but his visits to the leaders slowly changed his mind.[15] He realized that their beliefs were far from being Christian, especially concerning the person and work of Christ, and while

---

10. John, "In Memorium," 1–2; Gibbard, *Griffith John*, 36–37.
11. Thompson, *Fifty Years*, 51.
12. Ibid., 50–53.
13. Gibbard, *Griffith John*, 38–41.
14. Chesneaux, "Taiping," 38–39; Roberts, *Western Eyes*, 52–53.
15. John, "Journal," April 6, 1860–April 21, 1861.

the leaders were living in luxury, the people were dying of starvation. It is surprising that he took such a long time in changing his mind. As Broomhall said of him, "His optimism outstripped events."[16]

HANKOU

The city of Hankou was opened to foreign trade in 1860, and the Taiping rebels left early in 1861. John realized that there was an opportunity to pioneer mission work there and even expand from that center. He and Robert Wilson, another London Missionary Society missionary, arrived in Hankou on June 21, 1861. John settled down quickly and was out preaching on his first day in the city. A list of his early successes reveals his devotion to mission work:[17] on March 16, 1862, he baptized the first convert; on July 19, 1863, he opened the first chapel; on February 26, 1864, he opened the first school; on September 3, 1866, he opened the first hospital.

As in Shanghai, preaching was at the center of John's work in Hankou. He was careful to gather the converts together and form them into a church. He was church-centered in his thinking. John questioned the candidates for membership, and if satisfied, he would present their names to the local church. He divided inquirers into three groups, "1. Those who are actuated by pure motives only. 2. Those who are actuated by false motives only. 3. Those who are actuated by mixed motives."[18] Some have accused the missionaries in China of welcoming "rice Christians," that is, those who joined the church for its material benefits.[19] This was not true of John's practice in Hankou. He was a disciplinarian. Opium smokers and "renegade Roman Catholics" were refused admission, while a person could be disciplined for non-attendance.[20] As a Congregationalist, John argued strongly for infant baptism.[21] Denominational differences could be a problem for the Chinese, because they suggested a lack of unity amongst the missionaries. Furthermore, membership in denominations with overseas leadership placed Chinese believers under orders that were alien to their traditions.

Attention was also given to congregational singing. As early as 1862, John produced a hymnal of fifty hymns. The 1876 edition contained two hundred hymns, some of them translated from the Welsh by John and Evan

16. Broomhall, *Open Country*, 214.
17. Gibbard, *Griffith John*, 68–70.
18. John, "Present Aspect," 494.
19. Blake, "Foreign Devils," 238–39.
20. John, *Conference Shanghai, 1877*, 495; John, "Journal," March 28, 1868.
21. John, "Journal," February 6, 1857.

Bryant, another Welshman with the London Missionary Society.[22] The collection also reveals the influence of Ira Sankey's revival hymns on John.[23] Like other missionaries, he did not believe that Chinese singing was pleasing to the ear, but admired their enthusiasm and their desire to truly worship God. Unlike W. E. Southill, John did not advocate the use of Chinese melodies and Chinese instruments in church services.[24]

Unlike Arnold Foster, who believed that all appeals for money should be confined to the church, or Hudson Taylor, who advocated living "by faith," Griffith John had no qualms with going outside the church to seek financial support. He collected a monthly offering from the church, and between 1861–62 they had received enough funds to buy a piece of land for a cemetery and help two or three poor members of the congregation.[25] National workers, as well as the missionary, had to be paid a reasonable wage. Griffith John was angry when the LMS directors suggested lowering the wage of Chinese colleagues. He pointed out that Shen, the most efficient worker, only received two pounds and eight shillings, which was a "pittance."[26] Of the seven evangelists in 1879, five were paid by the Missionary Society, one was paid by the church, and others served voluntarily. John also had substantial help from the merchants of Hankou to build a chapel, two rooms, a house for an evangelist, and two schoolrooms, with a total cost of five hundred pounds. Half of the land that had been purchased was left ready to build a hospital.[27] John himself gave liberally to the work in central China, including about one thousand pounds to establish a theological college.[28]

---

22. MacGillivray, *Encyclopedia*, No. 2; Julian, *Dictionary*, 744.

23. Ira Sankey (1840–1908) was Dwight Moody's principal hymn composer and leader of singing during his highly influential meetings in England (beginning in 1872) and then in North America. [Ed.]

24. Southill, "Chinese Music," 228.

25. John, Letters, CWM, January 1, 1864, "Griffith John to My Dear Brother," box 3, folder 2.

26. John, Letters, CWM, December 6, 1879, "Griffith John to My Dear Mr. Whitehouse," box 4, folder 4.

27. Gibbard, *Griffith John*, 79, 119; Robson, *Hankow Mission*, 150.

28. Sparham, "Griffith John," 108. Known as the Divinity College.

PREACHING

John's advice to his fellow missionaries was, "Preach, Preach, Preach."[29] He was convinced that preaching was God's ordinary way of reconciling people unto himself. Although there were occasional declarations in the temples, the sermon was unknown in China. Some missionaries, such as J. L. Nevius, thought that the emphasis should be on teaching rather than preaching, since the latter method was alien to the Chinese.[30] The Roman Catholics concentrated on literature, teaching inquirers, and helping with social and legal problems.[31] For John, however, preaching the gospel was the greatest possible kindness to the Chinese, because it meant "dispensing the bread of life to perishing men."[32]

John adapted his preaching method to various situations. His aim was to reach the common people, unlike missionaries such as Timothy Richard, who aimed at reaching the scholars (although Griffith John was able to discuss with them as well).[33] During the week, he would be out in the street preaching and distributing tracts. He would enter a shop, gather people around him, and speak to them. On other occasions he would sit outside the preaching center and would speak and preach to those who were willing to listen.[34] The preaching center was open five afternoons a week, and people would come and go during the afternoon. The preacher could address the people briefly or could continue for a long time. Reports refer to John preaching for two hours, and one refers to a sermon lasting three hours. At the end of the first hour, the listeners asked him to continue and did so again at the end of two hours, but at the end of three hours, John had to stop because he was exhausted. Usually, he would have an evangelist to help him.[35]

Often, John would come down from the platform to join the people. He would throw out a question like, "Who is God"? Some would respond, and depending on the response, he would continue to expound Christian doctrine. This method of "familiar conversation," appealed to him.[36] If persons showed real interest, John would take them into the vestry, expound an

---

29. Thompson, *Fifty Years*, 187.
30. Nevius, "Methods," 59.
31. Gibbard, *Griffith John*, 46.
32. John, *China: Her Claims*, 59.
33. Richard, *Conversion*, 13; Gibbard, *Griffith John*, 48, 201.
34. Robson, *Hankow Mission*, 168; Thompson, *Fifty Years*, 185–87.
35. "Y Maes Cenadol," ("The Mission Field") 342.
36. John, *Conference Shanghai, 1877*, 91.

aspect of the gospel, and pray. On Sunday, he concentrated on the believers. The men and women would sit on opposite sides of the church. If a baby cried, mothers would either pinch the baby or press his windpipe. The congregation sang with gusto, swaying to and fro, although they were not very musical. They were drilled in the Bible and would have their Bibles open to check the verses quoted by the preacher.[37]

A visitor described John's preaching:

> Dr. John keeps his Bible in one hand, with a sheet of notepaper containing an outline of his sermon; with the forefinger of the other hand he enforces his points. Sometimes he forgets his book and notes, and in the fire of his earnestness he speaks with vehemence, pacing to and fro on the platform; yet always carefully repeating and illustrating and applying his lessons in every possible way. It is a grand and impressive sight to see his power over these people.[38]

The preacher could be scathing in exposing sin, but he did so in love. He knew his people personally—all their trials and temptations. The visitor mentioned above marveled at the fact that he was preaching in Chinese: "We forget that we are listening in Chinese. We feel the speaker is as grandly eloquent as ever he could be in his native Welsh or adopted English tongue."[39] Although his appeal was made to the people in general, John was happy to meet with scholars, because he had a thorough knowledge of the Chinese classics. Tung, one of the national workers, arranged a meeting for John. Describing the event, John wrote, "Whilst we were preaching Tung himself attended to the audience leading them to their seats and serving them with tea. In the midst of the service a number of scholars made their appearance, and they were led to their seats in front of the platform, where they sat for about an hour listening to the gospel as preached by us."[40] After the service, John dined with the scholars and they discussed Christian doctrine.

John delighted in the opportunity to travel and preach the gospel. Describing his itinerating experiences, he wrote, "Its reflex influence on both the missionary and the mission is most healthful and stimulating. It tends to enlarge ideas, deepen the longings, intensify the ardour, and brace up the nerves of both pastor and people. One often feels at the end of a hundred or two hundred miles' tour, having spent a fortnight or three weeks

---

37. Thompson, *Fifty Years*, 182–83.
38. Ibid., 183.
39. Thompson, *Fifty Years*, 183.
40. John, Letters, CWM, "Journal of Journey," April 23, 1880, box 4, folder 5.

in preaching from town to town and village to village, that he could dare anything and endure anything."[41]

John ventured on some remarkable journeys. In 1868, along with Alexander Wylie of the British and Foreign Bible Society, two Bible workers, and two servants, John travelled three thousand miles through Hubei (Hupeh) and Sichuan (Szechwan).[42] The purpose was to explore the land, preach the gospel, and distribute Scriptures. They faced many dangers on this expedition. Travelling meant spending much time on the river, a great deal of walking, climbing, and riding in sedan chairs. The main danger was the strength of the rapids. On one occasion, they miraculously escaped drowning when the captain of their boat refused to tie a rope to a rock in order to maneuver the river's rapids. If they had struck the rocks, the boat and all the travelers would have been lost.[43]

The greatest challenge that John had to face was taking the gospel into the bitterly anti-foreign Hunan province.[44] Having played an important part in suppressing the Taiping rebellion, the people of Hunan were proud and renowned for their courage. John knew that he would have to persevere for a long time in order to enter any place in Hunan, especially the walled cities. He was able to persevere, however, and over the span of twenty-four years, he visited Hunan on eleven occasions.[45] His early visits met with strong opposition, but there was a measure of success.

If he was not welcomed, a national worker had better hopes for success. A native of Hunan, Wang Lien-king, was converted when he heard John preaching during a visit to Hankou. On his return to Hunan, he shared the gospel with others, and a small fellowship of Christians was formed at Hangzhou (Hangchow). It was possible, therefore, for Griffith John to visit Hunan, knowing that the Christians would welcome him.[46] Wang, a self-supporting evangelist, shepherded the little fellowship in Hangzhou, but he wanted John to baptize the new believers. They knew very well that being baptized could make them open to more opposition, but they pressed the missionary to administer the ordinance, and John agreed to do so during his visit in 1897.[47] This was the beginning of the London Missionary Society's work in Hunan.

---

41. Thompson, *Fifty Years*, 221.
42. Wylie, "China," 49–51, 66–70; Gibbard, *Griffith John*, 81–88.
43. Wylie, "China," 68–69.
44. John, *Voice From China*, 220–45.
45. Ibid., 217–50.
46. Ibid., 225.
47. Ibid., 228.

Griffith John's optimism was being confirmed, and he continued to enter the province. Other stations were established, and in the spring of 1899, six evangelists and four Christian book sellers had been set apart for six of the most important stations, including Peng, a converted enemy of the Christian faith.[48] His career is significant, because he started as a voluntary worker and became a colporteur before being set apart as an evangelist.[49] When Yueyang (Yo-chow) was opened to foreign commerce, John saw it as, "an event of great importance in its bearing on the missionary work in Hunan."[50] Spread of foreign commerce opened the way for the dissemination of the Christian faith. Another key event was the signing of the deed in 1901, authorizing Griffith John to build a house in Changsha.[51] A chapel was opened there in 1902. In 1904, the Theological College was opened. Rather than training new Chinese preachers alone, he now taught courses in New Testament Studies and Pastoral Theology.[52] When a hospital was built, it included a Preaching Hall where the gospel was made known regularly.[53] A medical missionary was responsible for the medical work, and John's first wife, Margaret, and his second wife, Jeannette helped tremendously in the opening and maintaining of hospitals.[54] John also oversaw the work of mission schools, where Bible teaching was a central feature. He was jealous about keeping them as Christian institutions; he gave particular attention to them during the period from 1897–1904.[55]

OPPOSITION

Griffith John experienced much suffering in China. After a visit to Wei village, John said, "This was a proud day for me. I have shed blood for my Master when trying to tell the people of the love of God for them."[56] Even after obtaining passports from the Consul, signed by a Chinese official, and taking his visiting card with him, he sometimes found it difficult, and often impossible, to enter a city. Officials would deny him entry or tell him to

48. Like so many other Chinese evangelists, pastors, and helpers of the missionaries, he is known only by his surname.
49. Ibid. 245–48; John, *Voice From China*, 232.
50. John, *Voice from China*, "Hunan and Hupeh," 125.
51. John, *Voice from China*, 238–41.
52. Gibbard, *Griffith John*, 173.
53. Gillison, "Report," 399; Gibbard, *Griffith John*, 70–71.
54. Gibbard, *Griffith John*, 141, 121, 172–73.
55. Ibid., 172, 180.
56. Wilson, "Memories," 277.

come back later.[57] Officials and scholars would use placards to express their opposition to missionaries. Griffith John brought one home to Hankou that exhorted the people to look out for a foreigner, rob him, deny him food, and cut off his ears and nose.[58] Those in authority could incite the people to oppose foreigners, which could lead to attacks on missionaries. One square they entered was "thronged with thousands of people, among whom there were not a few who would have rejoiced to imbue their hands in our blood."[59] John was often greeted with the cry, "Kill the foreign devils!"[60]

During the 1890s, a number of uprisings took place in different parts of China, which meant more danger for missionaries. During 1891, much literature was produced that stirred up anti-foreign hatred. Griffith John helped Christopher Gardner, the British Consul in Hankou, to track down the source of much of this literature. He reported that the main instigator was a man named Chou Han in the capital of Hunan.[61] John helped to find Chou Han, and sent him Christian literature, which he was happy to accept.[62] The Beijing Court stopped the circulation of the literature and Chou Han was degraded from office[63] and, according to John, he was imprisoned.[64] Griffith John's wisdom in this matter could be questioned, as he was deeply involved in a political issue, which could have compromised his position as a missionary in China.

After the war with Japan in 1895, opposition to foreigners was renewed. Moved to action by patriotism and anti-foreign spirit, eighty members of the Vegetarian Society[65] attacked a missionary station in Sichuan (Szechwan); "one man and eight women were barbarously butchered." Elsewhere, much property was destroyed.[66] The uprising led to Western retribution.[67]

---

57. John, *China Her Claims*, 28; John, Letters, CWM, "Griffith John to Dear Mr. Cousins," April 20, 1897, box 10, folder 1.

58. John, *Voice From China*, 220.

59. John, "Hunan," 368.

60. John, *Voice From China*, 221.

61. Gibbard, *Griffith John*, 150–51; Thompson, *Fifty Years*, 472–73.

62. John, Letters, CWM, "Griffith John to Dear Mr. Cousins," April 20, 1857, box 10, folder 1.

63. Thompson, *Fifty Years*, 473.

64. John, *Voice from China*, "Hunan and Hupeh," 135.

65. On the Vegetarian Society, see Welch, The Vegetarians, 26–29. See also Cai, "On the Origins of the Gelaohui," 481–508. [Ed.]

66. John, Letters, CWM, September 9, 1895, "Griffith John to My Dear Mr. Thompson," box 9, folder 2.

67. Hudson, "Response of Protestant Missionaries," 132–33.

Another upheaval took place in 1900, during a prolonged drought and bad harvests, with the emergence of the Boxers.[68] They were determined to get rid of all foreigners. "The Boxer movement found the people ripe for lawlessness, under stress of circumstances which were sufficiently appalling."[69] Although most of the destruction took place in the north, Hunan and Hubei (Hupeh) were not unscathed. Griffith John mentioned the situation in Hunan: "I am afraid that most of our chapels in Hunan have been destroyed, and that in some places the Christians are sorely persecuted."[70]

John, like most missionaries, believed that those in authority were really responsible for these uprisings. "The Szechuan riots can be traced unmistakably to official influences," John noted.[71] There is no doubt that there were a number of times when the officials were behind the riots, but John tended to exaggerate and be sensational in his reports. The Vegetarians, for example, were not linked with either the local gentry or the local populace.[72]

When there were claims of persecution and loss of life and property, missionaries had to face the problem of compensation. All agreed that they should not ask for compensation for loss of life, but they disagreed regarding other matters. They could deal with lesser matters without much complication. Griffith John always defended the national Christians if they were persecuted, but he did so with care. He would first establish whether it was a religious case, and thus covered by treaty stipulations guaranteeing religious freedom to Chinese Christians, and if he was satisfied that it was, a national worker would make further investigation. Griffith John would then ask the accused to meet with him and would also appeal to their friends or family to plead with the accused. If all these steps proved futile, John would appeal to a Chinese official, and if needed, to the Consulate.[73]

More serious cases had to be dealt with as a result of riots. Griffith John had no doubt that indemnity should be asked for in serious cases, since he was a representative of the London Missionary Society and also a British

---

68. Gibbard, *Griffith John*, 161–65. The Boxer Rebellion was an uprising initiated by a secret society, the Yihetuan ("Society of the Righteous Fist") in 1900 against all foreigners in China. Since many missionaries lived in the interior, they and their Chinese converts suffered terribly. The rebellion, supported by the Qing government, was suppressed by an eight-nation coalition that captured Beijing. [Ed.]

69. Ibid., 162–64.

70. John, Letters, CWM, "Griffith John to Directors," August 10, 1900, box 12A, folder 2.

71. John, Letters, CWM, "Griffith John to Dear Thompson," August 12, 1895, box 9, folder 2.

72. Hudson, "Response of Protestant Missionaries," 132–33; Lovell, *The Opium War*, 278.

73. John, "Persecution?" 529–30.

citizen in China. His protection was guaranteed by treaty between Britain and China; he depended on that treaty for his own safety and the safety of others in Hankou. Griffith John he was glad that the gunboats were in the city.[74]

According to Griffith John, it was false policy not to claim indemnity. Immediately after the Boxer uprising, he busied himself securing what he regarded as the legal claims of the missionary stations, and in February 1901, he received indemnity from Hangzhou amounting to sixteen thousand taels (eighteen thousand pounds). As early as July 1900, he discussed the matter with some military authorities and reported the opinion of the magistrates and gentry, "I may add that the magistrates and the gentry think it quite reasonable that the Mission should be indemnified."[75] In doing so, Griffith John was asserting his authority, not only as a missionary, but also as a representative of England. Indeed, on an occasion prior to 1900, he had declared to his opponents, "I am an Englishman and a messenger of Jesus."[76] He knew that it would be pointless to mention the fact that he was a Welshman. To say "I am a Welshman" would have no effect at all.

Most missionaries would agree with C. C. Baldwin that in accepting indemnity, the "right is clear, the claiming of it not always advisable."[77] John's co-worker, Arnold Foster, disagreed with John, as did Hudson Taylor. He gave practical and Scriptural reasons for refusing indemnity. The outcome of many cases was uncertain, and even when there was success, they would be dreaded more than ever, and officials would be more convinced that they were political agents. Taylor argued that the example of Christ and the teaching of Scripture made it clear that indemnity should not be accepted (1 Pet 2:19–23; 3:13–18; 4:12–19).[78] Stephen Neill came to the right conclusion when he said, "Few missionaries followed his example, but the later history suggests that the greater wisdom was granted to Hudson Taylor."[79]

---

74. John, "Response to Directors," July 20, 1900, box 22, China East Outgoing, Council for World Mission.

75. John, Letters, CWM, "Griffith John to Thompson," July 17, 1900, box 12A, folder 2; John, Letters, CWM, "Griffith John to Thompson," November 29, 1900 and February 11, 1901, box 12B, folder 1.

76. John, Letters, CWM, June 26, 1864, "Griffith John to Directors," box 3, folder 2.

77. Baldwin, "Missionaries appeal to secular arm," 99–105.

78. Taylor, "Appeals for Redress," 576–78; Bickers, *Scramble for China*, 248–49.

79. Neill, *Christian Missions*, 288; Gibbard, *Griffith John*, 164.

THE MESSAGE

Missionaries were opposed not only because they were foreigner, but also because of the content of their message. They were in China to proclaim the Christian message. At the center of this message, according to Griffith John, was the love of God, which was not made fully known through nature, but through the Scriptures. At the center of that revelation was the Lord Jesus Christ: his unique person and his atoning work on the cross.[80] John declared, "I do not think of Jesus Christ as one among many, but as God's *one* message of salvation to a sinful world."[81] His atoning work on the cross was the basis for reconciliation between God and man. As to the extent of the atonement, John believed that it was sufficient for the whole world, and by faith, could be realized for all. "Jesus Christ on the Cross took my place, the just for the unjust."[82]

Closely related to the love of the Father revealed in his Son was the work of the Holy Spirit. Griffith John was Trinitarian in his theology. He expounded the different aspects of the Spirit's work. The Spirit is present everywhere, and the missionary should realize that the Spirit is already in the land to which he was going.[83] The Spirit is the author of general revelation. His saving work is conversion. In his evangelism, John always aimed at conversion, which led to holiness of life. The Spirit leads believers to a deeper knowledge of Christ, what John described as a "full vision of Christ," which he also described as the "baptism of the Spirit."[84] John was Christ-centric in his belief and experience. He dwelt much on a deeper experience of Christ, which gave him power for service. The influence of the Keswick teaching can be found in these aspects of John's teaching, although he did not follow it slavishly.[85] One other aspect of his teaching regarding the Holy Spirit was his emphasis on the phenomenon of revival. He prayed to see a manifestation of the Spirit that reflected what happened on the Day of Pentecost. News of the Welsh Revival of 1904–5 rejoiced his heart, and he

---

80. John, *Voice From China*, 95.

81. Ibid., 80.

82. Ibid., 97.

83. Ibid., 77.

84. Gibbard, *Griffith John*, 93; John, "Discussion," 269–70; Bryant, "Forty Years Ago," 113.

85. Gibbard, *Griffith John*, 93–96. "Keswick" teaching presented the possibility of a "higher" or "deeper" Christian life, often associated both with profound "rest in Christ" and more power for ministry. [Ed.]

sent a letter to Evan Roberts, one of the main leaders, entreating him to pray for China.[86]

With a clear, uncompromising message, and without a trace of syncretism, Griffith John had to engage the various belief systems that he encountered in China. Missionaries differed in their response to these beliefs. A. E. Moule stated dogmatically, "Other religions do not meet Christianity halfway."[87] William Muirhead acknowledged that there were real differences, but thought that it was possible to learn from the example of Paul's preaching in Athens, as recorded in Acts 17, how to interact with pagan philosophers.[88]

Griffith John's approach was not confrontational, but was to "acknowledge what is true and noble" in another religion before dealing with what he believed to be its errors.[89] He was able to say that he did not remember a time when missionaries in China "regarded the non-Christian Faiths as absolutely wrong to be condemned *in toto*," but rather they presented Jesus Christ as the "one Savior."[90] He regarded Confucianism as too conservative. Its moral emphasis could never change a person and make him a new creature. Mohammed was a remarkable man, but could not offer a Risen Savior or life in a glorified body in a new heaven and new earth. Laozi's *Dao De Jing*, with its emphasis on reason, could never lead to a real knowledge of God.[91] A recent work has claimed that only a few missionaries in China adopted a conciliatory attitude towards the Chinese and their religions. "In fact the frank attitude of the majority of Protestant missionaries to the whole Chinese value system was that of 'war to the knife.'"[92] In the light of Griffith John's statement, "majority" is an exaggeration, and the author should have included Griffith John's name among the few who appreciated what was true and noble in other religions.

Another problem that Griffith John had to face was the growth of liberal theology within the church. The rise of biblical criticism, which denied the divine inspiration of Scripture, and the appearance of Darwin's *Origin of Species*, which undermined supernaturalism, led to significant changes in the way many viewed the authority of the Bible, the atonement,

86. Ibid., 174–75.

87. Moule, *Half a Century*, 240.

88. Muirhead, *China*, 47–48.

89. John, Letters, CWM, "Griffith John to My Dear Sir," October 6, 1857, box 2, Folder 1.

90. John, Letters, NLW, "Griffith John to George," including letter he had sent to Robert Beer, January 26, 1907.

91. John, *Voice From China*, 79–80.

92. Hudson, "Response of Protestant Missionaries," 23.

and eternal life. For instance, John strongly disagreed with R. J. Campbell, who taught that God was present in all creatures, though to a greater degree in some than in others. In John's view, Campbell was denying the central truths of Christianity, particularly the uniqueness of Christ and the need for atonement.[93]

John was not always consistent in his theological conservatism, however. He had three motives for mission work. First was the commission in Matt 28:18–20, in the tradition of William Carey. Second was love for Christ, and last was the coming kingdom of Jesus Christ, which was a driving motive for his work as a missionary.[94] On the one hand, he looked forward to the end of time, when all the kingdoms of this world would belong to Jesus the King; every knee would bow and all languages would praise him.[95] On the other hand, he believed in "the progress of the human race," materially, morally, and spiritually.[96] Such an attitude seems very much like the liberal emphasis on the kingdom of God on earth,[97] and yet John would never accept the liberal implication of that belief, "that man was increasingly divinized and God humanized."[98] He found difficulty in harmonizing the Providence and sovereignty of God and his utopian view of the future. Victorian optimism infiltrated his teaching, and he did not present the concept of the Kingdom in terms of Christ's second coming, judgment, and salvation.[99]

DISTRIBUTION OF THE WORD THROUGH TRACTS AND TRANSLATION

Unlike the sermon, the tract was a well-known means of instruction in China, and missionaries made full use of this means to make their message known.[100] Initially, they created these tracts individually, but in 1875, The Hankow Tract Society (later called the Central China Tract Society) was established, with Griffith John as president. It was made possible by a gift

---

93. Jones, *Congregationalism*, 549–54; John, Letters, NLW, "Griffith John to Dear George," January 28, 1907, and letter, no date.

94. The same was true of J. Hudson Taylor and most missionaries with the CIM and other "faith" missions. [Ed.]

95. John, *Voice From China*, 46–47, 51–52, 267; George, "Evangelical Revival," 58–63.

96. John, *Voice From China*, 46, 48, 49, 266–67.

97. Ibid., 71.

98. Bosch, *Witness to the World*, 155.

99. In this he somewhat resembled Timothy Richard. [Ed.]

100. Martin, "Native Tract Literature," 330.

of fifty pounds from the Religious Tract Society in London.[101] Their new building, which was completed after John's death, was named the Griffith John Memorial Building.[102]

In his writing of tracts, Griffith John depended on the help of his pundit, Shen, with whom he wrote tracts on a variety of subjects.[103] Some were doctrinal or evangelistic, such as "On Atonement" and "Regeneration." Others were more practical teachings on morality, such as "The Moral Teaching of Christianity." John attempted to relate Christian doctrine and science, most notably in "The Truth Stated in Eight Chapters," which included chapters on Christian doctrine, chemistry, and astronomy. He also wrote a "Child's Catechism" and "Leading the Family in the Right Way."[104] "Leading the Family in the Right Way" is a significant work. Griffith John refers to it as a "sort of novel, specially adapted to the Chinese. I feel that I can ask the blessing of God on it."[105] The work appeared in 1882, one of the earliest attempts of missionaries to write this kind of literature in Chinese.

John devoted much of his writing to social and political causes as well, exemplified by such tracts as "Religious Toleration" and "Against Opium." He was strongly opposed to the opium trade and was appalled that Britain was making huge financial gains while the Chinese were suffering, physically and mentally. Like C. W. Mateer, A. E. Moule, and other missionaries, Griffith John believed that "nothing that is morally wrong can be politically right."[106] He chaired a committee to present a memorial to the Royal Commission on Opium and published his responses to their questions.[107] Some, like Kathleen Lodwick, write with sympathy when dealing with the missionaries and their attitude to opium-smoking,[108] while others have adopted a critical attitude, accusing the missionaries of being alarmists, sensationalists, and having lack of medical knowledge.[109]

After returning from Britain in 1882, John decided to produce a Wenli version of the New Testament.[110] He made use of the Delegates Version and

101. Lai, "Institutional Patronage," 39–61.

102. Martin, *Cycle of Cathay*, 25.

103. Lists of tracts found in Wylie, *Memorials*, 337–38; Wason, "Descriptive and classified," references 228–1002.

104. Lists of tracts found in Wylie, *Memorials*, 337–38; Wason, "Descriptive and classified," references 228–1002.

105. Thompson, *Fifty Years*, 335.

106. "Opium," *Shanghai Conference, 1877*, 248.

107. John, "Opium in China," 194–200.

108. Lodwick, *Crusaders against Opium*.

109. Newman, "Opium Smoking," 765–94; Dikotter, "Parient Zero," 1–6.

110. That is, using a literary, but not classical, style of Chinese.

B and C sources, and used the Mandarin dialect, completing the work in 1885, followed by a revised Mandarin version in 1889.[111] The 1885 version was recommended by William Muirhead and Archdeacon Moule. Moule's opinion was that, "All I see of Mr. John's version leads me to hope that it may after all become our, if not Authorized yet however Common, Version of the New Testament; always allowing our excellent Brother three or four years at least to perfect its rendering in communication with the brethren."[112] There was, however no "unanimous approval"[113] For example, the Rev. F. G. Fitch argued that a literal, word-for-word approach should have been employed, and that a panel should have been responsible for the work rather than just one man.[114] John responded by saying that a literal translation was impossible. The work of the translator was to "carry ideas and thoughts from one language to another," and to be true to the genius of that language.[115] This was one of his seven rules for translation. Calvin Mateer agreed with Fitch's opinion that a panel should be preferred to a single translator.[116] Griffith John was determined to continue single-handed.

In 1890, a conference was arranged at Shanghai to discuss a Union Version in Mandarin. Griffith John was invited to sit on some of the translation committees, but he refused the invitation, believing that the task was "gigantic," and the "scheme complicated."[117] Nelson Bitton commented, "The event proved Dr. John to have unduly magnified the difficulties and underestimated the spirit of his fellow-Translators."[118] By 1890, John had also completed the Psalms and Proverbs, and the New Testament in the Wenli and Mandarin, and continued to translate other portions of the Old Testament into Mandarin.[119]

---

111. *Annual Report*, NBSS (1885) 33; Editorial Correspondence, No. 25, 30, December 1889.

112. Moule, "Mr. John's New Testament," 53.

113. As Robson, *Hankow Mission*, 123; *Annual Report*, National Bible Society of Scotland (1885), 33; Editorial Correspondence, no. 25, 30, December 1889.

114. Fitch, "On a New Version," 298–99.

115. John, "Leading Rules," 381–82.

116. Mateer, "Easy Wen Li," 51; Foster, "New Testament," 25–26.

117. Gibbard, *Griffith John*, 135.

118. Bitton, *Story of Griffith John*, 129.

119. Ibid., 128.

A PIONEERING MISSIONARY

Griffith John returned to London due to ill health at the end of 1911. He died in 1912, and was buried in his native Swansea. He was a man of faith and an optimist; sometimes he was audacious in his defiance of difficult situations. On many occasions, he revealed exceptional physical courage and mental strength. In committing himself to the work of mission, he never neglected his own spiritual condition. Walking with God came before working for God. It is no wonder that two of the men he most admired were Elisha and Paul.

His optimism could be his weakness as well, as he occasionally failed to interpret events correctly. There is no doubt that he loved the Chinese and sympathized with the best in their tradition. By the 1890s, however, he fully supported the introduction of English and Western ideas into China. As a missionary, he served his Savior with untiring zeal, but at times, he could not hide an imperialistic spirit. After such a long ministry, during which he suffered physically and underwent a period of depression, perhaps it would have been better if he had retired in 1906. He probably would have avoided further suffering.

The strengths of Griffith John outweigh his weaknesses. He had contributed substantially to the growth of Christianity as a pioneering missionary in central China and the founder of the London Missionary Society work in that area. During his ministry, he planted numerous churches. Not only did he sow, but he also reaped a huge harvest. In 1904, one hundred London Missionary Society chapels had been built in Hankou and thirty-seven in Hunan. During the same year, the Central China Tract Society issued 2.5 million publications. The present-day hospital and college at Wuhan are clear reminders of his lasting legacy. John was highly regarded by missionaries and Chinese as an outstanding preacher, and deserves to be thought of as the Spurgeon of China. He served his Savior with untiring zeal, and during his ministry, not only did he sow, but he also reaped an abundant harvest.

5

J. Hudson Taylor
Advocate for China's Inland Millions

G. Wright Doyle

Arriving in Shanghai on March 1, 1854, a young man from northern England met with "completely unexpected problems."[1] He knew no one, and had no place to stay. Two out of three letters of introduction proved useless, for one man had died and another had left for America.

The city was at war, with rebels and imperial troops shooting at each other constantly, making life dangerous even for those living in the International Settlement, and much more so for anyone daring to venture into the no man's land between the fighting forces, as Taylor often did, both to evangelize and to treat the wounded. It was bitterly cold when he arrived, and coal was selling at wartime prices and had to be used sparingly, so he was miserably uncomfortable most of the time, and language study was quite difficult. Lack of funds impelled him to rent a house outside the foreign settlement, but the civil war made that situation untenable and he returned to the relative safety of the city after a few months. A man of intense emotions and strong affection, he suffered from almost unbearable loneliness, as letters to and from home took months to arrive, and as he waited in vain for encouraging words from the girl he hoped would marry him and come to share his life in faraway China.

1. Taylor, *Looking Back*, 54.

He had brought letters of credit from the Chinese Evangelization Society when he landed in Shanghai, but soon discovered that these had not been adequately covered; he was reduced to poverty and great embarrassment, since he had to rely on the generosity of other missionaries. They were kind to him, but he could not be unaware that they held his non-denominational sending agency in low regard and had little but pity for this seemingly directionless young visionary. For many, sympathy turned to scorn when he adopted Chinese clothing, even going to the extent of shaving the front of his head, dyeing his hair, and attaching a long pigtail. How could he so demean his English culture and civilization?

James Hudson Taylor is widely regarded as one of the most important and influential missionaries of all time, and certainly one of the most significant missionaries to China in the nineteenth century. His reputation rests largely upon the founding of the China Inland Mission, whose members were known for their penetration into parts of China where few, if any, Protestant Westerners had gone and hardly any had dared to live; for their dressing, eating, and living like the Chinese among whom they dwelt; by the very high standard of proficiency in the Chinese language that was required of them; their extensive evangelistic, medical, and educational work; and their refusal to seek protection from consular authorities when threatened with danger or even when attacked by local Chinese mobs. Behind this organization, however, lay the character and conduct of its founder, surely a remarkable Christian leader by any standard of measurement, though not without weaknesses and failings.

James Hudson Taylor was born at Barnsley, Yorkshire, England, of devout Methodist parents who introduced him early to a vital Christian piety. His father had been struck by the spiritual needs of China through his reading, and prayed that if God would give him a son, that boy would be "called and privileged to labor" there.[2] Hudson Taylor remained ignorant of this prayer and desire until he had returned from his first stay in China. In his youth, the inconsistencies of many professing Christians led him to become skeptical of Christianity and to drift from the faith. When he was fifteen, in a moment of boredom, he picked up a tract that he found in the house and began to read it just for entertainment. Unbeknownst to him, his sister Amelia had been praying for his conversion for a month, and at that very time his mother was moved to pour out her heart in asking God for his salvation. When he came across the phrase, "The finished work of Christ," he was powerfully struck by its meaning, which was, "A full and perfect atonement and satisfaction for sin: the debt was paid by the Sub-

2. Taylor, *Retrospect*, 9.

stitute; Christ died for our sins, and not for ours only, but also for the sins of the whole world . . ." He asked himself, What is then left for me to do? "There was nothing in the world to be done but to fall down on one's knees, and accepting this Saviour and His salvation, to praise Him forevermore."[3]

From this moment flowed all his subsequent life, which was dedicated to responding to God's love for him in Christ with gratitude and to spare no effort to share this marvelous Good News with everyone he could. His sense of leading as a missionary to China came later, in two stages. First, he had a remarkable time of earnest prayer to God when, as he says, "I besought Him to give me some work to do for Him, as an outlet for love and gratitude; some self-denying service, no matter what it might be, however trying or however trivial; something with which He would be pleased, and that I might do for Him who had done so much for me."[4] He continues, "The presence of God became unutterably real and blessed; and though but a child under sixteen, I remember stretching myself on the ground, and lying there silent before Him with unspeakable awe and unspeakable joy."[5] A few months later, he became convinced that God wanted him to serve in China, and began preparing himself. Convinced by reading Walter Henry Medhurst's *China*[6] of the usefulness of medical work, he apprenticed himself to a physician in Hull and commenced medical studies. At the same time, he did everything he could to improve his health and to inure himself to hardship. He discarded his featherbed, began to exercise regularly, and adopted a very simple diet. Tithing of his income became a set pattern, as did ministering to the physical and spiritual needs of the poor people among whom he chose to live.

More importantly, he began to practice living "by faith" in God to provide for his material needs without his telling anyone of his situation or asking assistance. He was often brought to the point of extreme poverty by this discipline, but God always supplied his lack, often at the last moment, and frequently through unusual means. Once, when the physician to whom he was apprenticed forgot to pay his salary, Taylor refrained from reminding him until he was down to his last crust of bread, while inwardly crying out fervently to God. The older man returned to his office late that night with a payment from a wealthy patient, suddenly remembered that Taylor's pay was in arrears, and handed the money over to him. By constantly exercising

---

3. Ibid., 12.
4. Ibid., 14.
5. Ibid., 15.
6. Medhurst, *China*.

faith in little things, he developed an extraordinary confidence that God, his heavenly Father, would not deny him the basic necessities of life.

Leaving Hull, he entered medical school in London, where he continued this austere and faith-stretching lifestyle. He restricted his diet to brown bread and apples, and walked eight miles a day to and from the college. "He deliberately cut himself off from possible sources of supply. It was God, the living God he needed—a stronger faith to grasp His faithfulness and more experience of the practicability of dealing with Him about every situation."[7]

Before he could complete his medical curriculum, an urgent plea for missionaries came from China, where the Taiping Rebellion was at its height. Hong Xiuquan, the leader of the movement, had expressed faith in Christ and a strong desire to work with Western missionaries to spread the Gospel throughout the land, so the time seemed ripe. The leaders of the Chinese Evangelization Society (CES), to which Taylor was attached, asked him to drop his degree studies and leave immediately, which after consultation with his parents, he did. CES was founded under the inspiration of Charles Gutzlaff, the brilliant, flamboyant, and very controversial German missionary who believed strongly that China should be evangelized by Chinese. The directors meant well, but were completely inexperienced in the administration of a mission society, and almost totally inept in caring for the workers whom they sent to China.

EARLY YEARS IN SHANGHAI

God had not forsaken Hudson Taylor, though things looked bleak enough when he first landed in Shanghai. The third letter of introduction when he brought with him led Taylor to Dr. Walter Medhurst, the veteran missionary whose book had made such an impression upon him, and who introduced him to Dr. William Lockhart of the London Missionary Society, who in turn invited Taylor to stay with him and help with his medical practice. Despite the obstacles and bitter disappointments of his first months in China, Hudson Taylor persevered in trying to learn the Mandarin language, with the help of a Chinese teacher, devoting many hours a day to this arduous task. In time, he realized that he also needed to gain fluency in the Shanghai dialect in order to communicate with most of the inhabitants of the city. Medhurst and Alexander Wylie, both excellent sinologists, also gave him advice and help in acquiring the language and culture.

Within a year, he had taken the momentous step of adopting Chinese dress. Roman Catholic missionaries had done this for centuries in order

---

7. Taylor, *Hudson Taylor's Spiritual Secret*, 44.

to escape detection, since they were forbidden to live and work in China, but almost all Protestant missionaries believed that they should continue to dress like Westerners. Dr. Medhurst, who enjoyed great prestige among other missionaries, himself suggested that Taylor depart from the usual practice, and the result confirmed the wisdom of it. Dressed like a Chinese, Taylor was able to move about much more freely than before, attracting much less attention from the people because of a strange appearance.

His financial frustration only doubled when CES sent new workers, Dr. William Parker and his wife, to Shanghai. They soon discovered that there was no hope of depending upon funds coming through CES; eventually, the Parkers and Taylor decided to leave the Society and become entirely independent. Taylor's earlier training in living "by faith" enabled him to trust God more readily than a group of men thousands of miles away. Repeatedly, his needs were met, often at the last minute, by donations that came to him directly.

As soon as he had acquired enough language ability, he began to share the gospel with Chinese, many of whom responded eagerly to this message of hope in the midst of a horrible situation. Though the Treaty of Nanking (1842) called for missionaries to restrict their activities to the a narrow area surrounding the city, Taylor and others believed that they should go further afield, since there were already so many Westerners working in Shanghai itself. His first forays were with the Rev. J. S. Burdon, of the Church Missionary Society, who later became the Anglican bishop of Hong Kong. Many of the people warmly received them and the Bibles and tracts that they distributed, which encouraged the missionaries, but others jostled and threatened. Taken to a high-ranking mandarin, they were courteously treated. Experiences like this, often repeated, convinced Taylor that he could venture far away from treaty ports without much danger or official interference, and with generally positive receptions by the people. Nine months after his arrival in Shanghai, he was taken on evangelistic journeys with Joseph Edkins, a veteran missionary with the London Missionary Society. Right from the beginning, he was receiving the best possible mentoring in pioneer evangelism outside the treaty ports, which had been his original dream and which became his lifelong passion.

For many months he also accompanied the experienced Scottish evangelist with the English Presbyterians, the Rev. William Burns, on extensive itineration by boat along the waterways in the region. Over a period of just fifteen months, he completed ten such journeys, preaching, distributing literature, and treating countless patients. When working in the Shanghai area became impossible because of the opposition of the British consul, they went south to Swatow (now Shantou), where Burns had lived before.

Under extremely uncomfortable living and travelling conditions, Taylor learned the local Fujian dialect; more than that, he absorbed a great deal from the godly character of Burns, whose zeal and skill in evangelism he greatly admired. He saw first-hand what a life of prayer that was soaked in constant meditation upon the Bible looked like. For his part, Burns became convinced that he, too, should adopt Chinese dress. Following a strategy that Taylor would later apply to the work of the China Inland Mission, they started on the outskirts of a major town, circling round it and becoming familiar to the people while drawing ever closer to the center. The goal was to obtain a residence within the city itself and make that a base for future work. Because Burns liked to go off on his own, however, Taylor was left by himself much of the time. A man with an intense desire to love others and to be loved, he had to grow in his sense of intimacy with God through Christ and come to know how to depend on God, not man, for emotional as well as physical needs. After seven months together, Burns asked Taylor to return to Shanghai to get more medical supplies, but the separation proved permanent when Burns was arrested. A new chapter was about to open in Hudson Taylor's already eventful life.

NINGBO

Returning to Shanghai, Taylor discovered that his house had been robbed and that all of his medical supplies were gone. He decided, therefore, to go to Ningbo, where Dr. Parker had moved and was practicing medicine among expatriates in order to support his ministry to the Chinese. John Jones and his wife Mary, also with the CES, were in Ningbo as well, so Taylor decided to make that city his new base. Ningbo, one of the oldest and most influential of the cities on China's southern coast, was one of the first five "treaty ports" that were opened to foreign residence as a provision of the Treaty of Nanjing. By the time Taylor arrived in 1856, it had been the site of foreign missionary activity for a number of years, and there was a small community of missionaries there. He rented the top floor of a house and settled into ministry.

Taylor's decision to resign from the CES was made in Ningbo as a consequence of two factors. The first was the society's continuing inability to supply him with the funds that they had promised him. The second was his growing conviction that Christians should not go into debt for any reason. "Owe no man anything" (Rom 13:8) became for him a general principle, one he could not violate without betraying his conscience.[8] John Jones

---

8. See Wigram, *The Bible and Mission*, 238–40.

joined him in separating from the CES and casting himself entirely upon God's faithfulness to supply his daily needs. He continued to write home and tell people what he was doing, and he continued praying for God to send whatever he required in order to serve in China. Despite manifold trials immediately following his severance of the connection with the CES and in the decades to follow, he was able to tell story upon story of how God had stepped in at the last minute to keep him and those for whom he was responsible from ever lacking what was necessary. He believed that, as heavenly Father, God cared at least as much about his children as earthly fathers do, and would no more let them starve than we would our own children. Besides, he reasoned, God is infinitely rich and has no shortage of anything needful for our life and service. The China Inland Mission was founded upon this principle, which has proven to be valid, even to this day.[9]

He learned the Ningbo dialect as soon as he could, while preaching in Mandarin before he had acquired facility in the local tongue. Taylor writes about the first convert there: "I was preaching the good news of salvation through the finished work of Christ when a middle-aged man stood up... He told... about his faith in the gospel's power. 'I have looked for the truth a long time, as my fathers did before me. But I never found it. I have traveled far and near, but without getting it. I have found no rest in Confucianism, Buddhism or Taoism. But I do find rest in what I have heard here tonight. From now on, I am a believer in Jesus.'"[10] Almost immediately after arriving in Ningbo, Taylor met Maria Dyer, who quickly fell in love with him, though keeping her feelings secret. Maria was born in the Straits Settlements on the southwestern shore of the Malay Peninsula, the daughter of Samuel Dyer, one of the first missionaries to the Chinese. Hudson Taylor soon noticed her godliness and zeal and, after observing her during the normal course of missionary gatherings, decided to court her. His lack of association with a mission organization and of formal academic credentials, along with his Chinese dress, seemed to disqualify him as an eligible suitor in the eyes of Miss Mary Ann Aldersey, the redoubtable headmistress of the school where Maria taught and her self-appointed guardian, but her resistance was eventually overcome and objections overruled by Maria's legal guardians, so the two young lovers were married 1858. Maria was his faithful helpmate until her death in 1870.

After their wedding, the Taylors plunged into missionary work, with Hudson preaching, teaching, and treating patients. A little church was formed, the nucleus of what would become a stable congregation. Though

---

9. The successor organization to the CIM is OMF International.
10. Taylor, *Looking Back*, 119–20.

he could have employed the new believers, he thought it was essential from the beginning to build an indigenous, self-supporting Chinese church. When Dr. Lockhart left Ningbo, he asked Taylor to take over his medical clinic, an experience that further expanded his knowledge and skill as a physician. After two and half years, however, Taylor succumbed to the strain of constant overwork and had to return to England, with no prospect of seeing China again.

BIRTH OF A VISION

Although forced live away from China for five years, Taylor had a continuing concern for the millions of Chinese living in provinces where no missionary had ever gone. He tried by every means possible to drum up support for China among denominational missions, but there was hardly any response. He resumed his medical studies, finally qualifying in surgery and in midwifery. During these years, he also revised the Ningbo vernacular New Testament, working with Frederick F. Gough, Maria, and Wang Laedjun, an early convert who had accompanied them to England. He also trained Wang in theology and medicine.

Finally, with his health restored, after a life-changing experience at Brighton Beach in 1865, he accepted what he considered to be God's clear leading and founded the China Inland Mission, with the express purpose of preaching Christ where his name had not yet been heard, in the unreached provinces of China's interior. Hudson Taylor was tormented by the thought that millions of Chinese were dying annually without a saving knowledge of God through faith in Jesus Christ. Not only the Great Commission (Matt 28:18–20; Mark 16:15; Luke 24: Acts 1:8; John 20:21) but also Proverbs 24:11–12 imposed upon him a duty to spread the Christian message as widely as possible and to mobilize others to do the same. In this undertaking, he was consciously departing from the strategy of current missions, which focused on settled work in the major cities. He was also deliberately seeking to avoid any competition with existing societies by striking out into virgin territory and by not allowing any appeals for funds to be made in public meetings.

A few months afterwards, he concentrated all his thoughts on the urgent task of taking the gospel to that land in his book *China's Spiritual Need and Claims*. He then put out an appeal for "24 willing workers" to take the gospel inland. Unlike other mission societies, the CIM would not limit recruits to graduates of the universities, but would accept artisans and farmers as well. Some of these turned out to be excellent students of Chinese language and culture, and distinguished themselves as missionaries, while others, limited by their lack of education, could not make the necessary adjustments. In time, the CIM attracted many educated people, especially after the stunning events surrounding the departure of "the Cambridge Seven" from England in 1885.[11]

In 1866, Hudson Taylor and Maria sailed with the first group of sixteen recruits in the *Lammermuir*, arriving in Shanghai after a harrowing voyage in which Taylor showed great leadership. The new missionaries were soon taken away from the treaty port to Hangzhou for language study and initial cultural adjustment. Soon, a local church was firmly established, which Taylor turned over to Wang Laedjun and John McCarthy, while he ventured further afield to open new areas for missionary work, leaving Maria to keep correspondence and mission affairs running smoothly.

In coming years, this pattern was repeated over and over, with Taylor's early experiences forming the basis for both his later career as a missionary and mission leader and for the CIM. He taught missionaries to rely solely on God for all that they needed each day, and not on any guaranteed salary, which he could not promise to provide, and to live among the Chinese and identify with them as much as possible. The failure of the directors of the Chinese Evangelization Society to guide and govern a work thousands of miles away led to Taylor's insistence that the headquarters of the CIM would always be in China, while home councils in sending countries would recruit and send workers and keep supporters informed of progress. In order not to compete with established denominational missions, and broadened by his own experience of being welcomed by, and learning from, missionaries from various societies, the CIM would be an inter-denominational organization, based on a common evangelical, nondenominational faith and an emphasis upon diffusing the gospel as widely as possible throughout all of China.

In coming decades, both Hudson Taylor and some of his colleagues would go on long and arduous journeys throughout the length and breadth of China, learning as much as they could about the land and its people, and scouting out possible centers for missionaries to settle. They were almost always accompanied by Chinese helpers, whom Taylor considered essential both for evangelism and for the nurture and leadership of local churches. Taylor and his fellow missionaries were nearly killed in 1868, when a riot

11. This was a group of prominent athletes, soldiers, and young gentlemen who responded to Taylor's appeals for missionaries to China's millions, and whose testimonies and dramatic choice to forsake promising careers to follow Taylor to China aroused immense popular applause and emulation. See Pollock, *The Cambridge Seven*, and Broomhall, *Assault on the Nine*, 354–66.

broke out in Yangzhou. Though he reported the incident first to the local mandarin and then to the British consul, he was aghast at the ensuing use of military force to cow the Chinese into protecting the foreign missionaries, and thereafter foreswore any dependence on foreign power, relying only on the providential protection of God.

He was feeling the strain not only of adverse and unfair publicity in England but also his own sense of spiritual dryness when a letter from one of his missionaries opened his eyes and his heart to the possibility of enjoying continuous intimacy with Jesus Christ simply through faith. "He had tasted the joy of 'union with Christ,'" and stated that God had made him "a new man."[12] Thenceforth, he evinced remarkable peace and joy in the midst of otherwise crushing trials, and amazed others at his calmness and cheerfulness even when pressed beyond limits. When those around him were worried, he was at peace. Even at the last, when his weakness and illness rendered him almost immobile, he evinced a quiet joy that would not be quenched. Not that he never experienced depression or sorrow; he did. When his extreme labors had depleted his physical resources, or when dissension within the CIM or declension from the faith or the work of missionaries seemed chronic and insoluble, he was sometimes overcome with discouragement. Always, however, his faith in God brought a speedy recovery, and his resilience surprised even those closest to him.[13]

Throughout his life, Taylor maintained a disciplined devotional life, reading the Bible through annually for forty years until his death. Traveling companions would remark upon his habit of rising in the middle of the night to study the Scriptures while others slept, before returning to bed until day broke. At the root of Hudson Taylor's labors and influence lay his strong faith in God, based upon unswerving confidence in the veracity of his Word. This trust in a loving heavenly Father supplied constantly-renewed resources of patience, inner peace, and persuasive influence over other people.

DEEP VALLEYS, GREEN PASTURES

Their son Samuel died of a lung disease in 1870. To protect his children from the extreme heat and rigors of life in China, he sent three of them home with Miss Emily Blatchley the next month. Four months later, the newborn son Noel died, and Maria, who had contracted cholera in childbirth, followed him to the grave on July 23, 1870. Devastated by this tragic loss, Taylor had

12. Chang, *Christ Alone*, 53.
13. See, for example, Broomhall, *Assault on the Nine*, 307–10.

to turn to Christ constantly for a fresh draught of the "living waters" that were promised in John 7:37-39.

He was exhausted, however, and matters at home were pressing, so he returned with a few other CIM folk, including Jennie Faulding, in 1871. During the voyage their close friendship blossomed into a romance and they were married shortly after arrival in England. Before returning to China, he formed the London Home Council of the CIM, with responsibility for recruiting, evaluating, and sending new workers, as well as for overall promotion and handling of finances. He made it clear, however, that leadership of the mission's field operations would always be in China, vested in himself as general director or in his appointed deputy there. Emily Blatchley would perform editorial work for the *Occasional Paper*, forerunner publication to the later *China's Millions*, which Taylor edited from 1875-95 (with significant help from his second wife).

Back in China, Taylor enunciated two key principles for the CIM: "Indigenous" and "interior." He wrote, "I look on all us foreign missionaries as platform work round a rising building; . . . the sooner it can be transferred to other places, to serve the same temporary purpose, the better for the work . . . and the better for the places yet to be evangelised."[14] Hudson Taylor's missionary strategy had clearly changed over time. Although at first he relied upon itinerant preaching and the sale of Christian literature, he quickly came to believe that settled work, cooperation with Chinese Christian evangelists, and preaching to explain the printed message were also necessary. His mature plan was to send out a Western missionary with an experienced Chinese worker to train him and demonstrate truly Chinese methods of preaching. As Taylor had done long ago with Burns, working systematically, they would circle a major city for some time, moving gradually closer as the people began to lose their fear and suspicion of the messengers of a new religion, and finally settle in the town. Eventually, a mission station would be opened, with a chapel, and often a school for children and a medical clinic. Frequent trips to the regions around the city formed an essential part of this plan. Contrary to frequent claims that he was an advocate of "blitz evangelism," Taylor always believed in methodical, repeated, and strategic work in a region until a truly Chinese church had been planted and local leaders raised up; then the missionary was to move on. Always, he aimed to plant Chinese churches presided over by Chinese leaders, with the missionary assisting until he was no longer needed and could move on to open another field.[15]

14. Chang, et al., *Christ Alone*, 57.

15. He worked out these principles with his good friend, John Nevius, who later applied them so successfully in Korea.

Wherever possible, he and his colleagues sought to make friends with the *literati* to share the Gospel with these influential members of the community, often by first engaging them as language teachers. Not a few of the mandarin class did become Christians, the most famous among them being Xi Shengmo, "Pastor Hsi," whose career is briefly described in this volume. Mostly, however, new believers came from ordinary folk, and often from those who had sought for spiritual reality in some of the "reform" sects of Buddhism. Since the CIM missionaries worked in the interior of China, they did not have many opportunities to mingle with the educated elite of the cities. Taylor and his team intentionally kept pressing farther and farther into places where other Western missionaries had not penetrated and probably would not wish to live.

Taylor's own experience treating sick Chinese convinced him of the value of medical work. As much as possible, he continued to combine evangelism and teaching with medical ministry to suffering Chinese, who were all the more eager to hear his message after seeing the love of God demonstrated palpably. That is why a chapel and a medical clinic frequently combined in holistic ministry. As the numbers of CIM workers increased, he served as the mission physician, often traveling long distances to tend to women in childbirth or nurse critically ill missionaries. All too often, he had to console grieving family members who had lost someone to disease. One later wrote, "Anyone who knew Mr. Taylor would understand how truly he entered into our sorrow. . . He seemed to lay aside everything else for the time being to be as a *father* to us."[16] Naturally, his loving care strengthened the bonds of affection between him and his fellow workers. He provided basic medical training to new missionaries, and eventually saw a number of medically-trained men join the CIM, including his son and biographer, Howard. From then on, the CIM never failed to attend to the sick among and around them. Clinics and hospitals eventually became a major aspect of the overall CIM operation in China.[17]

RETURN TO ENGLAND AND OPEN DOORS FOR WOMEN MISSIONARIES

Taylor suffered a back injury in 1874 and had to return to England, where he lay convalescing for six long months, during which time he prayed for

---

16. Chang, et al., *Christ Alone*, 72.

17. This policy has continued in the successor to the CIM, OMF International, and in a separate but related organization founded by James H. Taylor III, great-grandson of Hudson Taylor.

the nine provinces as yet unreached by any Protestant missionary. Finally, in 1875, he issued a call for eighteen missionaries to launch out as pioneers, men of strong faith, burning zeal, and a willingness to suffer. The response was dramatic, and two dozen volunteered for the new venture. He returned to China in 1876 to lead the fresh advance, energizing everyone with his own dedication, vitality, and faith. In coming decades, Taylor and his CIM colleagues would call for seventy new workers, then one hundred, and then, with all the other Protestant societies in China, for one thousand missionaries to join with an equal number of Chinese to take the message of Christ to every household in China. Each time, despite others' doubts, God brought in the requested number.

A terrible drought devastated large portions of China in 1876–1879, causing disease, famine, and the death of millions. Like other missions, the CIM set aside other tasks to pour everything into famine relief. This demonstration of love opened many doors for the gospel, including among women. Having returned to England in 1877, Taylor was prevented by ill health from leaving England to help, but both he and Jennie sensed God's leading for her to spearhead the CIM's part in the relief effort, so she left in 1878. Back in China she and other women plunged into both relief and evangelism, establishing an orphanage in Taiyuan in the process. Jennie's contribution confirmed Taylor's sense that women could do a great deal that men could not, and led him to form the unprecedented strategy of sending unaccompanied single women in pairs as missionaries to regions where no other foreigners lived.

Almost from the beginning, Hudson Taylor had acutely sensed the need for Western Christian women to reach Chinese women with the gospel. Chinese etiquette forbade men from talking with women except within the family, so they were essentially unreachable to him and his male colleagues. Both Maria and Jennie were exceptionally effective in communicating truth and love to women and girls. Taylor's policy of sending out unattended women evoked harsh criticism at first, because it was feared that unprotected Western women would fall prey to unscrupulous and even violent men, but hardly any such incidents took place, while dozens of women labored successfully in remote regions. Though he held traditional views about the subordinate role of women in the church, he gave them ample scope to exercise their gifts in encouraging Chinese male leaders privately, as well as evangelizing and teaching women and children.[18]

---

18. Wigram, *The Bible and Mission in Faith Perspective*, 209–14. Taylor's deployment of women sprang from pragmatic, not theological, convictions.

In keeping with contemporary British Christian values, Hudson Taylor considered his calling as a missionary to take precedence over family life, though he deeply cared for his wives and children. He believed also that a missionary wife should see herself as much a "missionary" as a "wife." When duty called, the family had to endure long separations, which were keenly painful to him, for he was a man of powerful affection, as many love letters to Maria and then to Jennie reveal.

FINAL YEARS OF MINISTRY

Taylor returned to China for the fifth time in 1879, but soon fell ill again and nearly died. He and Jennie sought refuge in Yantai (Chefoo), on the coast of Shandong. Small in stature, he struggled with the illnesses that often felled Westerners in China, including dysentery, which was frequently fatal. Headaches, kidney stones, and a variety of other ailments sapped his strength. Disease and injuries (such as two to his spine) laid him aside on occasion, sometimes for months and even years at a time. He took advantage of these periods of enforced rest, however, waiting upon God in prayer and seeking fresh strength and guidance.

This period of convalescence in Yantai was no exception, for Taylor saw the value of Yantai, with its more temperate climate, as a place where sick missionaries could recuperate and a school for their children could be established, the later famous Chefoo School, which opened in 1881. When his health improved, Taylor traveled more than fifteen thousand miles to visit his new workers and to find places for future mission stations. By 1885, the CIM had 137 missionaries in thirteen provinces, and had established forty-five churches, 141 mission stations and out-stations, and sixteen schools, with 1,764 baptized Chinese Christians.

During the next decade, even more dramatic growth took place. The famous "Cambridge Seven" joined the CIM, stirring up tremendous interest among educated people. After Taylor visited the United States at the invitation of D. L. Moody, a North American Council was established, with Henry Frost as director, and Americans and Canadians began filling the ranks of the mission, followed by members from Scotland and Australia as a consequence of Taylor's travels to those places. At the invitation of Continental friends, he journeyed to Europe with the message of China's spiritual needs and open doors, prompting the formation of no fewer than seven "associate missions" in Scandinavia and Germany. The CIM became an interdenominational, international organization and the largest Protestant mission society in China.

Whenever he was in Great Britain, he was in constant demand as a speaker. Always, he pled for China and for a deeper walk with God; everywhere, people were deeply moved by the evident presence of God in his life. During this period, also, the CIM China headquarters were established in Shanghai, where a commodious building, designed by Taylor, was constructed to provide rest for missionaries, welcome to new workers, and offices for the running of the mission. Back in London, the CIM headquarters and mission home moved into a large building on Newington Green.[19] In time, Taylor made provision for his eventual retirement by appointing John Stevenson as deputy director, then William Cooper as China director, and finally, after Cooper had been killed in the Boxer Rebellion and Taylor was clearly unfit to continue to carry the load, in 1903 he named D. E. Hoste as his successor as general director.

All of these travels and speaking engagements, not to mention constant prayer for his hundreds of workers by name, could not help but take a toll, and he suffered a stroke in Boston in May, 1900, a month after addressing the Ecumenical Missionary Conference in New York on "The Source of Power for Foreign Missionary Work." He and Jennie went to Davos, Switzerland, for his recovery, just as dozens of CIM missionaries and their children were being murdered by the Boxers along with more than two thousand Chinese believers in their churches. As news came in, Taylor's tender heart was broken. He eventually recovered enough to return to China in January, 1905, for the eleventh time, but not after Jennie had succumbed to cancer in 1904.

His last journey to the land that had completely claimed his love and his life for fifty years was almost a triumphal tour, as missionaries and Chinese Christians alike showered their love upon "the Venerable Preacher" with his long white beard, sparkling eyes, loving face, and undiminished zeal and spiritual vitality.[20] As often before, his son Howard and daughter-in-law Geraldine, who became his first biographers, accompanied him.[21] He passed away peacefully in Changsha on June 3, 1905, deeply mourned by thousands of Chinese, many of whom accompanied his casket much of the

---

19. My wife and I stayed in this impressive and historic place on our way to Asia with OMF in 1975.

20. Here, as in so many places, Alvyn Austin's portrait of Taylor in *China's Millions* is totally inaccurate.

21. Their two-volume biography has been regularly denounced as pious and romantic hagiography. True, it does not record Taylor's flaws, but this was typical in the era of the "great man theory of history." Furthermore, it is meant to be primarily a devotional and spiritual biography. As a work of history, however, it otherwise excels in its copious use of first-hand sources and eyewitness accounts, which are liberally quoted.

way to its resting place alongside Maria's grave in Zhenjiang, Jiangsu. He was survived by five children.

REASONS FOR HIS EXTRAORDINARY INFLUENCE

In addition to an evident affection for his fellow workers and a willingness to sacrifice himself for their welfare, Hudson Taylor combined extraordinary vision with unusual administrative ability. He knew how to train others and then to delegate authority and responsibility to them. A great deal of his impact on others flowed from excellent communication. As a speaker, he wielded unusual sway over large audiences; in person, despite a humble, quiet demeanor, he quickly won trust and allegiance; and as a writer, he reached many thousands of avid readers, especially through his many articles in the CIM's magazine, *China's Millions*.

Though adamant on principles of action, he was patient with those who opposed him. All who became members of the CIM knew that they were placing themselves under his authority as director. In that sense, his leadership was "authoritarian," but in no way did he act like a despot or tyrant. He led, rather, by example; prayer; clearly-enunciated principles; constant communication; and great forbearance towards recalcitrant members, including those who spread malicious slander and fomented open rebellion against him.

As a leader, Taylor was eminently approachable. He loved children and delighted in playing with them, all the more so when he keenly missed his own little ones. He cheered others by singing hymns that he had memorized and by playing on his harmonium, which he always took with him.[22] On journeys, he would regularly rise early and shoot fowl for small game to supply fresh meat for his fellow travelers. Prompt in business, he stayed up late at night to handle the increasing burden of correspondence, always making a copy for reference. In the early years, he would personally select appropriate supplies and equipment for new workers to take with them to China, and arrange their passage on ships. His attention to detail was matched only by his grasp of overall strategy, his concern for people, and his deep piety. In other words, he earned the love and respect of almost all those who served under him. As Griffith John said after Taylor's death, "Firmness and love procured him a moral sway over the hearts of men. . . God and His love; Christ and His Cross, the Gospel as God's *one* remedy for China and the

---

22. The harmonium is "an organlike keyboard instrument that produces tones with free metal reeds actuated by air forced from a bellows." *American Heritage Dictionary of the English Language*, 602.

whole world, were realities to him. His trust in God was implicit . . . He lived in Christ and Christ lived in him. . . His heart was full of love."[23] His successor as general director, Dixon Hoste remarked, "We can witness to his beautiful character . . . the sources of his influence lay . . . in his humility, love and sympathy."[24]

He never asked others to do what he himself had not already done. He set an example for others not only in tireless labors and travels, as we have seen, but also as a diligent scholar, though not an academic like James Legge. His daily Bible reading was done in Hebrew, Greek, and English. To gain entrance to medical school, he had to pass examinations in Latin, Greek, German, and French, as well as geography, mathematics, mechanics, chemistry, zoology and botany. After qualifying as a Member of the Royal College of Surgeons and then receiving his Licentiate in Midwifery, he continued his study of medicine, both Western and Chinese, but also read widely in mathematics, astronomy, chemistry, Chinese history and culture, and theology. He was an avid naturalist, observing and classifying the varied flora and fauna of China that so fascinated him. For his reports on such subjects and on the topography and cities of China, he was elected a Fellow of the Royal Geographic Society. He eventually learned not only Mandarin, but also Shanghainese, the Tiechiu dialect of Swatow, and the Ningbo dialect, the last well enough to revise a vernacular version of the New Testament that had been made for speakers of that tongue.

NOTABLE SAYINGS

Hudson Taylor's penetrating words issued from a mind saturated by the Word of God and a heart captured by the love of Christ. Here are a few of his notable utterances:[25]

> Christ is either Lord of all or He isn't Lord at all.
> Now when you are so possessed with the Living God that you are in your secret heart pleased and delighted over the peculiar, personal, private guardianship of the Holy Spirit over your life, you will have found the vestibule of heaven.
> Oh! For eloquence to plead the cause of China; for a pencil dipped in fire to paint the condition of this people!
> China is not to be won for Christ by quiet, ease-loving men and women . . . The stamp of men and women we need is such as

23. Quoted in Broomhall, *It is not Death To Die!*, 511–12.
24. Ibid., 512.
25. Chang, et al., *Christ Alone*, 170–85.

will put Jesus, China, souls, first and foremost in everything and at every time—even life itself must be secondary.

Shall not the eternal interests of one-third of our race stir up the deepest sympathies of our nature, the most strenuous efforts of our blood-bought powers? Shall not the low wail of helpless, hopeless misery, arising from half the heathen world, pierce our sluggish ear, and rouse us—body, soul, and spirit—to one mighty, continued, unconquerable effort for China's salvation?

We wish to see Christian Chinese men and women, true Christians, but withal true Chinese in every sense of the word. We wish to see churches of Christian Chinese presided over by Chinese pastors and officers, worshipping in edifices of a thoroughly Chinese style of architecture.

We do well to recognize that we are not here as representatives of Western Powers, and that our duties do not correspond to theirs.

There is a living God; He has spoken in the Bible. He means what He says, and will do all he has promised.

It is no vain thing to wait upon God.

You can work without praying, but it is a bad plan; but you cannot pray in earnest without working. Do not be so busy with work for Christ that you have no strength left for praying. True prayer requires strength.

Depend on it: God's work, done in God's way, will never lack God's supplies.

If I had a thousand pounds, China should have it—if I had a thousand lives China should have them. No! Not China, but Christ. Can we do too much for Him? Can we do enough for such a precious Savior?

CRITICISMS OF HUDSON TAYLOR

In his own day as well as now, Hudson Taylor had, and has, his critics. We must address some of their concerns in order to gain a balanced portrayal of him.

Like some other missionaries, but not most, Taylor believed that the Great Commission gave Christians not only the right, but the obligation, to disobey rulers who forbade the preaching of the gospel. For that reason, he transgressed the treaty stipulations that limited foreigners to five ports and their immediate environs. The debate over the propriety of Christians engaging in illegal evangelistic activity in China continues today. His early illegal itinerations were met with mostly warm welcomes by the crowds who came to hear him preach and to receive medical treatment, but angry protests by Chinese mandarins to the British consular authorities. He was willing to accept fines and even suffering for breaking the law, but not to endanger his Chinese coworkers and new converts, so he reluctantly abided by the orders of the British consul.

In recent years, with the huge gender imbalance in the Chinese church, Taylor's policy of using women without men to open new mission stations has come under closer scrutiny. Some have suggested that single women missionaries planted churches in which women and girls predominated, and that Christianity, like popular Chinese religion, thus came to be considered a thing for women and not men. Others point out the ways in which single women were able to encourage Chinese men to lead their own churches.

Similarly, the recent emphasis upon family life as an essential ingredient of effective Christian ministry has generated objections to Taylor's perceived over-emphasis upon "the work." Though he himself clearly enjoyed extremely close and loving relationships with his wives and children, as evidence by their intense affection for him and the entrance of several of his children into the CIM, not everyone was able to imitate him in this way. Missionary marriages could dry up under the pressure of constant ministry and long separations, and children could be adversely affected by having to live away from their parents most of the year. Regardless of how we evaluate Hudson Taylor's own family life, we can say that a precedent was set—and not only by him—for an over-emphasis upon "God's work" and a relative neglect of the family that caused many wives and children to suffer more loneliness and emotional dryness than might have been necessary. At the same time, we should note that prolonged separations from Maria and then Jennie frequently drove him to depths of despondency and loneliness. These times apart were "a great trial" for him; more than once, he would say, "My heart feels ready to break."[26]

Taylor's friends and family believed that overwork frequently contributed to his ill health. Both Maria and Jennie urged him not to overtax his strength and neglect his health, but to no avail, except when he had suffered one of his breakdowns and could not go on. Reading any of the biographies of him, but especially the seven-volume treatment by A. J. Broomhall, one cannot escape the impression that he may have had too much of a sense of responsibility and perhaps too little faith that God could do without him. To be sure, he often faced life-and-death situations and felt his physical presence was necessary. Nevertheless, the opinions of those who knew him best

---

26. Broomhall, *Assault on the Nine*, 308.

appear to be accurate; he did push himself too hard, attempted too much, and thus paid a high price. He probably should have paced himself better. In this, he did not set a good example.

Taylor's refusal to pour resources into higher education has also been seen as a major failure. From his earliest days as a missionary in Shanghai, Taylor demonstrated the high value of education by opening a school for Chinese children himself and then making primary and secondary education a major CIM strategy both of evangelism and of building up the nascent Chinese church. He did not think that higher education, especially that which aimed to spread Western civilization as a means of "Christianizing" China, a useful means of spreading the Gospel, so he focused on training young men to be Christian leaders and preachers, and girls to be wives for them. The history of Christian colleges in China confirms his evangelical convictions to a certain extent, since relatively few students became Christians, though as a group, the graduates of Christian colleges in China made a huge impact upon the modernization of China, and some did become outstanding church leaders. In general, however, the history of Christian higher education shows that it "secularizes" both students and faculty.[27]

A number of people have claimed that Hudson Taylor had a low view of Chinese culture, in contrast to men like James Legge, W. A. P. Martin, and especially Timothy Richard.[28] On the one hand, Hudson Taylor evinced unusual respect for many features of traditional Chinese culture, as we see from his adoption of local customs of dress, eating, dwelling, and etiquette, not to mention learning the oral and written language. He took an avid interest in all aspects of the China he encountered, including its history, religion, customs, and natural environment. He greatly respected James Legge, and prized his translations of the Chinese classics and commentaries upon them. On the other hand, like most other missionaries in the nineteenth century, he believed that Chinese religion would not lead either to eternal salvation or to ethical transformation, and he considered the lofty principles of Confucianism to be ineffective in changing lives. Taylor did not think that the Confucian rites of ancestor reverence were merely expressive of respect. For most Chinese, they involved also a belief in the continued existence of departed loved ones whose welfare depended upon constant offerings,

---

27. In *Evangelicalism*, James Davison Hunter wrote of "the radical and abrupt secularization of higher education" in American Christian colleges (168). For many reasons, "education secularizes" (171). For an insightful description of the process of secularization in the American academy, which had started even in the eighteenth century, see Aikman, *One Nation Without God?*, 130–51.

28. See, for example, the negative assessment of Taylor by Peter Ng in *Chinese Christianity*, 130.

and a profound fear of "angry ghosts."[29] He thus opposed W. A. P. Martin's motion to the Missionary Convention of 1890, and was supported in this by the overwhelming majority of delegates.[30] We might add that this stance was followed also by "almost all" Chinese Protestants, who have "followed Taylor in destroying their ancestral plaques on becoming Christians."[31]

LEGACY

When he died, not only had J. Hudson Taylor left behind the largest foreign missionary organization in China, but several other missionary societies had been brought into being largely as a result of Taylor's itinerant work of promoting the cause of China in Europe, North America, and Australia.[32] His son, grandson, great-grandson, and great-great grandson all followed him into lifelong ministry among the Chinese, who highly revere the memory of one who loved them enough to become one of them. Anyone who has served among the Chinese knows how the name "Dai Desheng" brings expressions of admiration, even reverence.

---

29. For a concise but excellent survey of this debate, see Broomhall, *Assault on the Nine*, 283–88.

30. Taylor's action at the conference has been misunderstood and misrepresented, however. He did not intend to "call the question," as others around him thought; he really wanted the debate on Martin's motion to be continued to the next day. See Broomhall, *It Is Not Death To Die*, 140–42; and G. Wright Doyle, "*Hudson Taylor's Attitude towards Chinese Culture: a Critique*," http://www.globalchinacenter.org/analysis/christianity-in-china/respect-for-chinese-culture-the-example-of-hudson-taylor-part-two.php.

31. Pfister, "Rethinking Mission," 211.

32. At the time of his death, the CIM had 828 missionaries; there were 1152 Chinese workers, 18,625 baptized Chinese Christians, 418 churches, 1424 mission stations, and 150 schools.

6

William A. P. Martin
Pioneer of Progress in China

G. Wright Doyle

"Early in the morning of April 10, 1850, we were startled by the cry of 'Pirate! Pirate!' from our Dutch cabin-boy; but instead of those freebooters, so dreaded in the China seas, we were boarded by a pilot, who soon brought the good ship 'Lantao' to anchor in the harbor of Hong Kong, after a voyage of one hundred and thirty-four days from Boston—a voyage which may now be made in one fifth of the time."[1] With that light-hearted beginning, W. A. P. Martin's long and illustrious career as an American missionary in China commenced. When he died, he was honored both by his fellow missionaries and by scholars and officials in China for his remarkably influential sixty-six years as a "pioneer of progress" in China.[2]

---

1. Martin, *Cycle of Cathay*, 17.

2. The title of the definitive biography of Martin by Ralph Covell is *W. A. P. Martin: Pioneer of Progress in China*. That book, along with Martin's two volumes, *Cycle of Cathay* and *The Lore of Cathay*, provides most of the information on which this chapter is based.

EARLY YEARS

William Alexander Parsons Martin was born on April 10, 1827, in Livonia, Indiana, the son of an evangelical Presbyterian pastor, William Martin, whose "example of sacrificial labor to bring religious progress to Indiana's frontier was not lost on his son, who later integrated his many activities in education, science, and diplomacy with aggressive evangelism."[3] Not only did the frontier pastor engage in the usual activities of a Christian minister, but he also promoted education, believing it essential for the total wellbeing of settlers in the expanding frontier. He taught both his children and the children of others at his home, using a broad curriculum that included both the natural sciences and biblical and religious studies.

Martin and his siblings were not unaware of happenings around the world, or of the growing American missionary enterprise. His sister went to South Africa as a missionary, and he and his brothers were named after missionaries. His names derived from his uncle William Alexander, who served in the Sandwich Islands, and Levi Parsons, a missionary to the Jews in Palestine. His own "interest in China was first awakened in 1839 by the boom of British cannon battering down her outer walls,"[4] during the First Opium War, one in a series of conflicts in which western powers forced open the gates of China to commerce, diplomacy, and the spread of Christianity.

Though brought up in a disciplined and godly home, he did not experience any dramatic conversion, or at least did not refer to one in later years. Perhaps this absence of an emotional encounter with God through faith in Christ points toward his later almost total focus on intellectual apprehension of truth—and thus the necessity of education; the absence of what might be called a "devotional" tone in his writings; a very marked self-confidence; and a strong reluctance to admit that he might be wrong.

He and his brother Samuel went to Indiana University at Bloomington in 1843. By that time, the university was essentially secular in character. Martin was profoundly influenced by Professor Andrew Wylie, who had left the Presbyterian Church over doctrinal conflicts. Wylie believed in Manifest Destiny, namely that "America's mission was to bring 'science, liberal principles in government, and the true religion to the peoples of Asia.'"[5] Wylie also followed the Scottish school of Common Sense philosophy, which held that the external world is real and that the existence of cause and effect

---

3. Covell, *Martin*, 6.
4. Martin, *Cycle of Cathay*, 19.
5. Covell, *Martin*, 15.

could be used to prove the existence of God and therefore encouraged a spirit of scientific inquiry.

In 1845, having learned of missionary work in China through reports from missionaries, Martin decided to go to China as a missionary. He entered New Albany Theological Seminary in preparation for ordination as a Presbyterian minister. At New Albany, he was introduced to William Paley's *Natural Theology*, which he later used in the composition of his Christian Evidences. He taught school for a while to earn money for seminary, thus gaining experience as an educator. The theme of his graduation oration points clearly to his later career as a missionary: "The Uses of the Physical Sciences as an Equipment of the Missionary." Already at this early age, he thought that the missions enterprise necessarily included a variety of activities and goals, including general education. He applied to the Presbyterian Foreign Mission Board in January, 1849, and was ordained as a Teaching Elder in the Presbyterian church in October 1849. One month later, he married Jan VanSant, thus fulfilling what was then considered to be a requirement for male missionaries. He and his bride immediately set sail, along with his brother and wife and others, to join other Presbyterian missionaries in Ningbo (Ningpo).

NINGBO

"Ningpo appealed to missionaries because it was less anti-foreign than Canton, had extremely pleasant surroundings, was thought to be healthful, and was inhabited by people disposed to listen to the Gospel."[6] The first American Presbyterian to arrive in Ningbo, Dr. Divie McCartee, had settled there in June, 1844, and was soon joined by other missionaries. Although the missionaries of various societies enjoyed harmonious relations with each other, meeting monthly for a prayer meeting and exchanging pulpits, the American Presbyterians found it difficult to get along with each other. They disagreed among themselves about whether to start a boys' boarding school, for example. In contrast to Martin's later position, they disparaged ceremonies to ancestors as idolatry.

When Martin and his party arrived, the Presbyterian Missionaries in Ningbo were "already experienced in the work, well-versed in the Chinese language and accommodated to established policies and attitudes."[7] As new arrivals, William Martin and his brother were assigned to senior missionaries to learn from them. They immediately began the arduous process

6. Ibid., 47.
7. Ibid., 51.

of learning Chinese, in this case the Ningbo dialect. An avid and gifted student, Martin soon enjoyed language study. Employing two teachers so that he could study both day and night, he found that after "a few days the mists began to rise, and our further progress, from an irksome task, became a fascinating pastime."[8]

Since the Ningbo dialect could not be accurately represented by Mandarin-based Chinese characters, Martin devised a phonetic system, using Roman letters, to write it out, and soon had formed a society to produce it, as an aid for missionaries in acquiring the language. They also taught some Chinese to use the phonetic system. One missionary produced a hymn book in the phonetic alphabet, to which Martin and his brother contributed a few hymns. Using the phonetic script, the "Chinese saw with astonishment their children taught to read in a few days, instead of spending years in painful toil, as they must with the native characters. Old women of three-score and ten, and illiterate servants and laborers, on their conversion, found by this means their eyes opened to read in their own tongue wherein they were born the wonderful works of God."[9] Martin hoped that this way of teaching Chinese to read would spread throughout China, but was disappointed in that aspiration. By the end of a year he could preach in the local dialect, and within five years, he had also "read the nine chief works which form the basis of Chinese literature" and had begun to "employ the learned or classic language [literary Mandarin] for the purpose of [written] communication."[10]

Soon after arriving in Ningbo, he and his wife moved into the Chinese city. "I wanted to be near the people. . . There I spent six years, the most fruitful of my life; and there I came to know the people as I could not had I been content to view them at a distance."[11] He later criticized missionaries who stayed in their fortress-like compounds. He took a part in the construction of a new church, built with Corinthian columns, in the center of the city. The people were receptive, because the British had treated them well and even protected them during the recent war. "They never tired of telling how Dr. Gutzlaff, formerly a missionary in Hong Kong, had been installed in the *yamen* of the prefect, and how careful he was to see justice done."[12]

8. Ibid., 53.
9. Ibid., 56.
10. Ibid., 56.
11. Martin, *Cycle of Cathay*, 65.
12. Ibid., 66–67. Karl Friedrich August Gutzlaff (1803–51), anglicized as Charles Gutzlaff, was a German missionary to the Far East. Remarkably brilliant and learned, he wrote a number of widely read books about his travels. He served as interpreter for the British diplomats during and after the Opium Wars and served as a magistrate in Ningbo for a while. He was one of the first Protestant missionaries to adopt Chinese clothing.

Martin records that this made "it safe and pleasant for us to promenade the streets—it opened to us the doors of many families," and visits from local officials prompted him to learn the official dialect of Mandarin. "Its acquisition was easy," he reported.[13] Though their association, his teacher became a Christian.

Soon, Martin engaged in preaching, teaching in the church schools, and "writing or translating a variety of books and pamphlets."[14] He spoke to a congregation of about two hundred, mostly artisans, in the city chapel, and to a larger, more educated audience in the larger downtown church building to which his home was attached. He also engaged in itineration in the nearby area, sometimes preaching to thousands of people at a time. He traveled frequently to surrounding areas both to preach and to take his family on vacations, especially to escape the awful heat. City life affected his health, as well as his family's, which eventually led him to return to American for rest and recuperation, but also played a role in his decision to move to northern China.

While serving in Ningbo, he was involved in many disputes with his fellow Presbyterian missionaries, some of whom accused him of being contentious. Martin was perceived to be lenient on admission of candidates for baptism, and he often crossed verbal swords with Dr. McCartee, who "[felt] that Martin was too ready to accept a man whose conversion was purely intellectual rather than spiritual."[15] Perhaps his own mostly rational commitment to the faith influenced his perceptions of Chinese with similar experiences. On one occasion, when three converts were presented for baptism, their answers to questions about the hypostatic union in Christ brought charges of heresy against Martin.[16]

EVIDENCES OF CHRISTIANITY

In the church, where his audience was usually more highly educated, he lectured on Christian apologetics. These lectures, based on William Paley's work, were later published in 1854 as *T'ien-tao su-yuan* (*Evidences of Christianity*). In a move to gain a hearing among China's elite, Martin suggested that "the *ta-tao* (great doctrine) was not the property of either East or

---

13. Martin, *Cycle of Cathay*, 67.
14. Covell, *Martin*, 58.
15. Duus, "Science and Salvation in China," 19.
16. Covell, *Martin*, 69. The hypostatic union is that between Christ's deity and his humanity. Later investigations by ecclesiastical authorities affirmed Martin's basic orthodoxy.

West—its origin was in Heaven with a personal God who, he argued, might be referred to as shen, t'ien-chu, or shang-ti."[17] Over the course of several decades, this book reached thousands of intellectuals, and decades afterwards, was judged by his fellow missionaries as "the most popular Christian book ever published in China."[18] The book was divided into three sections: evidences of Christianity, natural theology, and revealed theology.

The first part appealed to "an orderly world and the reliability of man's rational capability of perception," to show the existence of God.[19] For each point of his argument, he engaged a particular Chinese concept in order to make contact with his readers. Examples include the five elements, the idea that each form of life has its heaven-bestowed nature, the obedience of Jesus as an example of filial piety, and the Christian religion as one of "morality and rectitude," a fundamentally Confucian value.[20] He also sought to answer typical objections posed by educated Chinese, and sprinkled his argument with allusions to Chinese literature. We may reasonably suppose that Martin's remarkable familiarity with, and obvious respect for, Chinese classics and contemporary writings and customs played a great part in the amazing influence and popularity of this book.

The second part of the volume, on natural theology, relied more on Scripture to show man's need for revelation, as well as on evidences to show the truth of that revelation. Martin pointed to the "historic triumphs of Christianity as it was propagated throughout the world," as well as ways in which it had made the Western nations strong, as evidence of its universal truth.[21] Indeed, "Martin identified his Christian faith with Western civilization and used the latter as an evidence of the former."[22]

He also related Christianity to Confucianism and Buddhism, though without fully endorsing them. For example, he showed that Christianity, like Confucianism and Buddhism, considered the inward transformation of character important. He made clear that Confucianism, "although

17. Ibid., 110.

18. Ibid., 59.

19. Though he claimed not to have consulted any "authority," in this, as throughout the book, Martin followed William Paley's *Natural Theology; or Evidences of the Existence and Attributes of the Deity. Collected from the Appearances of Nature*, first published in 1802, and widely used in the Protestant world for many years. Covell, *Martin*, 110. In addition to William Paley's *Natural Theology*, Covell thought that Martin may also have been consciously following Matteo Ricci's famous work, *A True Disputation about God*.

20. Covell, *Martin*, 115.

21. Ibid.

22. Ibid., 123.

correct and beautiful in his view, was not complete, for it had completely neglected the Divine dimension in doctrines of the *wu-lun*, the five human relationships,"[23] but Chinese did not need to turn their backs on Confucius entirely. "Confucianism and Christianity may be distinguished in terms of breadth and narrowness, but not in terms of truth and error."[24] On the other hand, Jesus is God-man and thus the only savior. Martin also, like other Christian authors, freely employed Buddhist words to translate such terms as heaven, hell, and the Scriptures, but he invested them with Christian meaning.

In the third and final section, he used much Scripture to expound the biblical doctrines of redemption and future life. He spoke plainly of human sin, a notion not congenial to most Confucianists, and pointed out the need for regeneration and new life by the power of the Spirit. In his section on ethics, he stressed individual responsibility more than social relationships. He stressed the importance of prayer; but not much on "getting things from God" through prayer, in stark contrast to Chinese religions. His treatment of sacraments and rites made it clear that Christians could engage in only those allowed by the Bible, not the worship of ancestors. Christians can, and should, express their filial piety in other ways, including some form of ritual in memory and respect of departed loved ones. The doctrine of the Trinity came last, and was fully orthodox. Perhaps significantly, he did not mention the second coming of Jesus Christ, a theme often found on the lips of some other missionaries, like J. Hudson Taylor.

Beyond lecturing on this material while in Ningbo, Martin also participated in the translation of the New Testament into the colloquial Ningbo language, using the Romanized script. He contributed translations of Matthew, John, and some of the Psalms.[25] He also wrote a book on the evils of opium. "At this stage of his life, Martin viewed science as valuable for presenting the Gospel, but science took second place to evangelism among the masses, and to a system of general apologetics for the intellectuals."[26] Later in life, in the last years of the Qing dynasty, he noted that "along with [Western] science came the Christian religion, and with it a spiritual force which is destined to effect a profound revolution in the inner life of the Chinese."[27] Others disagreed, thinking that missionaries should focus on expounding the Bible.

23. Ibid., 117.

24. Ibid., 118.

25. J. Hudson Taylor would later spend several years with another missionary revising this translation and adding references to other parts of the Bible.

26. Covell, *Martin*, 61.

27. Martin, *Cycle of Cathay*, 264.

ATTITUDE TOWARDS CONFUCIANISM

He received criticism, also, for his perceived approval of Confucianism. He stated his general position clearly: "There is no necessary conflict between Christ and Confucius."[28] Like James Legge, he believed that the biblical words for "God" (*Elohim* and *Theos*) were best translated by the ancient Chinese term Shang-ti (Shang Di), which meant "Supreme Lord."[29] He received a letter from his mission board in America saying, "The Executive committee of the Board objected strongly to Martin's avowed position that 'the Chinese classics teach the worship of the true God.'"[30]

What he said was, "In contrast, however, with our Holy Scriptures, the religious element in [the Confucian classics] is so frail and feeble as to suggest the aurora borealis rather than the life-giving sunshine. They recognize, under the names of Shangti or Tien, a Supreme Power, who presides over the destinies of men and dispenses rewards and punishments; but they do not inculcate the worship of that august Being. He is consequently forgotten by the people, and his place is usurped by idols."

On the other hand, "so pure are the moral teachings of these ancient [Confucian] writings that no nation, with one exception [i.e. the Hebrews] ever received from antiquity a more precious heritage."[31] Martin considered Confucius to be "one of the most human of sages—a sort of wiser, better Solomon," and noted that Confucius was not deified; "he is never invoked in the character of a tutelary divinity. The homage paid to him is purely commemorative. It is not, therefore, a direct obstacle to the acceptance of the Christian faith. . . Among the sages of the pagan world he comes nearest to Christ in virtue and influence."[32] "Few men have ever been more penetrated with reverence for the Supreme Power of the universe, whom, to avoid irreverence, he calls by the vague designation of Heaven." To Confucius, Heaven had personality, and could receive prayer. "To him it is due that the worship of Heaven still survives, for which the emperor officiates as high priest."[33]

Confucius was guilty, however, of allowing into *The Book of Odes* a poem disparaging the worth of girls. (Parenthetically, but of great

---

28. Ibid., 455.

29. For my view of this thorny question, see Doyle, "Problems in Translating the Bible into Chinese: The Name(s) for God," http://www.chinainst.org/en/articles/christianity-in-china/problems-in-translating-the-bible-into-chinese-the-names-for-god.php.

30. Covell, *Martin*, 68.

31. Martin, *Cycle of Cathay*, 58–59.

32. Ibid., 78, 287.

33. Ibid., 288.

importance, we should note Martin's estimation of Chinese women. Chinese culture taught women to consider themselves inferior; on the contrary, when Martin once saw 3,000 women praying together, and learned that they were praying that in the next life they would be born men, he wrote, "so unhappily, as well as inferior, are they taught to consider their present condition. Morally, however, they are China's better half—modest, graceful, and attractive. Intellectually, they are not stupid, but ignorant, left to grow up in a kind of twilight, without the benefits of schools. What they are capable of may be inferred from the fact that, in spite of disadvantages, many of them are found on the roll of honor as poets, historians, and rulers. Some of the brightest minds I ever met in China were those of girls in our mission schools. Woman ignorant has made China Buddhist; will not woman educated make her Christian?")[34]

"Confucius was above all a teacher of morals. So consonant is his system with that of Christianity that the golden rule, in a negative form, is its first law, and charity and humility among its leading virtues. He was not a Christ, but Moses. The chief defect of Confucianism is one that is inherent in the [Mosaic] 'law,' which, though 'holy, righteous, and good,' is yet 'weak through the flesh.' It is lacking in spiritual life."[35]

Confucius had immense practical wisdom, but "ignored, if he did not deny, . . . the immortality of the soul and the personal existence of God."[36] He substituted a rather impersonal Tian (heaven) for the very personal Shang Di. Furthermore, in his writings, "not a line can be found inculcating the pursuit of truth. Expediency, not truth, is the goal of his system."[37] His teachings were meant to be memorized, not pondered, unlike Christ, who "appealed to evidence and challenged inquiry."[38] "It was a philosophy, not a religion, that claimed to propagate."[39] Now it has become an idolatrous system, "worshiping the powers of nature, ancestors, and heroes."[40] And yet, though "in view and practices, the Chinese of to-day are polytheistic and idolatrous. . . Yet, . . . [there are] traces of a religious sentiment, deep and real, which is not connected with any of the objects of popular worship—and veneration for T'ian, or heaven, and a belief that in the visible heavens there resides some vague power who provides for the wants of men

---

34. Ibid., 82–83.
35. Ibid., 288.
36. Martin, *Lore of Cathay*, 176.
37. Ibid., 177.
38. Ibid.
39. Ibid., 178.
40. Ibid.

and rewards them according to their deeds."[41] Despite these problems with Confucianism and the "formalism and hypocrisy" of most of Confucius' followers,[42] Martin believed in an approach of "Confucius plus Christ," not Confucius or Christ."[43]

BUDDHISM

He saw Buddhism in a very different light: "No longer doing anything to strengthen or renovate Chinese society, Buddhism clings to it as ivy clings to a crumbling tower, deriving its nourishment from the rottenness of the structure."[44] He notes that "the philosophy of Buddhism, like that of the Stoics, has for its aim to protect the soul from suffering rather than to arm it for conflict with moral evil. Their method consists in a course of mental discipline, involving an elaborate system of metaphysics and a comparatively pure code of morals. . . Their ideal is light without heat."[45] Their monks "theoretically contemplative, pious, and virtuous, as a matter of fact most are . . . lazy, ignorant, and immoral."[46] Of original, philosophical Buddhism, he wrote: "It dries up the sources of life, wraps the soul in the cerements [cloth used for wrapping mummies] of the grave, and aims to convert a living being into a spiritual mummy which shall survive all changes without being affected by them."[47]

On the other hand, Buddhism has prepared the way for Christianity, for it "has given the Chinese such ideas as they possess of heaven and hell; and of spiritual beings, rising in a hierarchy above men. . . It has given them all their familiar terms relating to sin, to good works, to faith, to repentance, and, most important of all, to a righteous retribution, which includes the awards of a future life. . . Half the doctrines of Christianity are introduced to the Chinese in a dress borrowed from Buddhism."[48] In addition, they have introduced to China the notion that God is "a vigilant and merciful Providence."[49] Buddhism also has a sort of triad of faith, hope, and love.

41. Martin, *Lore of Cathay*, 165–66.
42. Martin, *Cycle of Cathay*, 289.
43. Duus, "Science and Salvation in China," 33.
44. Martin, *Cycle of Cathay*, 38.
45. Ibid., 229.
46. Ibid., 227.
47. Martin, *Lore of Cathay*, 186.
48. Ibid., 261.
49. Ibid., 255.

Faith that "keeps in view the realities of the unseen world."[50] Hope is seen in the "constant endeavors of a devout Buddhist to secure the rewards of the life to come"[51] in anticipation of the Pure Land or Western Paradise. Love is found in their emphasis upon compassion.[52] Finally, Buddhism has introduced the precedent of receiving a foreign religion and making it Chinese.

Martin thought less of Daoism: He said that *the Dao De Jing* "abounds in acute apothegms, and some of its passages rise to the character of sublimity; but so incoherent are its contents that it is impossible for any literal interpretation to form them into a system."[53] In this short work, the Dao is impersonal, not personal, though there are some superficial resemblances to Christianity. Daoists originally believed in Shangdi, but this faith degenerated later into polytheism. As a philosophy, it is materialistic. They believed the body might survive death if perfected by discipline or the elixir of life.

Ancestor Worship

Very early, Martin realized that ancestor worship held a place of supreme importance for the Chinese. "It is the leading element in the religion of the people. . . It constitutes the very heart of the religion of China."[54] Among civilized nations, the Chinese "alone have shaped their offices for the dead into an all-pervading and potent cult which moulds the social and spiritual life of every individual in the Empire."[55] Worship of ancestors "also strengthens the ties of kinship, and binds together those family and tribal groups on which the government so much relies for the control of its individual subjects." The local temple shrine to ancestors served as a "church, theatre, school-house, counsel-room . . ."[56] It motivated people to good in this life and inculcated a faith in the next life.

The question, therefore, was what the attitude and teaching of missionaries should be regarding this issue. At some times, the element of worship was clear, as when worshipers prayed for blessing upon themselves.[57] Could anything good be found in this system? Most missionaries said no. On the Chinese side, "Nothing has ever aroused such active [Chinese] opposition

---

50. Ibid., 259.
51. Ibid., 260.
52. Ibid.
53. Ibid., 180.
54. Ibid., 266–67.
55. Ibid., 268.
56. Ibid., 272.
57. Ibid., 273.

to Christianity as the discovery that it stands in irreconcilable antagonism to the worship of ancestors."[58]

W. A .P. Martin thought that Christians should "prune off [idolatrous elements] and retain all that is good and beautiful in the institution." The tablet with ancestors' names on it could be kept, and offerings of flowers could be substituted for incense and food. Going further, he maintained that even prostration before the tomb of the departed could be allowed, because other missionaries agreed that there was nothing wrong with bowing before living elders. Remove geomancy and "invocation of departed spirits" in prayer, and Chinese believers could keep the rest of the rites with a clear conscience.[59]

Likewise, Martin held that the Emperor, when officiating at the sacrifices at the Temple of Heaven, was "like Melchizedek of old . . . a priest of the most high God."[60] He approved of the action of James Legge, who took off his shoes before ascending the steps to the altar.[61] Unwittingly revealing what some would consider a lack of theological perception, he claimed that there was no necessary conflict between Christ and Confucius, any more than there was between Paul and Plato. Martin believed that all the religions of China had left room for "a fourth stage in the progression—one which China is waiting for. Christianity alone can supply the defects of all the systems, and present one harmonious unity." The other religions were materialistic, and only asked, "Is it good?" and not "Is it true?,"[62] but Martin believed that Christianity could emancipate Chinese from their neglect of God as the standard and source of ethical excellence and stimulate a spirit of inquiry.

TAIPING REBELLION AND AFTERWARD

When the great rebellion led by the semi-Christian Hong Xiuquan broke out, Martin was perplexed by the relatively slow progress of Christianity in China and wondered whether the Taipings were God's means of bringing faster growth, either by establishing a new Christian dynasty or by bringing down the old one and forcing it to allow missionaries to travel freely. He remained supportive as the revolt continued. Sympathetic to their Christian intentions, he looked gently on their doctrinal deviations as marks only

58. Ibid., 276.
59. Ibid., 277.
60. Ibid., 168.
61. Ibid., 167.
62. Ibid., 195–96.

of immaturity. As the true character of the rebels and their beliefs became more evident, however, he wrote, "To them the restraints of morality were as flax in the flames; and what purpose would it serve to attempt to mould the theology of a people who received revelations from heaven?"[63]

Despite his disappointment with the Taipings, he wrote letters to the US Government and to newspapers advocating US neutrality, not support for the Manchus, whom he considered effete, corrupt, and incorrigibly anti-Christian. "He saw his duty—participation in one more phase of making China a Christian nation—and he acted upon it."[64] He said of the rebellion's failure, "who can tell by how many centuries it has postponed the adoption of Christianity by the Chinese people?"[65] He lamented, "More than once, when the insurgents were on the verge of success, the prejudices of short-sighted diplomats decided against them, and an opportunity was lost such as does not occur once in a thousand years."[66] Though the Manchu government was able to combat the Taiping rebels, their simultaneous war with Britain and France ended in disaster.[67] During the "Arrow War," Martin believed that the British were in the wrong, but that the process was God's way of opening the empire to the gospel.

Martin applied for, and received, a post as helper in the treaty negations of 1858 in order to "promote the missionary cause in the treaty renewal and have some weight in securing the desired provisions for liberty of

63. Martin, *Cycle of Cathay*, 131.
64. Covell, *Martin*, 87.
65. Martin, *Cycle of Cathay*, 133.
66. Ibid., 142.

67. Variously called The Second Opium War, the "Arrow" War, and the Second Anglo-Chinese War, this conflict was fought between 1856 and 1860. It originated when Chinese soldiers boarded a ship near Guangzhou, which the British claimed was registered as one of their own, and seized the crew. Though the Chinese later released the crew, the British used this incident as a pretext for attacking Guangzhou and then later to take the campaign north to Tianjin and Beijing. The French joined them after a French missionary was murdered. The first phase ended in 1858 with a treaty, but the Europeans reopened it in 1860 when their efforts to send a diplomatic legation to Beijing were forcibly resisted. During this phase, European diplomats were detained by the Chinese. Most of them were tortured and mutilated beyond recognition. Enraged by this flagrant breach of international law, the allied powers decided to burn the Summer Palace after they captured the capital area. They chose the Summer Palace in order to target the Empress Dowager and her court, rather than to make the citizens of Beijing pay for imperial perfidy. The resulting treaty called for opening more ports, legalization of the opium trade, permission for merchants and missionaries to travel within China, ceding Kowloon to England, and other concessions by a thoroughly humiliated China. Chinese have never forgotten, or forgiven the destruction of the Summer Palace, though few of them know what motivated the allies to wreak such destruction.

conscience."[68] During the negotiations, he met several ranking officials who later became friends when he lived in Beijing. He clearly disapproved of the British and French for their aggression, but also thought that the arrogance, rudeness, and stubbornness of Chinese leaders helped to provoke aggression from the West. He thought that if foreign Christians had been better witnesses in earlier years, the whole conflict might have been avoided.

When the Chinese did agree to certain freedoms for missionaries and toleration and protection for Chinese believers, Martin believed, at first, that they had seen the light; when they repudiated these concessions, he lost all faith in the Chinese leaders. Still, he sagely understood their objection to allowing missionaries to propagate their faith in China: "They fear that it may be made the pretext for political interference. They seem too, to perceive that an element so antagonistic to the institutions of a pagan country as Christianity necessarily cannot be compatible with the continuance of the present state of things."[69]

He also served as secretary and interpreter for American negotiators of the Tientsin treaty revisions in 1859. During the campaign by the British and French before the treaties were concluded, Martin observed that they had been "clearly wrong" in the whole matter, as in their three previous wars against the Chinese. He concludes, "What estimate will a Chinese statesman on such a retrospect form of the morality of England?"[70] On his way to Beijing with the American minister, he shared the gospel with the Chinese who were accompanying them, with the permission of the minister. "My experience, as I assured him, was that the more freely I spoke to the Chinese on the subject of religion the more friendly they showed themselves."[71]

Soon after the treaties were signed, anti-missionary riots began to break out, the number totaling more than four hundred within fifteen years. Many historians believe that this anti-foreign violence was due to missionary involvement in the negotiations. After his stint as an interpreter, Martin went home in 1860 on a two-year furlough, with his family, all in poor health, suffering from malaria. Four sons had been born to the Martins in

---

68. Covell, *Martin*, 90. Several American missionaries were "closely linked with their own government in political and diplomatic activities." They included Dr. Peter Parker and Elijah Bridgman in 1844 and later. Samuel Wells Williams helped draft the treaty of 1844 and "later occupied a number of positions with the United States government in Peking." D. B. McCartee, Richard Way, and John Quarterman also entered diplomatic service for shorter or longer periods of time. Covell, *Martin*, 79.

69. Martin, *Cycle of Cathay*, 181.

70. Ibid., 193.

71. Ibid., 197.

Ningbo: Pascal (1850–82), Winfred Robert (1852–1915), Newell A. (1854–1941), and Claude (1856–?).

NEW DIRECTIONS

While in the United States, Martin mulled over his future work. His work in the north had awakened him to the needs and opportunities there. Another factor was his desire to get away from constant conflict with Dr. McCartee. Ralph Covell believed that he also wanted to "satisfy his compulsive desire to pioneer" by charting a new course.[72] Easton College awarded him an honorary Doctor of Divinity degree (D.D.), which his literary labors had certainly earned for him, and which he appended to his name thereafter. He put two of his sons into Philips Academy; promoted missions; and asked his board to be given permission to open a high-grade school to train ministers as well as other professionals in literature, theology, science, and medicine.

Returning to China with his two younger sons in the summer of 1862, he landed in Shanghai, where he was asked to stay and help. There, Martin "reopened the two Presbyterian chapels, took over the management of the press . . . , made plans to reinvigorate the school program, and sought to revive the local Presbyterian church, which had added no converted members in ten years."[73] He also began training the missionaries in classical Chinese, using new materials.

After a while, however, his wife became ill and they had to move north. They moved into a house in Beijing, where they lived for two years. Evangelism continued to be his main priority. Taking the advice of a friendly official, he used low-key methods. He spoke in homes, held private conversations, and reached out especially to tradesmen who lived in the area of his home, but he also spoke regularly in a Presbyterian chapel. The famed Scottish missionary W. C. Burns co-labored with him some of the time, and Mrs. Martin opened a class for women and girls in their home. Separate women's meetings were also held, with a Chinese preacher instructing them in the gospel. The church grew slowly, the members coming mostly from poorer classes, but with some high-class inquirers. Martin remarked wryly, "They came seeking admission from all motives but the right one."[74] On at least one occasion he made a five-week evangelistic trip into the interior, where he preached freely and sold Christian literature. Like Matteo Ricci, whom

---

72. Covell, *Martin*, 99.
73. Ibid., 135.
74. Martin, *Cycle of Cathay*, 238.

he greatly admired and desired to imitate, he sought out the remaining Jews in the area, and explained the gospel to them also.

Martin opened a school for boys in 1864, with the invaluable assistance of Robert Hart.[75] Students were mostly poorer folk, whose conversion was Martin's principal aim, but few professed faith. The school taught geography, mathematics, science, and Chinese classics and offered Sunday lectures on Christianity. In a foretaste of future frustrations for Martin, the mission board at home was not very supportive.

During this period he joined the team of missionaries translating the Bible into Mandarin. The committee included S. I. J. Schereschewsky, J. S. Burdon, and Henry Blodget. Martin worked mostly on John's Gospel. He also translated Henry Wheaton's *Elements of International Law*. "I was led to undertake it, without the suggestion of anyone, but providentially I doubt not, as a work which might bring this atheistic government to the recognition of God and his Eternal Justice; and perhaps impart to them something of the spirit of Christianity."[76] He also wanted to explain to them why the Summer Palace was burned: They had violated a truce, tortured and killed diplomatic emissaries, and imprisoned one of the negotiators. The Chinese government assigned four scholars to Martin for this project. The book increased his stature and opened doors for future service in the government. It also introduced Chinese to the fact that Western nations had another principle than brute force in their dealings with each other. His Board questioned the missionary value of this work, but he pointed to the chance to share Christian books with helpers and conversations with them in his home and elsewhere.

Continuing to write for a Chinese audience, he prepared a seven-volume work on natural philosophy for use in his school. Its aim was to establish "the fundamental truth, the being and unity of God as author and law-giver of nature."[77] He aimed, also, at showing the incorrectness of the Chinese theories of "dual forces" (yin and yang) and "five elements," which underlay a great deal of popular Chinese religion. Revealing his great faith in the persuasive force of scientific knowledge, he optimistically prophesied, "The power that shakes these pillars will bring down the whole edifice of

---

75. Sir Robert Hart (1835–1911), was a British consular official in China, who served as the second inspector general of China's Imperial Maritime Customs Service from 1863–1911. A man of exceptional ability and integrity, he managed the customs service with utmost honesty and efficiency, earning revenue for China and a great reputation for himself.

76. Letter to Board 1863, in Covell, *Martin*, 146.

77. Covell, *Martin*, 151.

superstition."[78] Printed at government expense, the set went through many Chinese editions.

Lack of funds from home led him to find paying jobs, including teaching English at a government school for interpreters and writing letters about current affairs to the *New York Times*. Later, he was offered a job as "chair of International Law and Political Economy" at the T'ung Wen Kuan ("School of combined Learning"), with a salary, but the Board disapproved. Tired, he returned to the United States with his family in 1868. He had already begun to move in a different direction.

"PIONEER OF MODERN STATE EDUCATION IN CHINA"[79]

When he returned from his second furlough in 1869, he was invited to be president of the T'ung Wen Kuan, now given more prestige and support from the government. He resigned from the Presbyterian Board of Foreign Missions on December 1 of the same year. The Board had stopped supporting him, was sending no more people to Beijing, and was apparently opposed to all non-religious work. His new salary was ten times what he could receive as a missionary, and his family was in critical financial straits. He also thought he could pursue literary work better as a scholar, a position he thought was essential to reach the Chinese literati. "The role of the teacher gave him a natural context for Christian witness."[80]

After only a few months, Martin tried to resign, thinking that teaching only ten boys wasn't worth his time, but the Chinese mandarins urged him to stay on in view of the potential of these boys and of the school. "Who knows?" they said. "One of the graduates might eventually tutor the Emperor." "A view so gratifying to one who regards effective influence for good as the first object in life decided me to stay. . . I retained it [the headship of the school] as promising to open a field of influence much wider than I could find in the wayside chapels of Peking."[81] But when he composed *Cycle of Cathay* many years later, he wasn't sure whether he had made the best choice.[82]

Even after his resignation from the Board, he said, "I would like to be considered as possessing a life [missionary] membership . . . in spirit I am

78. Martin, *Cycle of Cathay*, 236.
79. This is the title of Chapter 7 of Covell, *Martin*.
80. Covell, *Martin*, 175.
81. Martin, *Cycle of Cathay*, 298.
82. Ibid., 298.

still a missionary and labor, as I believe, in what is *for me* the most effective way, for the good of this people."[83] That is, he thought the conversion of China should be undertaken from the top down. Graduates of his school served in the government, especially foreign service, but also elsewhere, some of them in high positions. In time, one of Martin's former students did indeed become the emperor's English tutor.

"Martin brought academic flair, a high ideal of duty; very considerable literary skill; the gift of eloquence both in English and in Chinese; a charming simplicity of manner combined with much natural dignity, and the complete confidence of his employers—the Tsungli Yamin—to his task as head of the school. He concentrated on teaching, writing, and control of academic affairs, and left administrative decisions to others."[84] He was wise enough to accommodate himself to Chinese concerns in education. Outside the classroom, he made his Christian commitment clear, but never in an obnoxious way. The faculty and students translated many technical books into Chinese. Martin himself was involved in translating and producing nine books on science, international law, and political economy. As a reward for his faithful service, he was given the Mandarin rank of the third degree.

While serving as college president, he continued to write political articles for the *New York Times*, organized the Peking Oriental Society, composed books and articles to acquaint the West with China, and served as an informal political adviser to the Chinese government. The government sent him to Europe, America, and Japan to study educational methods and policies from 1880–82. Despite all this effort, however, he did not succeed in reforming Chinese education: "Neither had the T'ung Wen Kuan contributed measurably to advancing the Kingdom of God in China."[85] As for his influence, it has been said that "the Chinese were willing to use his scientific knowledge and to adopt the reforms he advocated but they neither needed nor wanted the Christianity he preached."[86]

The Martins sailed to the United States for a rest again in 1895, returning in 1897. During the famous "Hundred Days' Reform in 1898, he was made dean of a new Imperial University, which survived that year's coup. Because several faculty and assistants were from Christian schools, they were given permission not to observe the Confucian rites at the opening ceremony, but Martin and some others took off their hats and made bows to the tablet of Confucius, causing consternation among many missionaries.

83. Covell, *Martin*, 175.
84. Ibid., 177.
85. Ibid., 183.
86. Duus, "Science and Salvation in China," 31.

All educational work stopped during and following the Boxer Rebellion, so Martin went home in 1900 for a year.

When the school reopened, he was dismissed, along with all foreign faculty. They had demanded and received back pay, and Martin had also denounced the Empress Dowager and her government during the siege of the legations, comparing her to the "Jezebel of Samaria" and urging that she be replaced by the young Kang Hsi emperor and that his policies be continued. His ideas were not implemented, and Martin, disappointed and feeling that his time in China had been wasted, went back to America again briefly in March, 1902. But that very year, he returned to China, accepting an invitation to be president of Wuch'ang University, a position in which he served for three years, after which he re-settled in Beijing.

MARTIN AS REFORMER

While in Beijing, Martin did not cease traditional missionary work: "He often preached on Sundays, led Bible classes, helped in the organization and work of the Peking Presbytery, and gave advice to the Presbyterian Board on a variety of missionary matters."[87] On visits into the countryside he found that "away from great cities the people always exhibit a friendly and unsuspicious disposition. 'He speaks our language,' they said; 'if his whiskers were shaven off he would be as good-looking as we are.' They asked me not from what country but 'from what province' I came, and occasionally inquired whether I was Tartar or Chinese."[88] Even more encouraging, "When I spoke to them on the truths of religion they listened respectfully."[89]

His work as a reformer came partly as a response to the violent anti-missionary sentiment that broke out in 1870 with the massacre of Roman Catholics in Tianjin. To avoid unnecessarily provoking Chinese sensitivities, he urged care in evangelism, such as sending only single men, not married men, into the interior. He believed strongly that much anti-missionary rage came from superstition, which modern scientific knowledge would dispel. For that reason, in 1872, he and some other Protestant missionaries organized The Society for the Diffusion of Useful Knowledge, purposing to overthrow superstitious beliefs that "constitute the most formidable barriers in the way of material and social development" and "to prepare the way for

---

87. Covell, *Martin*, 199.
88. Martin, *Cycle of Cathay*, 271.
89. Ibid., 271.

inevitable innovations by rendering the idea of such changes familiar to the public mind."[90]

In June 1872 they published *Chung-hsi wen-chian-lu (Peking Magazine)*. It was not financially self-supporting, and the Chinese did not write enough articles, so most of the essays were composed by Martin, Joseph Edkins, and John S. Burdon, who had all worked together translating the Mandarin New Testament.[91] Martin carried the heaviest load for the last two of the magazine's three years. It was the first magazine dedicated entirely to reform. To continue its influence, he later published four volumes (thirty-six issues) of selections from the magazine, totaling almost six hundred pages, on "Geography, popular science, edited news articles, and miscellaneous items."[92] There was no religious content. He still blamed China's failure to develop essential aspects of modern industrial life on superstition. He was partly right, but should also have noted their fear of foreign influence and domination by those who could use the new technology, and their desire for China to be economically self-sufficient, among other motives.

By avoiding Christian content and stressing the outward features of Western material civilization, he may have given the impression that China did not need Christianity in order to become stronger and more modern. He omitted religious material partly because he did not think the literati would read a religious journal; he wanted to create a "'wedge' to create a desire for Western culture, which Martin hoped would lead to an interest in the Gospel." Furthermore, "the editors believed that the Christian message and European civilization were but two aspects of the one message of salvation and progress."[93] At the same time, in his English writings, Martin contrasts China with the West, where Christianity provides moral energy and life, by "the renovating power of the Holy Spirit, which in due time may be expected to put new life into the dry bones of the old systems of China."[94]

His portrayal of Western nations' scientific and technological power only threatened the Chinese, who saw Western countries as morally suspect. He presented "new types of morality, free world trade, schools with new aims and different kinds of students, a new attitude toward the world, and many other features of Western life with intensity and with little sensitivity

---

90. Covell, *Martin*, 200.

91. Other missionaries who promoted reform included Young Allen, Timothy Richard, and Gilbert Reid. Chinese reformers of various types, like Kang Youwei, who gave credit to Martin's influence, rose to propose new measures to make China stronger.

92. Covell, *Martin*, 203.

93. Ibid., 117.

94. Martin, *Cycle of Cathay*, 290.

to Chinese feelings... Chinese needs, *as the Chinese perceived them*, were either unconsidered or casually dismissed."[95]

INTERPRETING CHINA TO THE WEST

In order to promote greater understanding as the two civilizations engaged in more and more commerce, diplomacy, and people-to-people contact, Martin wrote two learned, witty, and scintillating books. *Cycle of Cathay* contains fascinating descriptions not only of ordinary Chinese life, but of religious sites, architectural monuments, and customs, as well as providing comments on religion and a brief but lively sketch of Chinese history. Clearly, he was a brilliant Sinologue with keen observation and ready wit. *The Lore of Cathay*, equally brilliant, focuses on the intellectual life of the Chinese.

With these books, Martin sought to explain China to the West, for "if China is to be a part of the family of civilized States—Chinese thought, the principles at the basis of Chinese history and life must be understood."[96] "Never have a great people been more misunderstood. They are denounced as stolid, because we are not in possession of a medium sufficiently transparent to convey our ideas to them, or transmit theirs to us; and stigmatized as barbarians, because we want the breadth to comprehend a civilization different from our own. They are represented as servile imitators, though they have borrowed less than any other people; as destitute of the inventive faculty, though the world is indebted to them for a long catalogue of the most useful discoveries; and as clinging with unquestioning tenacity to a heritage of traditions, though they have passed through many and profound changes in the course of their history."[97]

Defending them against these stigmas, he pointed out their venerable tradition of international diplomacy and their many scientific and technological discoveries and inventions. He presented yin and yang as predecessors of the ideas of negative and positive charges. He respected their past achievements, and even the contemporary situation, in Chinese education, and with great intensity, he commended their system of civil service exams to the United States, which was considering establishing something similar at the time.

He felt, however, that missionaries had the right to be in China, and that this should be protected by force if necessary. He and many other foreigners

---

95. Covell, *Martin*, 218. Emphasis original.
96. Martin, *Lore of Cathay*, 2.
97. Ibid., 8.

had been besieged in the British Legation during the Boxer Rebellion. After the allied victory and occupation of Beijing, when foreign troops began pillaging, he "did a little looting on their [i.e., Chinese Christians who had lost everything] behalf."[98]

He left for New York in 1900, where he wrote, *Siege in Peking*, in which he expressed his outrage and advised America to take Hainan Island as part of their "God-given destiny in the Orient."[99] In Shanghai in 1900, missionaries met and resolved that the Kuang-hsi emperor should be restored, Manchu officials punished, and missionary rights assured. They argued that the rebellion was anti-foreign, not anti-missionary, ideas that Martin fully endorsed. In newspaper articles, he urged indemnity, punishment of bad officials, restoration of the Emperor (whom the Empress Dowager had removed and kept under house arrest), and troops for the foreign legations. He especially decried the Chinese violation of international law in killing or attacking diplomats. Though he failed to influence American policy, he did confirm the suspicions of the Chinese that missionaries were merely agents of Western powers.

RETURN TO MISSIONARY LIFE—LAST YEARS IN BEIJING

When Martin returned to Beijing 1906, he was encouraged by the rapid reforms being instituted by the Empress Dowager, and changed his previous censure to praise, but he was alarmed by the attempt to restore Confucianism to its previous place of honor. After the civil service exams were abolished in 1905, ceremonies of worship to Confucius were made mandatory in schools and in the performance of public duties. Martin saw this is a deification of Confucius and a direct challenge to Christ, since it would probably prevent Christians from serving as teachers or in the civil service.

Nevertheless, he kept busy preaching and lecturing, often on the changes taking place in China, but also on comparative religion. Martin was optimistic that most officials were beginning to be sympathetic to Christianity, and just needed imperial sanction to come out as supports of Christ. Consistent with his broad views, he supported ecumenical activities. Literary work was still prominent among his endeavors. His last work, *The Awakening of China*, had a cool reception, because most thought he was naively optimistic about China's future. He was also impressed with the progress of Christianity in China, however. He revised earlier works and

98. Covell, *Martin*, 238.
99. Ibid., 238.

also wrote *A History of the Revolution*, on recent changes, although it was never published. A revised version of *Chinese Legends and Other Poems* was published as *Chinese Legends and Lyrics*. He also wrote a memoir.

After the 1911 revolution, he was optimistic about Yuan Shikai, whose son (Yuan Keting) he had tutored in political economy, international law, and Christianity.[100] By now an elder statesmen among his fellow missionaries, Martin was happy to attend the 1907 Centenary Missionary Conference in Shanghai, where he served on two committees and, as usual, took controversial opinions on several issues. He still believed that Western military power was necessary to ensure the freedom and safety of missionaries, and said that, until religious toleration was granted by the government, "China ought to be made to feel that she is regarded by the civilized nations of the world as rather more than semi-barbarian."[101] Somewhat ahead of his time (but in agreement with Hudson Taylor's consistent policy) he supported new moves for independence of Chinese churches from foreign control.

As his strength declined, he lectured less to large groups and spent more time with older students or smaller groups of students, but still taught small classes for an hour or two each day. Political events interested him less and less, and he did not comment on them in public. In his later years he served on the International Reform Bureau, which worked for the abolition of opium, liquor, cigarettes, and gambling.

Many honors were paid to him as a great missionary and friend of progress in China. Always consistent in vigorous daily exercise, he remained physically and mentally strong and alert up to the time of his death. He finally succumbed to pneumonia, dying in Beijing in December, 1916, the oldest foreigner in China, with the greatest number of years (sixty-six) of continuous service. At his funeral, Li Yuan-hung, president of the Republic, sent a statement to be read by his secretary, saying that Martin "enjoyed an exceptional popularity as well as the respect of the scholars and officials both in the government and elsewhere in the country."[102]

---

100. Yuan Shikai (1859–1916) was a Chinese general and politician who exerted great influence during the late Qing Dynasty; served as the first President of the Republic of China; and made an abortive attempt to restore the monarchy, with himself as Emperor.

101. Covell, *Martin*, 264.

102. Ibid., 266.

MISSIONARY STRATEGY

All that Martin did during his six decades in China was aimed at winning the nation to the Christian faith. He perceived no conflict between direct proclamation of the gospel and secular education and reform efforts, since "he saw salvation as a coin with two sides—the material and the spiritual—but the spiritual was always the more important."[103] In his words, "Science might wing the arrow, but religion should be its point."[104] Despite perceptions of him to the contrary, he did not think that education must come first in reaching China; he also thought the Christian message itself was the most effective means of bringing intellectual enlightenment. To gain a hearing for the Christian message, missionaries should produce secular literature in Chinese.

Martin believed that missionaries had done well in promoting progress in China. Meanwhile "the seeds of a higher civilization are being sown" by missionary work, for "the gospel of Christ . . . redeems human nature from its wild state, and enriches and sweetens this life as a foretaste of that which is to come!"[105] He thought that missionaries must show that they know more than the Chinese about the universe. Even more important, "They require to be strong in faith, and full of the Holy Ghost."[106] Thus, the Western church should send only their best.

His stance on Confucianism brought much criticism, along with agreement from a few missionaries, such as Timothy Richard and Gilbert Reid. As for the ancestor cult, he came to believe that it should not be abolished, but that functional substitutions should be made in some of the rites. Like Matteo Ricci centuries before, he focused on the historical and social role of the practices, while opposing obviously idolatrous elements in them. In time, he came to believe that his earlier insistence of abandoning ancestral tablets was altogether wrong. His new ideas were read for him by Gilbert Reid at the General Missionary Conference at Shanghai in 1890. Martin had criticized J. Hudson Taylor for "leading his followers to make war on ancestral worship, instead of seeking to reform it."[107] Actually, at the earlier conference in Shanghai in 1877, Taylor had "warned against negative attacks on the error" of Confucianism, "when positive presentation of

---

103. Ibid., 245.
104. Ibid.
105. Martin, *Cycle of Cathay*, 457.
106. Ibid., 455.
107. Ibid., 214.

Christian truth was Christ's commission."[108] After Martin's paper asking for toleration of ancestor worship was read (with some modifications), strong objections were raised by a number of learned speakers. Martin's position was defended by Timothy Richard and Gilbert Reid, but this approach was finally rejected in an almost unanimous vote.[109] The debate continues into the twenty-first century.

Martin hoped to win the nation of China through mass conversions. Contrary to both Roman Catholic and Protestant practice, he thought that baptism should be administered as soon as people committed themselves to some form of Christian teaching, however imperfectly they might comprehend it. In his mind, teaching could follow baptism. Additionally, he believed that evangelists should focus on the head of the family or the clan. In time, large numbers of converts would make a powerful impact on their communities. To remove the charge of being unfilial or even traitorous, evangelists should teach loyalty first to the emperor and the family, and then to God. Martin's main insight, one that should be observed, is that Christian teachers should relate their message to the principal tenets of Chinese culture as much as possible. On the other hand, "he did not seek 'common ground' with Confucianism or Buddhism but a 'point of contact' that utilized terms and concepts as a framework that made communication possible."[110]

He thought that evangelism yielded "immediate, but limited, results. More important... was the preparation of foundations for a later, but more widespread, reception of Christianity. Such foundations rested on the reshaping of China's culture in those areas where it was incompatible with the beliefs and practices of Christianity, sweeping aside superstitions, immoral social customs, and sterile ways of thinking. And in this task Christianity and science were inextricably bound to one another."[111]

EVALUATION

Martin was much like his hero, Matteo Ricci. "Neither of them seems to have had an intense religious experience. In short, it might be said that their emotional commitment to Christianity was less strong than their emotional commitment to Western secular culture. They both had a faith more

108. Broomhall, *Assault on the Nine*, 110.

109. For a full account of the debate, including Hudson Taylor's role in it, see Broomhall, *It is not Death to Die!*, 139–43.

110. Covell, *Martin*, 275n3.

111. Duus, "Science and Salvation in China," 33.

philosophical than religious in nature and were consequently less rigid and dogmatic in their approach than was the soul-winning evangelist."[112] In light of his future focus on education and reform, might we take his autobiographical evaluation of his early years in Ningbo as "the most fruitful" period of his life as a mild indication that perhaps Martin came to believe that preaching the gospel and teaching the Bible were, in the long run, ultimately more profitable than secular education and political reform.

Though his theology remained far more orthodox than that of Timothy Richard, he diverged from other evangelicals in some important respects. He did not believe in a personal devil, and never spoke of eternal punishment in hell for unrepentant sinners. Not surprisingly, his messages, in print and orally, did not sufficiently emphasize the necessity of Christianity for individuals or the nation. Reading his autobiographical narrative, one is struck by the almost total absence of a sense of his own sin and a corresponding lack of expressions of gratitude for forgiveness and reconciliation with God through the work of Jesus Christ.

The concluding assessment of Ralph Covell, who is on the whole quite sympathetic, is that Martin was a "loner" "with all the ambivalent characteristics of the pioneer. . . . A man with boundless energy, a creative spirit, and iron will, and brilliant abilities as a teacher and writer."[113] When his ideas were resisted, "he revealed a caustic intolerance of 'conservative' opinions, took positions designed to accentuate differences with his colleagues, and sometimes deliberately provoked them. Impatient of those with minds less brilliant than his, he frequently showed an impetuous spirit given to hasty decisions and the articulation of only partly-developed ideas."[114] Nevertheless, in his writings, Martin frequently mentions Chinese scholars and officials with whom he formed lasting friendships. This may have been an essential part of his success in being accepted by Chinese leaders. His relationship with his brother S. N. D. Martin was also very close. Despite their differences, Martin and Hudson Taylor, whom Martin praised highly, remained friends. He posed together with Taylor and Griffith John in a famous photograph just before Taylor's death in 1905.[115]

He possessed "abounding optimism," and in his Chinese writings, he projected an "image of a tolerant scholar ready to build his faith within the context of their 'heavenly doctrine.'" Covell comments that this might have

---

112. Ibid., 34.
113. Covell, *Martin*, 271.
114. Ibid.
115. His commendation of Taylor can be found in *Cycle of Cathay*, 214.

led them to think they did not need this faith.[116] He also gave the impression that Christian faith and Western civilization were inextricably linked. "One could not be had without the other... The power of Western civilization was implicitly used to coerce faith."[117] In the end, Covell thought that Martin's emphasis upon progress, both spiritual and material, led him to become "more the agent and interpreter of an alien culture than of the Biblical faith."[118] In short, "The American missionary message in China was always a mixture of Biblical faith and American culture."[119]

Martin was clearly correct to predict that a science-oriented education would diminish the hold of rank superstition upon the minds of Chinese, and to believe that the introduction of science and technology would confer great benefits upon the population of China. He erred, however, in supposing that the diffusion of science would also foster the growth of biblical Christianity, or eradicate general belief in traditional Chinese religion, including ancestor worship (which flourishes in Taiwan and even now in Mainland China). Under the influence of secular scientific education, promoted by both Nationalist and Communist governments, a massive shift in the mind of Chinese intellectuals did take place, but it was not towards theism, but atheism. Only when the simple message of the Cross began to penetrate the halls of academia did large numbers of educated Chinese begin to turn to Christianity.

Though he may have failed in his primary objective, he left an example of perseverance; hard work; broad-mindedness; and knowledge of, and appreciation for, the finer elements of Chinese culture. His continuing friendship with J. Hudson Taylor and Griffith John demonstrates that even those who disagreed with him could recognize him as an orthodox brother in Christ and an esteemed co-laborer in the great task of bringing the gospel to China. No one can doubt his lasting contribution to education China; in that arena, his legacy endures.

---

116. Covell, *Martin*, 271.
117. Ibid., 272.
118. Ibid., 275.
119. Ibid., 5.

7

"Pastor Hsi"—Xi Shengmo
"Overcomer of Evil" through Prayer and Preaching

Yading Li with G. Wright Doyle

When Pastor Hsi—known also by his assumed Christian name, Xi Shengmo[1]—died, he was beloved by hundreds who had heard of Christ from his lips and been rescued from opium and sin through his loving, patient efforts. He had for many years poured forth his very life in the service of others, often sacrificing time, health, home, and every comfort to help people come to know Christ and be delivered from opium addiction. What began as a small effort to serve a few addicts from his home had grown, until several regular refuges had been opened, which gradually developed into centers of missionary activity, with many men and women being led to Christ.[2]

---

1. Though older writings called him "Pastor Hsi," we shall hereafter employ the modern pinyin spelling "Xi."

2. The following pages rely mostly on the biography by Mrs. Geraldine Taylor, with reference also to some materials by D. H. Hoste, who for the last ten years of Pastor Xi's life was his fellow worker and most valued friend.

EARLY LIFE

In 1836, the fifteenth year of the Emperor Daoguang, Xi Liaozhi was born into a family of above-average financial means and culture in Western Zhang village, Shanxi province. Both his grandfather and father were scholarly men, and had built up the family fortunes by careful management of their property and diligence in the duties of public life. They had gained reputations also as skilled physicians. Liaozhi was the fourth son of his parents.

Though he seemed to be cheerful even in early childhood, Xi was troubled by questions about the purpose of life and the fate of those who die, and the fear of death darkened the future with mystery and terror. Sometimes Xi went with his brothers to the temple on the mountains near his home, where he saw hideous idols, along with their horrible depictions of the tortures of the Buddhist hell. These sights turned into dreams that tormented him at night. He somehow sensed that he possessed a soul that came from Heaven, but did not know how to escape future punishment. Usually, however, he was animated and bright. Because of his intelligence and force of character, he became his father's favorite son. He studied hard in school, hoping to earn the *Xiucai* degree that would qualify him to become a mandarin (government official). His bad dreams continued to fill him with fear, however.

At the age of sixteen, he was married to a girl slightly older than himself, whom his father had arranged for him to marry, and whom he had never before met. They continued to live in his parents' house. In the same year, he won his academic degree, which was a "remarkable achievement," to the joy and honor of his father.[3] In time, he became both prosperous and respected. He seemed to be a man of character and determination, wholly absorbed in the pursuit of power. Fearless, resourceful, and determined, he combined shrewd judgment with powers of ready speech, and possessed a fearsome temper. Gradually, he was increasingly trusted to manage difficult matters and settle quarrels among villagers. His wife died, however, while he was still young, leaving him a widower and childless. Deeply grieved, he returned to the old questions that had previously vexed him, about the meaning of life and his ultimate destiny, but found no answers in Confucianism, Buddhism, or Daoism.

Xi married again, when about thirty. His second wife was a bright young woman about sixteen or eighteen years old from a neighboring village. In a desperate search for an escape from the vanity of life and emptiness of earthly things, he had plunged more deeply into Daoism.[4] The result was

---

3. Austin, *China's Millions*, 173.

4. Austin states that Xi became a follower of the Golden Pill (Jindan) sect at this time, but without citing the source for this claim. Austin, *China's Millions*, 166.

only a gradual but steady deterioration of his previous good health. In the depths of despair, he yielded to the suggestions of his friends that he try a little bit of opium to relieve his pain. He could always give it up later, they said.

The drug helped him at first, but soon each period of rosy exhalation was followed by deeper depression, the only remedy for which was more opium. He lost his appetite and couldn't sleep. A craving for opium consumed him, until he had totally forgotten his studies, business matters, stewardship of his property, and the pursuit of his career. For a year and a half he lay in bed, a total wreck. When he was lucid, he plumbed the depths of misery, remorse, and despair. Occasionally, he would try to conquer the deadly craving, but he could not. His original illness gradually worsened, until he seemed close to death. At one point, his wife and friends dressed him for death, convinced that the end was near.

FIRST CONTACT WITH MISSIONARIES

Like many Chinese, especially the literati, Xi connected opium with the Christian religion brought by the missionaries from England and America. Thus, he was thus quite upset when two foreigners suddenly appeared in the village. Though they wore Chinese clothes, said they were teachers of a religion from the West, and claimed to have nothing to do with commerce or opium, Xi distrusted them and would not even see them.

A terrible famine was devastating Shanxi at the time. Many homes in Xi's own village were empty, the owners having died of starvation. Somehow, he managed to stay alive and maintain his own household. He was unaware that the English missionaries, David Hill and Joshua Turner, had written letters home about the famine, and that money had been wired to them so that they could help relieve the sufferings of the people. They belonged to the China Inland Mission (CIM), which, along with other missionary organizations, was doing all it could to demonstrate the love of God by distributing food and other necessities.

As the famine raged on, in early summer of 1878 two missionaries came to settle in Pingyang city, not far from Western Zhang village, where Xi lived. They had come to distribute food and money among the famine sufferers, and to preach the Christian gospel. Wearing Chinese garments, their heads properly shaved, with their hair plaited behind in the required queue, they possessed the polite manners of proper gentlemen. They were constantly doing works of mercy, and seemed to live virtuous lives, neither indulging in wine nor tobacco. They rescued thousands of people who would otherwise have perished. Though he was sick, depressed, and impoverished, Xi still had no interest in seeing them, and would not accept the gifts they sent.

Then David Hill, desiring to reach out to the influential literati, conceived the idea of holding a literary contest, with a substantial sum of silver offered for the winning essay, the theme for which would relate somehow to Christianity.[5] After some hesitation, Xi entered the contest, submitting three essays under different names, and winning the top three prizes. When he went to collect the prize money, he was very favorably impressed with Hill's gentlemanly bearing and obvious ability and intelligence. As he later wrote, "One look, one word, it was enough. As daylight banished darkness, so did Mr. Hill's presence dissipate all the idle rumours I had heard. All sense of fear was gone; my mind was at rest. I beheld his kindly eye, and remembered the words of Mencius: 'If a man's heart is not right, his eye will certainly bespeak it.' That face told me I was in the presence of a true, good man."[6] In time, despite strong reservations, but needing employment and income, he accepted Hill's request to become his Chinese language teacher. To make a long and very interesting story much shorter, Xi's residence in the missionary's home and daily contact with him led to his serious consideration of the Christian faith. He read the New Testament that had been placed on the table in his room, and increasingly became convinced of its truth. From long and close observation, Xi believed that Hill embodied the Confucian ideal of "the Princely Man." This respect was joined with a love that lasted as long as they both lived. On his part, Hill sought to impart as much Christian teaching to Xi as he could before he had to move on to another place.

> Finally, one evening, the consciousness of his unworthiness became so overwhelming that he could bear it no longer, and placing the book reverently before him, he fell upon his knees on the ground, and with many tears read the Gospel accounts of Jesus' death and resurrection. Eventually, the very presence of God overshadowed him. In the silence he seemed to hear the Savior's cry, "My soul is exceeding sorrowful, even unto death," and into his heart there came the wonderful realization, "He loved me, and gave Himself for me." Then, suddenly, as he himself records, the Holy Spirit influenced his soul, and "with tears that flowed and would not cease," he bowed and yielded himself, unreservedly, to the world's Redeemer, as his Savior and his God.

5. Austin, *China's Millions*, 170, states that the idea was suggested first by a Chinese convert, "Gatekeeper" Sung.

6. Taylor, *Pastor Hsi*, 64.

Then came the vision of the risen Christ. Silently, and with deep solemnity, the very presence of the living Christ overwhelmed his soul. He saw Him then, not only as his Savior, but as his absolute Owner, his Master, his Lord.[7]

With characteristic energy and decisiveness, Xi at once begged to be allowed to join the Christians in their Bible study, prayer, and worship, and to be identified as one of them. Hill hesitated at first, but then realized that a profound transformation had taken place in Xi's inner being, and welcomed him warmly. Soon afterwards, Xi realized that his opium addiction was wrong, and decided to break the awful habit. Immediately, however, he was overwhelmed with the terrible agonies of withdrawal.

In his most suffering moments he would frequently groan out aloud: "Though I die, I will never touch it again!" In utter weakness, he cast himself on God, and cried for the gift of the Holy Spirit. Suddenly a tide of life and power seemed to sweep into his soul. Anguish and struggle ceased, the conflict was completely ended. The Holy Spirit came, flooding his heart with peace. "He did what man and medicine could not do," records the liberated soul. "From that moment my body was perfectly at rest. And then I knew that to break off opium without real faith in Jesus would indeed be impossible."[8]

Many times in later years Xi would say, "If you would break off opium, don't rely on medical help, don't lean on man, but trust only in God."[9] Though he always used medicines to help opium addicts persevere through the period of withdrawal, he never trusted in medicine alone, but always pointed the addicts to the risen Christ and his divine power.

He was baptized by CIM missionary Joshua Turner in November, 1880, David Hill having left Pingyang. Turner thought that it was a bit too early for this momentous step, but Xi insisted, saying, that "his desire to 'worship God is not because of Mr. Hill, but because of God's own teaching; I know for myself; I have read his word; I know my sins are great; I ought to go to hell. I know, too, that Jesus is able to forgive my sins, able to save me from sin, able to save me from hell, and to give me to live in heaven forever."[10]

---

7. Ibid., 69.

8. Ibid., 77.

9. Ibid.

10. Austin, *China's Millions*, 176, citing the records of the Hong-t'ung Conference, "Testimony of Mr. His," 6.

BECOMING A MINISTER OF THE GOSPEL

Xi made rapid progress in his growth as a Christian and soon became a powerful preacher of the Scriptures. Several experiences of the filling of the Spirit further deepened his faith in the living God and the presence of Christ in the life of the believer. It was not long before he also sensed that God wanted him to become a full-time minister of the Word and prayer. Without being prompted by the missionaries, he quickly also realized that idolatry was wrong, and tried to explain to his family why they had to get rid of their images and cease their worship of ancestors and false gods. Of course, he was met with fierce resistance, but his wife could not help but see the remarkable change that had occurred in her husband. As head of the household, he removed all vestiges of false religion, then returned to Hill's home.

At this point, Xi decided he must assume another name, one that expressed the transformation that had taken place in his life. His experience of liberation from the power of opium, which he saw as a victory over Satan, led him to take on "Sheng Mo"—"Overcomer of demons"—as his new self-appellation, one that reflected not only his past but also his purpose to wage spiritual warfare in the power of God for the rest of his life. He wanted also to share his newfound faith with others, so he wrote two tracts: "How to Obtain Deliverance from Calamity," and "The Ten Commandments of God," which were widely circulated.

Meanwhile, his wife, watching him become less irascible and more gentle, kind, and considerate, began to soften in her opposition to his new faith. Though previously he had never wanted to teach her or any other woman anything, now he was leading worship in their home and doing his best to explain Christianity to her and the other women, as well as to others in the village who had begun to be drawn to the truth that could effect such a remarkable alteration in a man known for his haughtiness and uncontrollable temper.

Just as Xi's wife seemed to be about to trust in Christ, she fell victim to a terrible depression and to paroxysms of rage, in which she would rush into the household worship services screaming horrible curses and blasphemies. This went on for a while, as neighbors mocked Xi, the so-called "overcomer of demons," for the obvious hold of evil spirits on his own wife. He finally called for a three-day fast, after which he laid his hands on his wife's head and commanded the demon to leave her. Immediately, she was delivered, and dedicated herself to Christ as her only savior, while relatives and friends marveled.

In April, 1883, Xi's wife, her mother, and Xi's aged stepmother were all baptized, to the amazement of others in the village. Xi redoubled his efforts at evangelism and Bible teaching, relying on the Holy Spirit to instruct him. People who had heard his testimony began to ask him to pray for those who were sick or possessed by demons, which he did, with faith and efficacy. Soon, small groups of believers were formed in surrounding areas, and his own home had become the location of a growing church, with Xi as the effective pastor, though he had not been ordained.

Not surprisingly, persecution followed in the wake of this expansion of the gospel into virgin territory. Non-Christians spread false rumors and aroused the ire of the people against those who were not worshiping their ancestors or the local gods anymore. At one point, Xi had to use his influence to protect a group of believers who were about to be tortured until they joined in idolatry during an important festival. He quickly realized that suffering is a normal part of the Christian life, however, and instructed his hearers to expect it as a consequence of following Jesus Christ. Rejection by non-believers could be used to test and even strengthen the faith of new believers, and to demonstrate that they really were committed to their new Lord and Savior; this, in turn, drew more people to Christ. Xi was not immune to attack either. When they could not force him to recant his faith, the local scholars "prevailed upon the corrupt literary chancellor of the province to disgrace Hsi by depriving him of his degree. He refused to pay bribes or take his case to law, but [CIM missionary S.B.] Drake laid the facts before the provincial governor who saw that justice was done. Hsi's degree and honors were restored."[11]

Of course, without close association with missionaries, he had to learn many things on his own. It took him a while, for example, to realize that he should take down the tablet to his deceased wife, which he retained though he had ceased to burn incense before it. Likewise, he continued to grow and sell opium, which brought him a great deal of income. When the Holy Spirit convicted him of the wrongfulness of selling to others what had been so deleterious to himself, however, he immediately broke off entirely from everything connected with opium. He also forbade the planting or use of tobacco on his property.

Not only was he unusually careful about personal cleanliness and orderliness in the home and in the management of all business affairs, but he kept himself spiritually alert at all times. He writes,

> On account of many onslaughts of Satan, my wife and I for the space of three years seldom put off our clothing to go to sleep,

---

11. Broomhall, *Hudson Taylor and China's Open Century*, vol. 6: 401.

in order that we might be the more ready to watch and pray. Sometimes in a solitary place, I spent whole nights in prayer: and the Holy Spirit descended. Frequently my mother noticed a light in our bedroom toward midnight, by which she knew that we were still waiting before our Heavenly Father. We had always endeavoured in our thoughts, words, and actions to be well pleasing to the Lord, but now we realised more than ever our own weakness, that we were indeed nothing, and that only in seeking to do God's will, whether in working or resting, whether in peace or peril, in abundance or in want, everywhere and at all times relying on the Holy Spirit, we might accomplish the work the Lord has appointed us to do. If we had good success, we gave all the glory to our Heavenly Father, if bad success, we took all the blame ourselves. This was the attitude of our hearts continually.[12]

After a while, the village elders came to him and asked Xi to become the headman. The headman was responsible for the gathering of taxes, the maintenance of law and order, the defense of local rights, the care of temples and public buildings, and of the festivals proper to each season of the year. Energy and experience were required, and moral rectitude according to Chinese standards. They were unanimous in their choice of him, but Xi insisted upon two conditions: First, he would have no dealings with ancestor worship or the worship of the local temple. Second, the temple must be closed and no one must worship pagan gods. They objected at first, but later agreed, so Xi became headman. After the year was over, everyone agreed that things had gone well for the village, better than ever before, in fact, and asked him to continue in his position. At the close of the third year Xi was once more unanimously chosen. But by this time his evangelistic and other labors had so increased, that he could no longer properly attend to the needs of the community. He declined, but commented that perhaps the idols had by now starved to death, and needed no more maintenance.

MINISTRY TO OPIUM ADDICTS

Xi put all his resources at the disposal of his ministry to Christians and seekers. He disposed of all superfluous possessions and donated the money to the work. He provided tea and refreshments for the weekly meetings, and often gave to the poor. As requested, he prayed for the sick, dispensed medicines free of charge, helped opium addicts gain freedom from their

12. Taylor, *Pastor Hsi*, 111.

bondage, and offered whatever assistance he could. When his own assets were exhausted, his wife sensed that she should sell parts of her dowry, she was so fully a partner with him. As they prayed about how the work could be made self-supporting, they came upon the idea of opening a drug store, for Xi had received training in Chinese pharmaceuticals from his father. They acquired premises in the village and opened a shop, which also served as a preaching hall and place of worship.

At the beginning, Xi relied on medicine procured from the missionaries to help addicts through the awful period of withdrawal from the drug. One time, however, a number of men were desperate to break the habit and had applied for help to Xi's coworker, Fan, who had opened a work in a nearby village. After praying for a long time, Xi sensed that God had given him a "recipe" for a drug that he himself could concoct. Following what he thought was divine guidance, he produced the pills, which proved to be remarkably effective. Soon, he had perfected a method of turning them out in sufficient quantities to meet an ever-expanding network of opium refuges under his overall supervision. Still, he relied more on prayer and the Word of God than on the pills he dispensed to addicts. He "had no confidence in medical treatment alone to accomplish a permanent cure."[13]

Both in his own time, and more recently, some have questioned the use of these anti-opium pills, as well as those dispensed at many refuges run elsewhere by missionaries and Chinese Christians, contending that their main ingredient was morphia, or morphine, and that no one was cured by this method. Medical missionaries and others expressed their concern about the use of this drug to cure opium addiction, and gradually the practice was discontinued. The CIM was aware of this criticism and moved cautiously to require supervision by missionaries, but there is not enough information to make a judgment about the pills which Xi concocted. At any rate, Pastor Xi and the missionaries always insisted that freedom from bondage to the drug resulted from the work of the Holy Spirit, through prayer and faith in a loving community, and they had the presence of many truly cured addicts in their churches to prove that God could bring full relief.[14]

13. Taylor, *Pastor Hsi*, 139.

14. See Lodwick, "Missionaries and Opium," 356–57, and Austin, *China's Millions*, especially 365–75. Austin's assertions must be taken seriously, especially since they are supported by documents from missionaries, but they also must be seen as part of an overall portrait that paints Hudson Taylor, Pastor Xi, Henry Frost, and the CIM generally in the darkest possible hues, and from the worst possible angle. His book is replete with instances of suppressed sources, twisted interpretations of cited materials, and outright fabrication, all of which combine to make it a highly unreliable resource.

It seemed to him as if the Lord had opened for him the way to achieve several purposes at once: Spread the gospel throughout the region through opium refuges; employ recovered addicts and others in the ministry; and sustain the entire ministry through the sale of the medicines. In cases of real need, Xi was happy to give the pills away free of charge, but ordinarily people were willing and able to pay for them, and in this fashion a number of opium refuges were opened and hundreds, later thousands, of sufferers found lasting relief.

From his own experience, he knew that the real power of opium addiction came from sin and from the temptations of Satan, so he always emphasized the necessity of prayer, fasting, and faith in God for lasting cures. Worship services were held twice a day in all the refuges, with attendance required. Enough men returned to their habit soon after leaving one of the refuges to demonstrate the truth of Xi's oft-repeated statement that real deliverance would come only through faith in God, exercised by prayer. After a period of failure, many of these men returned to the refuges and cast themselves upon the mercy of God. In this way, over the years, thousands of people were set free to serve God and their fellow citizens. Several of Xi's most valued lieutenants came from the ranks of former addicts who had once been destitute, without health or hope in this world. Because they had known the power of God, they were able to walk with others who were suffering and to encourage them to cry out in faith to the only one who could deliver them. As the number of worshipers and helpers in his household grew, Xi designed and erected several buildings to serve the needs of the expanding community; he also refurbished the barn and turned it into a chapel. His main concern was always the deepening of spiritual life, however, so he gave himself constantly to the exposition of God's Word in order to help everyone grow in faith and holiness.

Though, of course, he needed the refuges to be self-supporting, Xi never fell prey to the love of money. Everyone could tell that his heart burned with passion for the salvation of sinners and for their growth into Christ-likeness. Not only did he seek no personal gain, but he would not accept donations that did not seem to come from a pure heart and a sincere faith. On more than one occasion he even turned down substantial sums because he could perceive that the donors had ulterior motives.[15]

Once, when his accounts were in serious deficit, he maintained his firm posture against borrowing money to make up the need, and turned instead to fasting and prayer. A few days later, an invitation came from

---

15. Alvyn Austin's insinuations that Xi sought to make money are without basis in fact.

missionaries in a nearby town to participate in a contest for a large prize for the most beautiful Christian poetry. Xi had for a while been composing songs for use in the worship in his home church and outlying refuges, but this time he poured all his literary talent into composing elegant poems that could also be sung. The silver that came to him for the best poetry satisfied their financial need, but more importantly, Xi had found a new way to serve God. "From that time he continued, like the Psalmist, to weave all vicissitudes into songs of praise and prayer. Lessons learned amid joy or trial, defeat or deliverance, flowed from his pen in simple, often beautiful verse."[16] In coming years, his hymns and songs were used not only in the gatherings connected with his network. A collection of them, with more by CIM missionary Stanley Smith, was published, and entered into the hymnody of the Chinese church, encouraging thousands. Some of them were translated into English by Francesca French, also a member of the CIM, and published in a book entitled, *Songs of Pastor Hsi*. Some of the tunes were Chinese, while others originated in Europe but were adapted so that they sounded indigenous.

One by one, new refuges were opened, not only in country villages but also in the capital of the county, and then even farther away. Each time, Xi was guided by what seemed to be God's leading as he prayed and fasted for direction and for the expansion of the kingdom of Christ among his people. Once, after he had shared his burden for one city in daily worship for several days, he was surprised and overwhelmed when his wife presented to him all her wedding jewelry, insisting that it be used to open a new refuge there.

PASTORAL STRENGTHS AND WEAKNESSES

We must not suppose that Xi had no faults, or that these were trivial. His usually admiring biographers were candid on this point:

> And those failings, as with most strongly marked characters, were very apparent. For one thing, Xi was a born leader, and could not but feel it. Others felt it also, and in spite of his tendency to be too masterful at times, were ready to follow him anywhere. This weakness, however, gave rise to a good deal of friction that might have been avoided. But he deeply felt his need of more humility, the meekness and gentleness of Christ, and prayed for it accordingly.
>
> Then too he was very independent showed itself in his attitude about money matters. He never accepted a salary of

16. Taylor, *Pastor Hsi*, 177.

any kind, or looked for financial help even to the mission with which his work was connected. But it showed itself also in ways that could not but cause anxiety. He was none too teachable, as we have seen already, and his faith and devotion led him to go ahead at a rate that was sometimes alarming. His preaching lacked balance and sobriety, and his enthusiasm needed to be tempered by experience. But he was not easy to advise in early days, much less, control.[17]

This sort of man would not be easy to work with, and the China Inland Mission missionaries with whom he collaborated sometimes offended him deeply, as he did them. Forbearance and forgiveness on both sides kept them together, but not without a great deal of prayer and patience. Fiercely independent and confident in God, Xi at first sought to work entirely without help from foreigners, but when he saw that many new converts had come from refuges where CIM missionaries helped, he changed his mind and warmly welcomed them. Stanley Smith and Dixon Hoste remained Xi's faithful coworkers for many years. Of Stanley Smith it was said, "The more he was willing to let Pastor Hsi keep his natural position, the more God seemed to bless him."[18]

With his constant communication with God through prayer, fasting, and poring over the Scriptures, Xi was not totally unaware of his besetting sins, as we see in this except from a brief autobiography that he left:

> The devil, seeing that God was using me during these three or four years by the power of the Holy Spirit, sought to involve me in pride and self-consciousness. He caused ignorant men to address me as "Pastor," and I could not stop them. Some even behind my back went so far as to speak of me as the "Living Jesus." I knew that all this was just the devil's scheme to get me to take glory to myself and forsake the cross of Christ. Therefore, I humbled myself still more, and sought to have in all things the heart of a bond-slave, exerting my whole strength to lead men to repent and forsake sin, and thus yield no place to the devil. Not that I was able of myself to do this, it was all and only through the grace of God.[19]

The fruits of such piety could not be hidden from anyone with spiritual sensitivity. When J. W. Stevenson, the deputy director of the CIM, went to

---

17. Taylor, *Pastor Hsi*, 190.
18. Broomhall, *Hudson Taylor and China's Open Century*, vol. 6: 409.
19. Taylor, *Pastor Hsi*, 192.

see Pastor Xi in preparation for an upcoming visit by the director, J. Hudson Taylor, he was immediately aware of Xi's outstanding qualities:

> He came over several times, and stayed for days together at Pingyang. We had many long conversations. . . . I watched him too in the management of practical affairs, and the more I saw of him the more I was impressed by his grace, wisdom, and ability.
>
> It was impossible to be with Xi without having prayer. His first instinct in everything was to turn to God. Long before daylight, those summer mornings, I used to hear him in his room across the courtyard, praying and singing by the hour together. Prayer seemed the very atmosphere of his life, and he expected and received the most evident answers.
>
> Travelling with him on one occasion, we reached a little inn, and I remember a poor woman coming to him with a child in her arms who was ill and in great suffering. The people used to come to him like that everywhere. They knew he was a man of God and could help them. It was most remarkable how naturally they gathered round him with their troubles, taking it for granted that his time and sympathy were at their disposal. This mother, for example, came in great distress, as soon as she knew that he was in the inn.
>
> Xi rose at once to meet her. "It is all right," he said, "don't be troubled. The little one will be better directly." There and then he took the child in his arms and prayed for his recovery. The woman, greatly comforted, went away. And a few hours later I saw the little fellow running about, apparently quite well and happy. One got accustomed to such things, with Xi.
>
> One scene I shall never forget. It was after the conference at Pingyang, Xi was still there, and a number of Christians. Late at night, Mr. Cassels called me out to see what was going on.[20] I went with him, quietly, to the front courtyard. As we drew near we heard sounds of weeping, and voices pleading in low tones. There they were, dear fellows, a whole lot of them, down upon their knees, with Xi in the midst, crying to God for the conversion of loved ones, relatives and friends at home. Many were weeping. And the earnestness and simplicity of those prayers in the power of the Holy Spirit was most remarkable and touching.[21]

In an interview with Xi's biographers, Stevenson was asked, "As a preacher, what were his chief characteristics?" He answered:

20. William Wharton Cassels was a CIM missionary.
21. Taylor, *Pastor Hsi*, 211–12

> He was fearless and convincing, preaching even on the streets with great boldness. His style was cultured, and most interesting. He always used plenty of good Chinese illustrations, but even in addressing heathen audiences, he rarely referred to the classics. His one weapon was the Word of God. The people loved to hear him, heathen as well as Christians, he could hold them for hours. His sermons were chiefly expository, and I was often surprised at the way he unfolded the truth, bringing new meanings to light. I heard him give one address on temptation that was most remarkable, the temptations of Christ. The solemn impression remains with me to this day.
>
> But it was as a pastor he excelled, he was so naturally the shepherd. People opened their hearts to him, and he was so vigilant in his solicitude for their spiritual welfare. I was specially struck with this. He had everybody's burdens to bear.

His preaching benefited greatly from his pastoral work. Because Xi was constantly with his people, visiting them in their homes and praying with them about their daily lives and darkest trials, he knew them well. He was, therefore, able to speak to their particular conditions as he expounded the Scriptures in his regular teaching. Though he preached systematically through a passage, verse by verse, he always applied biblical truths to the concerns that he knew were burdening, or tempting, his listeners. In short, his preaching was both spiritual and practical.

The interviewer continued, "Through suffering and temptation of his own, I suppose, he had learned the secret of helping others?" Stevenson replied:

> Yes, he had lived through much himself, and was still in the midst of the conflict.[22]
>
> He knew well what temptation meant. He dealt with God, and if one may say so, dealt with Satan too. For he had strange experiences at times, that used to remind one of Luther in the Wartburg. But in all such conflicts he had learned to overcome upon his knees. With prayer and fasting he fought the tempter. Indeed, whatever the trouble was, he seemed to resort at once to this scriptural practice.[23]

The missionary noticed, too, Xi's energy, decisiveness, and amazing influence with people. To be sure, he could be dogmatic, and not easily

---

22. Ibid., 213
23. Ibid., 214

persuaded to change a course of action that he thought had been shown to him by the Holy Spirit. Stevenson concludes, however, with this assessment:

> But the most remarkable thing of all was his spirituality of mind and intense devotion. To him there was nothing at all in life, nothing in the world, but that one thing—love for Christ and for the souls of men. All he had was on the altar: time, money, home, friends, life itself. One could not be with him, as I was privileged to be that summer, without gaining a wholly new ideal of Christian life and service.[24]

After years of hearing about Xi and his expanding ministry, Hudson Taylor was eager to visit him personally, and Xi was no less desirous of meeting the man who had sent missionaries into the deep interior of China and to live so humbly and simply among the people. Finally, "the Venerable chief Pastor," as the Chinese termed Taylor, arrived, along with Stevenson. The two outstanding leaders took an instant liking to each other, and the following days were spent in long conversations about the current state of Xi's ministry and ways in which it could be strengthened and further extended.

Taylor recognized Xi as a man raised up by God to shepherd the flock of Christ, and as a leader who could supervise others well. His own gift for organization made him realize that these *de facto* churches and their *de facto* pastors needed to be brought into some sort of formal association with each other, and the leadership regularized according to biblical principles. In the end, elders and deacons were ordained by Taylor and the other missionaries, with Xi being appointed as lead pastor or, in effect, "bishop" of the region. He was at first unwilling to take such a title and position, but accepted the arguments of Stevenson that they were only formalizing something that had been a reality for some time.

During that same conference, Xi told Taylor of the multitudes of Chinese women who, because of social conventions, could not be taught by men. He asked for foreign women to be sent to share the gospel with them, and specified that single ladies, free from the duties of home and family, would be the most appropriate agents of this fresh advance into the Chinese home. Taylor, who had long ago seen the value of female missionaries, agreed to pray for God to supply this need, and in time they came, bringing great blessing.

A letter written by Mr. Stanley Smith[25] further unfolds Xi's character:

---

24. Ibid., 215.

25. Stanley Smith, one of the famous "Cambridge Seven" who joined the CIM in 1884, was a well-educated man from an upper-class family, so he was qualified to make these judgments.

Socially, Xi was a thorough gentleman, and a most interesting companion. Intellectually he had mental gifts of a high order. His powers of imagination, organization, oratory, memory, and judgment were uncommon. In temperament he was enthusiastic, bold, and decided. In his spiritual character, when I first knew him, amid much that was loveable and attractive, there were some points in which he was decidedly weak. Since first believing in the Lord, he had not had the advantage of any spiritually-minded man, taught in the Word, who could be a help to him in this respect, consequently his exegesis of Scripture was often at fault and fanciful. In those days, too, there was a want of subjection to the Word of God, and a tendency to exalt ideas Chinese, as well as not a little under-estimation of the foreign missionary. His prayer life, however, was full and intensely real. All matters were with him subjects for prayer, and as time went on he became a powerful exponent of the Bible, giving addresses marked by great originality and much spiritual insight.[26]

He had strong temptations, which were sometimes yielded to, in a direction which was a weak spot in his character, the love of power, though it would be very unfair to put this down as ambitious pride, pure and simple. He believed that God had given him a position like Moses, that of leader, and in expecting the subjection of others to his authority, he thought he was carrying out the Divine Will. He had, however, some humbling experiences, and in the two years I was with him his progress in humility was marked, and afterwards deepened as time went on. His love for the Master and for souls was characterised by constant labor and self-denial.[27]

FAN'S REBELLION AND OTHER TRIALS

The elements mentioned in Smith's letter, and many others, combined to bring about the "great gathering" of April 1887, in which hundreds of believers and inquirers took part, and more than fifty people were baptized. After that came a time of trial that threatened to undo all of Xi's work thus far. Some of his coworkers had been quite upset by the way he had been honored by the foreign missionaries, and resented his being placed in a position which they perceived to be above themselves, though the missionaries had done all they could to avoid this by giving only the title, "pastor,"

26. Taylor, *Pastor Hsi*, 243–44.
27. Ibid., 244.

not "bishop" or "superintendent." "As long as he was on their own level, they were content to follow him, but the moment he was placed above them, though it was a change only in name, they were filled with envy and suspicion."[28] He gave them an opening for criticism when, by invitation, he moved into the home of Stanley Smith when he was away. The idea was to give him time for rest and reflection, as well as to put him in a location from which supervision of the scattered refuges would be more convenient.

But Xi handled the move ineptly, by saying that this brief enjoyment of more comfortable quarters was a sort of reward for many years' selfless service, and that it illustrated the principle that recompense for faithful obedience to God sometimes comes in this life. His coworkers, who had been resenting and envying him for several years already, and who were themselves burning with covetousness, accused him of self-aggrandizement and embarked on a vicious campaign of slander, charging him with misuse of funds and many other transgressions. Many were led away from Xi by these lies.

Elder Fan gathered a few others around him, and began systematically to compete with Xi's opium refuge work by selling his medicines far and wide at lower prices, opening new refuges close to his, and spreading false rumors to cause disaffection among his supporters. On one terrible occasion, Fan even tried to take Xi's life, and would have succeeded, had not Benjamin Bagnall, the missionary before whom they had accused Xi, intervened physically to restrain him while Xi escaped. For a while, their plot succeeded, causing Xi indescribable pain and bringing confusion to many others.

To add to his distress, disasters of all sorts fell upon various refuges in different places, seeming to lend credence to the accusations of his detractors that God was not with Xi and his work. Most of his workers remained loyal to him, which was a great comfort but "[i]n those dark days Xi was brought to an end of himself and all human resources, and learned the deeper meaning of that 'sentence of death in ourselves' that drives us to trust 'not in ourselves, but in God which raiseth the dead.'"[29] Time and again, he resorted to prayer and fasting, and the Lord intervened to save him from utter ruin.

When D. E. Hoste returned from a long absence, he and Xi conferred as to whether strict discipline should be meted out to the offenders.[30] Wisely,

---

28. Ibid., 250.

29. Ibid., 254.

30. Dixon Hoste, one of the famous "Cambridge Seven" who joined the OMF in 1885, went on to become the general director of the CIM.

they decided to leave the whole matter in God's hands, certain that the truth would eventually come out for all to see. After several more months, the dishonesty and unchristian conduct of Fan and his partners came to light, while the humble, patient, and godly demeanor of Xi and his people stood out in stark contrast. The rebellion collapsed from its own internal rot, and Xi was vindicated. Meanwhile, the faith of the believers had been tested, showing some to have been shallow or false in their profession, while others proved to be genuine followers of Christ. The church was cleansed and purified. Xi had been humiliated, but this turned out for his spiritual benefit, for his proud spirit did need pruning so that he might bear even more fruit.

Of this harrowing period Xi wrote later,

> At that time the Heavenly Father allowed Satan to buffet me, and tried me with fire, in a manner quite different from anything I had before experienced . . . Each time I met with heavy trials, all of which I received from the hands of my Heavenly Father, I used to fast for three, four, or five days, and the tears that I shed were beyond knowledge. But the Lord opened a way of escape for me. And although I endured much loss of means, weariness, and alarm still, in the end, it was peace. For, in the midst of it all, the Lord comforted and strengthened me, and kept me from growing coldhearted and going back.[31]

Another good result ensued: Xi began to appreciate the help and cooperation of D.E. Hoste and the other CIM missionaries, whose presence he had sometimes resented. Independent by nature, he had often chafed at having to collaborate with foreigners. During the Fan crisis, however, he came to see the value of association with those who had more experience in spiritual things and more awareness of church history, Christian ministry, and the Christian life generally. He also discovered "rich treasures of sympathy and friendship he might otherwise have continued to ignore."[32]

Of all the missionaries, D.H. Hoste "was surely the most fitted to win his confidence in such a crisis. With the deepest appreciation of Xi's character and work, he was not blind to his faults. Yet he stood by him as few others could have done, always at hand when needed, but letting him bear his own burdens, wise in counsel, steadfast in purpose and in prayer. . . Until the end they lived and worked together, in fellowship that had not a little to do with the deepening and mellowing of Xi's character, that so markedly began in the dark days of 1887."[33]

31. Taylor, *Pastor Hsi*, 268.
32. Ibid., 263.
33. Ibid., 263.

Even while the "gang of Fan" was causing so much turmoil, God moved Xi to open refuges in new places, often in response to an urgent call for help. In all, twenty were started over the next few years, with hundreds, then thousands, of addicts finding release and new life, some of whom went on to become trusted coworkers. As Xi would later write, "Truly, it is God that gives the increase. While we are ready to faint through many afflictions, He is working out in new and unexpected places His purposes of grace. The Lord is never weary and never discouraged. Oh, that we may more closely walk with Him."[34] The collaboration with the China Inland Mission became closer when several CIM missionaries came to live in some of the newer refuges. Eventually, three of these refuges became full-fledged mission stations, where churches were planted and believers taught the Scriptures.

Within six years of the troubles caused by Fan's rebellion, a total of forty-five new refuges were receiving opium addicts in several provinces, and hundreds were being treated for their affliction. It goes without saying that all this imposed heavy responsibilities upon Xi. Dozens of men were being employed; the refuges required a great deal of financial outlay; the business operation had to be monitored closely; conflicts among the Christians must be mediated, and persecuted believers comforted. And all this in addition to the normal busyness of running Xi's household, church, and refuge. His biographers tell us how he shouldered all these burdens without crumbling:

> In this spirit Xi went stedfastly forward, laying each difficulty before the Lord, as it arose, seeking His guidance at every step, and then counting unwaveringly upon it, daily and hourly cast upon God by needs he had no power to meet, but always finding His grace, His power sufficient. The stedfastness of conviction and conduct was one of Xi's strongest characteristics. He was cautious, unusually so. He made very sure of his ground to begin with. But when once he was satisfied as to the guidance of God, he was prompt in action and unfaltering in spirit. He moved carefully, but one may almost say he never went back.[35]

Once he was convinced that God had directed him to open a new work, he never abandoned it, even if it proved unprofitable or apparently unfruitful for years at a time. A wise businessman, he nevertheless placed his faith completely in God to provide, and was never disappointed. His fame as a doctor brought many to him who could not pay, but he never turned anyone away, and frequently dispensed his medicines, some of which were costly foreign products, without charge. He never became rich, but never

---

34. Ibid., 274.
35. Ibid., 285.

lacked, either. He practiced the strictest economy: "Xi had now and then to part with personal possessions to provide for some pressing need. His own habits were of the simplest. The silks and furs of former days had long since disappeared. He now wore plain, blue cotton garments, cotton, instead of satin shoes, and wadding did duty for comfortable fur linings in winter."[36] He told the missionaries that these experiences helped him to identify with poorer folk more easily.

Supervision of his many outstations required constant travel. In earlier years, he used a cart with "Holy Religion of Jesus" emblazoned in bright red characters on the side. The front of his own garments bore six characters that meant, "Jesus came into the world to save sinners." Later he made his visitations on foot, carrying his baggage himself. He journeyed far and wide, sleeping in dirty inns or even outside, partaking of the same simple fare as other travelers, and often engaging them in conversation about Christ. Many were first drawn to the gospel by his simple, straightforward manner of speaking and living. Never a strong man physically, he drew upon the energy that God supplies as he trekked along winding mountain paths to distant locations.

D. E. Hoste, who loved him and was with him constantly, wrote, "I always felt, that Xi had a bodily strength not his own. He was a man whom God specially sustained for the work. He had given him to do. I have known him walk thirty miles at a stretch, in case of need, quite a remarkable feat for a man of his age and training, and after fasting entirely for two days, he was able to baptize by immersion as many as fifty men at one time."[37]

His labors were made more difficult by criticism from some missionaries in Shanxi who thought he went forward too fast and had too much influence over the people. They would have preferred the whole operation to come under foreign control. This misunderstanding went on for about ten years, greatly taxing his emotional resources. He would not give in, however, responding, "Your exhortation I will keep in my heart. Had it been a question of my own wishes, I should never have opened one Refuge. But if the Lord desires to do this work through me, can I refuse? I dare not say I will or will not continue. I must be quiet in His hands."[38]

The rumor that he was getting rich never seemed to go out of circulation, despite patent evidence to the contrary. His response? "Yes, I am engaged in a profitable undertaking. My business sign is my Master, the Proprietor, is Lord of All. The profits I seek and obtain are the priceless souls

---

36. Ibid., 290.
37. Ibid., 300.
38. Ibid., 297.

of men, those who enter the Refuges, hear the Gospel, believe, and obtain salvation."[39]

A HELPER SUITABLE FOR HIM

Once she was converted, Mrs. Xi's hunger to know the Scriptures motivated her to learn to read. It was not long before she studied both the Bible and other Christian books on her own. Her growing mental capacities made her an increasingly valued comrade to Xi in all facets of the work, until he felt comfortable in turning over the entire operation of their local ministry to her when he had to be away.

Though he loved and respected her, Xi found himself unable to control a very nasty temper when he was irritated with his wife. Others he could treat kindly and patiently, but somehow he just could not keep himself from speaking harsh, angry words to her on too many occasions. They prayed about this together for years without seeing much change, to Xi's great humiliation and self-reproach. Finally, however, God gave him the victory, and their relationship exhibited a sweetness and harmony that moved all who saw them together.

One great hindrance to lasting deliverance of addicts remained: when they went home cured, they often had to endure the odor of opium being smoked by their addicted wives. For many, the temptation proved unbearable, and they sank back into their former slavery. How could this be prevented? Only by bringing the gospel and the healing work of the Christian refuges to women as well as men. Men could not perform such a ministry, however, because of binding social conventions. After years of prayer, both Xi and his wife came to the conclusion that she must sacrifice the relative comfort of home and take to the road to introduce the love and power of Christ to multitudes of degraded women.

For the next several years, their ministries parted them from each other, sometimes for months at a time. When he could, Pastor Xi accompanied his wife, but many times their paths diverged, and he had to let her go, trusting God to care for her, protect her, and use her to bring deliverance to entire families through the salvation of women. We might now question the wisdom, or even the Scriptural warrant, for such extended separation of husband and wife, but we cannot doubt the depth of their commitment to God, each other, and the mandate that they believed their Lord had given them. One unexpected blessing was that "as they trod this pathway, they found their immediate reward in a love so deep and tender that all that

---

39. Ibid., 295.

had ever come between them was forgotten."[40] Occasionally, they enjoyed unexpected times together.

> Sometimes on the main road through the province she would meet her husband's cart, or at one of the larger Refuges she would find him announced to lead the Sunday services. Those were little foretastes of heaven. Sometimes they would spend a week or two together at home, and almost forget, in the joy of such reunion, that they were pilgrims and strangers. But that would not be for long.
>
> "Do I not love my wife?"wrote dear Pastor Xi. "Often she is in the north, and I am in the south, and for several months at a time we are unable to see each other's faces, and can only mutually weep and pray, seeking those things which are above and the reward promised to every man according as his work shall be. The Bible says: 'The time is short, and it remaineth that both they that have wives be as though they had none.' My wife and I, remembering these words of Scripture, are comforted, and our hearts are kept in peace."[41]

ALL TO THE GLORY OF GOD

In time, many of the refuges turned into mission stations, with gifted men exercising pastoral oversight and feeding the flock with the Word of God. Meanwhile, back at the home base, which they called Middle Eden, affairs were put into the hands of Elder Si when Pastor Xi was gone. To make his task easier, as well as to promote order and harmony, Xi drew up a set of rules and regulations. These covered not only spiritual matters such as worship, teaching, and pastoral discipline, but also included detailed instructions for daily life, such as preparation of food, managing the estate, making the medicines for opium patients, and the division of labor among all residents, including the old and the very young.

His biographers write:

> It illustrates the way in which Xi carried his Christianity into daily life. There were no unimportant matters with him. "Everything has a great truth underlying it," was one of his characteristic sayings. He believed that the highest principles should be applied to the smallest details of everyday affairs, and that the true state of the heart shows itself in just these little things.

---

40. Ibid., 307.
41. Ibid., 308.

It is a deeply earnest view of life, and means, "whether ye eat or drink, or whatsoever ye do, do all to the glory of God." Thus it is possible to be filled with the Spirit, because nothing is kept back from His control. Xi was remarkable for discernment in the matter of character, that amounted almost to intuition, and his judgment of those with whom he had to deal, was largely based upon such indications. It was this genuine consistency in little things that gave his own life its practical power. For he was more strict with himself than with anyone else, and strove, unremittingly, to attain the ideals he set before others. At the same time there was nothing forbidding about his presence. Children loved him. He had a genuine sense of humor, and a pleasant laugh. Genial and bright at all times, he was specially so at home, and to none did he give himself more freely than to the members of his own large household.

In later years he adopted the precaution of receiving those who wished to come to him for a probationary three months to begin with. This conquered many difficulties, and made matters work more smoothly all round. But though his requirements were rigorous—no fairs, theatricals, wine, smoking, gossip, or resting in the daytime—few, if any, desired to leave The Middle Eden at the close of that period. They had found practical Christianity at work in a Chinese home, and were glad to be under its loving, wholesome influence.[42]

We have noted before that Xi was a man of prayer. This attitude toward life extended to everything, including farming. When some sheep died during an exceptionally cold winter, he prayed about the matter, asking for wisdom to care for his animals better. Sure enough, he was guided to an accurate analysis of the cause of their deaths, which was lack of adequate nutrition in the warm months. He called the household together, explained the situation and charged them with the duty of making sure that the flock received enough food before winter came. Not having stored up enough fat when food was available, they perished during the period of want.

Because he saw the hand of God in everything, he also discerned a spiritual lesson. He confessed that he should have exercised better supervision over the sheep, and compared the sheep to Christians. If we do not meditate daily upon the Word of God, and receive grace from him through prayer, how can we be ready when trials and temptations come? He admitted that he had not been diligent enough in caring for their spiritual needs, and asked for their forgiveness.

---

42. Ibid., 325.

In his later years, in great contrast to his early days, when his proud spirit would not allow such frank admission of wrong, Xi often confessed his faults to his brothers and sisters in Christ, and even to his non-Christian neighbors. No wonder that when he died, his people loved him dearly, for they could see how God had changed him into a kind and loving shepherd of their souls.

We should not be surprised to learn that his relationship with D. E. Hoste also improved over the years, as each of these strong men learned greater humility, forbearance, and love. Naturally, the work also grew, so that by the time of Xi's death more than seven hundred people had been baptized, and there were refuges in three provinces[43] where the gospel was preached and people were being rescued.

Finally, after years of over-work and the resulting strain on his body and mind, Pastor Xi collapsed, utterly exhausted. Six months of lingering in bed ended when he died, peacefully and surrounded by weeping friends and family, on February 19, 1896, at the age of sixty.

The affection of those he left behind can be explained by this description of him:

> He was a born leader, nothing escaped his keen eye, and he was ever ready to rebuke, instruct, or succour as occasion required. And with these sterner characteristics he possessed also a deeply affectionate heart, and true humility of spirit that could only be fully recognized and appreciated by those who knew him well. As years went by, his masterful character grew more and more mellowed and softened, until, when he passed away, it is no exaggeration to say that hundreds wept for him as for a father or elder brother.[44]

---

43. Shaanxi, Henan, Zhili (modern Hebei).
44. Taylor, *Pastor Hsi*, 12.

8

Timothy Richard
A Missionary Who Impacted the Late Qing Dynasty

Wenzong Wang

When passing seventy years of age, in 1916, Timothy Richard published his autobiography *Forty-five Years in China, Reminiscences*. Looking back at his missionary life of nearly half a century in China, Richard wrote, "The problem before the missionary in China, as I found it forty-five years ago, was not only how to save the souls of a fourth of the human race, but also how to save their bodies from perishing at the rate of four millions per annum, and to free their minds, more crippled than the feet of their women, from a philosophy and custom which had lasted for many centuries and left them at the mercy of any nation which might attack their country."[1] Starting from the year when he arrived in China as a twenty-four-year-old young man till his senior age of over seventy, Richard had thrown himself into the task with great enthusiasm and thoroughness. His life in China falls into two main chapters: first, twenty years' evangelism in Shandong and Shanxi; second, twenty-five years' literary work in Shanghai.

In his early years of missionary service, while studying the language, religious and moral ideals, and character and customs of Chinese people, Richard devoted himself to many kinds of service. He preached in a street chapel and provided western drugs in villages. Later, Richard distributed

1. Richard, *Forty-Five Years in China*, 7.

relief to farmers in the great famine (1876-81), introduced western science to Chinese scholars, and made suggestions to officials for preventing future famines. Through all of these efforts, some local people were converted to Christianity. Richard trained them to be local church leaders and helped to establish Christian communities. He was one of the founders of the Baptist Mission in Shandong, as well as the sole founder of the Baptist Mission in Shanxi.

In the second half of his missionary career, Richard mainly dedicated himself to Christian literature work. As the General Secretary of the Christian Literature Society (CLS), Richard shouldered the chief responsibility of the CLS to enlighten the minds of educated Chinese, both younger and those in high positions. Richard dreamed of establishing a modern Christian university for each province of China. He hoped that the leaders of this great nation would be brought to accept the Christian faith and would give themselves to winning their fellow countrymen to Christianity and to utilizing the knowledge and technology of the West in further the welfare of the Chinese and in bringing the Kingdom of God to this land. His efforts, along with those of many others, contributed to the uplifting of China in various ways: better religion; better science; better means of communication; better international commerce; and the establishment of a modern press and new industries and manufactures.[2] In his later years, in every province, in every city, and in towns and villages without number throughout the Qing Empire, the name of "Li T'i-mo-t'ai," (Richard's Chinese name) was known and respected. From the Emperor on his throne to the village student on his hard wooden stool, his writings were read, his love for Chinese people appreciated, his contribution to China was recognized in the entire country.

Indeed, Richard impacted the entire late Qing Dynasty. The Qing Empire conferred upon him the First Red Button Grade of the Mandarin in 1903, later followed by ennobling his ancestors for three generations to equal rank. In 1907, he was decorated with the Order of the Double Dragon. Richard was the only Protestant missionary who was so highly honored. Kenneth S. Latourette described Timothy Richard as "one of the greatest missionaries whom any branch of the Church, whether Roman Catholic, Russian Orthodox or Protestant, has sent to China."[3]

---

2. Ibid., 7–8.

3. Latourette, *A History of Christian Missions in China*, 378.

A DEVOTED YOUTH FROM WALES

Born on October 10, 1845 in a small village of Wales, Timothy Richard was the youngest child of a family of nine. His father, who was not only a farmer and a blacksmith, but also a narrator of stories, a veterinary surgeon, and a secretary and deacon of two small Baptist churches, He was also was often called upon as a peacemaker. His mother's family were also farmers and Baptists, and his mother was remembered for her guilelessness and sweetness of disposition. In his autobiography, Richard wrote, "I spent my early days on the farm where my parents lived, and there I had practical experience of every work on the farm, from plowing and reaping to thrashing on the flail and thatching the corn-stack, from herding the sheep on the mountains, to cutting peat and carting lime for the fields."[4]

The first school Richard attended until he was fourteen was built in the fields belonging to his father's farm. His father wanted him to help on the farm when he turned fifteen, but his mother and brother thought he should continue his education. Richard told his father that if he were supported for one year at school, he would never ask for further help. At the end of that year, Timothy was offered a teaching position, enabling him to support himself and further his education in any way he could. One of these ways was to borrow every book in the village that he could find. . From his early years, Richard showed great keenness in acquiring knowledge, and all his life he had a great love of learning. By the age of eighteen, he had become schoolmaster of an endowed school, with 120 pupils under his care.

During the great revival that swept like a prairie fire over America, Northern Ireland, Wales, Scotland, Norway, and Sweden from 1858–60, Richard had made a profession of faith in Christ at age of twelve and was baptized in the river near his home. Shortly after this, while listening to a sermon on the text, "Obedience is better than sacrifice," he felt as if a voice was commanding him to go abroad as a missionary. After a period of teaching school, in 1865 he entered the ministerial training college of Haverfordwest.

As he was finishing his ministerial training, Richard applied to the Baptist Missionary Society, desiring to be sent to northern China. He argued that the Chinese were the most civilized of the non-Christian nations and would, when converted, carry the Gospel to less advanced peoples. By working in the North Temperate Zone, Europeans could stand the climate, and the natives of northern China could then, when converted, win those living in the rest of China. Richard was already thinking in terms of

---

4. Richard, *Conversion by the Millions in China*, 7.

all China and displaying positive ideas of his own. He was accepted in the spring of 1869 and was appointed to the province of Shandong, in northern China, as he wished. At the last moment before sailing, Richard was asked if he would pledge himself to remain unmarried for ten years. That question took him by surprise, as he had not thought much of that subject, but had merely considered it would be risky to take a wife into the interior, then as little known as the wilds of Africa. He replied that whether he would marry in ten days or ten years would depend on what was best for the work. As it turned out, he did not marry for nine years.

Timothy Richard sailed for China on November 17, 1869, and reached Shanghai on February 12, 1870. Two weeks later, he arrived in Chefoo (today's Yantai), the only port in Shandong that was open to foreign residence at the time.[5]

THE BEGINNINGS OF MINISTRY

China was not open for Christian mission work when Robert Morrison arrived in 1807. From then until 1842, foreigners were not allowed to reside anywhere but on a narrow mudflat outside of Canton (today's Guangzhou). As the result of the Opium War that year, the then worthless Hong Kong was ceded to the British, and the five southern ports of Canton (Guangzhou), Amoy (Xiamen), Foochow (Fuzhou), Ningbo, and Shanghai were opened to foreign trade and residence. The north and interior were still forbidden territory. About twenty years later, northern ports were opened under another treaty between China and Western powers,[6] and for the first time, foreign legations and residents were admitted to Beijing (Peking). Even so, the interior remained closed to residence by foreigners. In 1870, when Richard arrived, his sole colleague[7] soon died of typhus, leaving him for several months the only representative of the British Baptist Missionary Society in China. Since he was left entirely alone, his own experiences formed his only guide, and from them he learned what course to follow and what mistakes to avoid in the future.[8]

After having learnt the language sufficiently, Richard started his evangelism work. He went to the street chapel to preach every day, as was the custom of all the missionaries in those days. Local residents rarely came, and he did not find the preaching very productive. In 1871, he took a number

5. Richard, *Forty-Five Years in China*, 19–31.
6. Treaty of T'ien-tsin (Tianjin), 1858.
7. R. F. Laughton.
8. Richard, *Forty-Five Years in China*, 32.

of journeys inland distributing the Christian Scriptures, and experienced hardships, including narrowly escaping being captured by bandits. Later, Dr. William Brown, a medical missionary from Scotland, came to work with Richard, and they set off on a tour of healing and preaching. Their willingness to visit remote villages and their medical services won the confidence of the people wherever they went. In April 1874, Brown left for New Zealand, and Richard was again left the sole representative of the Baptist Missionary Society in China. He continued his preaching ministries, distributing Christian tracts among local people, but making very few converts.

Around that time, Richard came across a missionary sermon by Edward Irving, the nineteenth-century preacher whose name is associated with the Catholic Apostolic Church. It pointed out a more scriptural and far more effective way of winning converts than by preaching in the street chapels through a more literal following of the instructions in the tenth chapter of Matthew. There, the Bible taught "to seek out those that were worthy." in other words, men who were not far from the Kingdom of God, and who hungered for something better than what their own religion offered. In such men he found the "good ground" in which to sow the seed of the gospel.[9]

By carefully studying the Scriptures, Richard found that the usual gospel preached by ordinary evangelists was only a fraction of the glad tidings of great joy which are to regenerate the whole earth. It was on the Kingdom of God that Moses and the prophets dwelt. It was on the Kingdom of God that John the Baptist preached. It was the Kingdom of God that Jesus Christ preached and sent forth his Apostles to proclaim. It was for the Kingdom of God to come and His will be done on earth as it is in Heaven, that Christ commanded his believers to pray. His Kingdom contains all that is good in the kingdom of this world, and something more. It is a kingdom of peace on earth and good will to men. It is a kingdom of righteousness, a kingdom of salvation of the poor and needy, even in this world. Starting from his early years in Shandong, these two convictions of "seeking the worthy" and "the Kingdom of God" became Richard's principles of practicing his missionary work.[10]

Before long, Richard realized that he could not remain content with life at the coast. By hard study of the New Testament, other religions, the sacred books of China, and China's various secret religious sects, he prepared himself for his future work. In January of 1875, he decided to move to Qingzhou, two hundred miles inland, where he had heard there were several religious groups seeking higher truth than was to be found in the

---

9. Richard, *Conversion by the Millions in China*, 81.
10. Ibid., 85–86.

religions of China. After eight days on the snow-covered dirt road, through a terrible blizzard and strong wind, Richard arrived in Qingzhou. He lived in a small inn for a while before moving to a rented house. In his foreign dress, Richard was a great curiosity and very often people came to see him out of curiosity. Because of this, he decided to put on the native dress, shave his head, and wear an artificial queue. This made him less conspicuous and more like an ordinary Chinese person. In the autumn of 1875, after the rainy season, there was an immense amount of suffering due to ague. Richard had a good supply of quinine and gave it out freely. Cholera was very dangerous then, carrying people off suddenly. Richard was able to save many lives by using spirits of camphor. The following year, Richard started an orphanage there.

Before moving to Qingzhou, Richard had studied some of the Confucian classics. Now he turned his attention towards the popular religious literature of the devout sects, including Daoist tracts and two volumes of the Buddhist Diamond Classic. Through the study of these books, he acquired a vocabulary of religious terms in common use among the Chinese. Using this knowledge, he prepared a catechism, a hymnbook of thirty carefully-chosen hymns, and brief tracts with only six to eighteen characters. In the catechism, hymnbook, and tracts, he avoided terms invented by foreigners and rather employed Chinese terminology. Richard used these to teach the main principles of the Christian faith in such fashion as to appeal to the Chinese conscience. That was another example of Richard's character and independence. He sought to clothe Christian ideas in Chinese dress, following the example of the Jesuit Matteo Ricci, who came to China in the late sixteenth century. Both endeavored to appeal to the Chinese from the authority of nationally acknowledged truth, rather than from an external authority which was not recognized.[11]

In 1875, within Richard's first several months in Qingzhou, three converts asked for baptism. In early 1876, Richard administered baptism to fifteen converts. Surely this was not a bad record for pioneer mission work. Richard realized that the best method was to visit leaders of thought and character. He also made an effort to distribute Christian literature to locals. He was always looking for the best, and believing the best of everyone, so that he brought out the best in all the Chinese with whom he made and kept contact. Moreover, the strength of his work lay in his regular meeting with, and encouragement of, his newly converted leaders. In this way, Richard prepared native converts to become local church leaders.[12]

---

11. Soothill, *Timothy Richard of China*, 76–77.
12. Ibid., 92–93.

FAMINE RELIEF AND WORK IN SHANXI

Then a great famine came to Northern China. Many millions of people starved to death during the years 1876 to 1878. Richard saw it as his manifest Christian duty to spare neither his means nor himself in relieving the suffering people. He administered relief in Shandong, using funds from compassionate foreigners living in Shanghai and other coastal cities. He established five orphanages, each maintaining one hundred boys, and distributed relief whenever fresh funds arrived. A few times, Richard took great risks to bring the relief funds to those who needed it the most. People's hearts were moved by Richard's compassion. They came to visit him and believed that his compassion for the suffering people must be based on his religion. When they came, Richard gave tracts away to all inquirers, and presented his catechism and hymnbook to those who promised to commit them to memory. The result was that in a number of places, the nuclei of new churches were formed. In less than three years, Richard had gathered together a church of seven hundred members and over one thousand inquirers in Qingzhou. Much of this growth was accomplished through Chinese whom Richard trained, and who were self-supporting. There were no "rice Christians" from the beginning. The evangelistic work took deep root in the good soil of Shandong.

In 1877, the worst famine on record struck the province of Shanxi. The Famine Relief Committee in Shanghai heard about Richard's experience in famine relief and asked if he would go to Shanxi and distribute relief there. On receiving the letter from Shanghai, Richard discussed and prayed about the matter with another missionary, Alfred Jones. They "felt convinced that it was a direct leading from God to open up the interior of China."[13] The Chinese might not receive written evidence of the truth of Christianity, but help rendered to them in distress would afford unanswerable evidence of the motives of this religion. At the close of their prayer and discussion, Richard was so profoundly impressed with the deep feeling that God was giving him an opportunity of exercising influence over many millions of people, that a powerful physical thrill affected him so that he could hardly walk back across the courtyard to his own room. With the church under the oversight of Alfred Jones and the Chinese pastor, Mr. Ch'ing, Richard decided to proceed to Shanxi and begin Christian work there.[14]

In January 1878, Richard set out on a tour with a servant to investigate the extent of the famine in southern Shanxi. It was a dangerous journey to make, for many of the starving had turned to murder and cannibalism. Day

---

13. Richard, *Forty-Five Years in China*, 125.
14. Ibid.

by day, he passed the dying and the dead on the roadside, some naked, some well dressed, some being devoured by dogs, crows, and magpies. For more than a year, Richard and several other missionaries aided nearly 160,000 persons, using funds coming from foreigners in the coastal cities and from Britain.[15] He sent letters back to England, appealing for help. The Mayor of London decided to open a Mansion House Relief Fund. These funds were cabled out to Shanghai, and then were sent to Tianjin. The Viceroy Li Hongzhang then arranged for soldiers to guard and transport the silver to Shanxi. At that time, the ignorance of foreigners was so great that the officer over one of the Viceroy's military escorts addressed Richard on arrival, and all the time he was there, as "Gui-Zi-Da-Ren," or "Your Excellency the Devil." Richard courteously refrained from correcting him lest he be shamed.[16]

During this time, Richard came to see that not only was it the Christian's duty to relieve famine, but perhaps even more important, to provide education to avoid future famines. If it was good to save a few thousands from this dreadful suffering, it was even better to prevent millions from so great a terror.[17] In Richard's mind, education was of utmost importance, for it could enlighten people about all the wonderful works of God, for body, mind, and soul. He was always alert, puzzling about how best to work for the people's welfare. He went so far as to suggest to the government a plan to re-locate people from Shanxi to Manchuria, to employ those suffering from famine to build railways for quick transportation of grain. He pointed out that Western science and industries could help to prevent future famine. He also wrote a pamphlet for the Chinese gentry declaring that famine was not, as Chinese tradition declared, due to the displeasure of Heaven because of the sin of the Emperor, but could be prevented if the country would adopt modern education and gain advanced knowledge and skills like Western countries.

For the education work in Shanxi, Richard spent nearly £1,000 on books and instruments, much of the money coming from friends in Wales. For three years, Richard delivered monthly lectures on the religion, history, education, and science of Christendom to the hundreds of mandarins, scholars, and students living temporarily in Taiyuan. In this way, he had so secured their goodwill that by the end of eight years, there were fifty

15. The missionaries included Wesleyan David Hill, Joshua Turner of the China Inland Mission, and Albert Whiting, of the American Presbyterian mission (until he died of famine fever in April, 1878), and afterward by Hudson Taylor's second wife Jennie, along with Miss Horne and Miss Crickney and later Mr. and Mrs. James, all of the CIM. [Ed.]

16. Richard, *Forty-Five Years in China*, 139-40.

17. Soothill, *Timothy Richard of China*, 105-6.

Protestant missionaries living throughout the province in perfect peace without a single riot—a thing unheard of in the opening of work in any other province in China before. In this fashion, Richard not only aided in the introduction of Western science to China, but promoted social intercourse between influential Chinese and missionaries. Among Richard's high-ranking friends was the governor Zhang Zhidong, who within a few years was to be a leader in attempts to "reform" China by introducing much of Western science and education. In appreciation of his services in the famine years, the governor sent Richard a letter of hearty thanks and invited him to join in his service. To a man like Richard, with his experience of the people's deep poverty, and his breadth of sympathy with their needs, it was not an easy decision to refuse the governor's invitation. Richard knew his call was to the prophetic ministry of the Christian faith and there were greater things laid up for him to do, however.

While gaining the respect of the people of Shanxi through the provision of material things, which they could see and understand, Richard offered them the less tangible but more potent influences of his Christian faith, for their temporal and eternal good. In the years after the famine, Richard and his co-workers distributed portions of the Bible and tracts in all the major towns and marketplaces of the province, 107 counties in all. They also handed out specially prepared pamphlets to the seven thousand scholars from each county who gathered at the provincial capital, and thus, Richard began to sow the ideas of the Kingdom of God in every part of the province. He supervised Christian schools in villages, conducted services in town and country, and either in person or through Chinese colleagues, spread the knowledge of the gospel through much of the region. In Taiyuan, the capital city of Shanxi, Richard established a flourishing center of the Baptist mission.

In October of 1878, Timothy Richard married Mary Martin, a missionary of the Scotch United Presbyterian Mission, whom he had first met in Chefoo (Yantai). "I had come to the conclusion," he wrote in his autobiography, "that I could do more effective mission work in this newly opened service if I were married." Their honeymoon was the journey back to Taiyuan through desolate Shanxi, and within four months Richard had to travel to the south of the province to administer relief. But he had chosen his companion well. "No missionary ever had a more devoted wife," said Richard many years afterwards. Few missionaries, it may be added, have had such a gifted wife. Mary Richard started an orphanage of sixty boys, and together with Richard, established seven elementary schools in surrounding villages. Once Mrs. Richard wrote in a letter to her brother: "... we make it a rule *not to pay any native agent*. If the native church chooses to do so, good and well, but the Christians are instructed it is the bounden duty of each one to do what in him or her lies for the spread of the truth they have themselves received. They know it to be their duty and they do it nobly in very many instances."[18]

CONFLICTS

After ten years of working in China, Richard understood that denominational divisions could hinder the spread of the Gospel. To avoid causing confusion, he suggested establishing a united Chinese church for locals. Large-hearted, sympathetic, and courteous, he always opened his home to newcomers from different mission societies and had good relationships with fellow missionaries. For quite a few years, they prayed together and worshiped in one church. By 1871, however, differences of theology and missionary strategy and practice between him and the China Inland Mission became so sharp that further cooperation became impossible.

After fifteen years of unbroken and unique service in China, Richard decided that it was his duty to return to England. For most of his life in China, he had been a pioneer in missionary service, first for eight years in Shandong, then seven years in Shanxi. Now he would take his experience home and discuss new projects for the extension of the Kingdom of God in China with the Baptist Missionary Society. Richard had a wider vision than even the two provinces of Shandong and Shanxi, and wanted all the missionary societies to unite in establishing a missionary college in each provincial capital, in the hope of influencing the leaders of the Empire to accept Christianity. In England, he laid this plan before the Baptist Missionary Society, but the plan was not approved because of a lack of funds. This refusal of his proposal was a heavy blow to Richard. He had built his hopes on opening the eyes of his own people to see the need of adopting a better method of evangelizing Chinese.

Though the object of his return to England had failed, Richard determined to fit himself more fully for influencing the leaders of China. Before returning to China, he took a course in science and went to Berlin and Paris to study their education systems. In Berlin, Richard visited the Minister of Education. He told the minister that he was anxious to see the best education system and wanted to introduce it to China. After hearing this, the minister looked angrily at Richard and cried, "And when you have educated the Chinese nation what will become of us?" Richard went to Paris and learned that the education minister of France wanted to strike out the name

18. Ibid., 131.

of God from all the government textbooks. During this trip, Richard felt that the pressing need of the world was for the so-called Christian governments to convert to real Christianity.

After returning to China in 1886, Richard experienced another painful period of his missionary career. During his absence on furlough, new colleagues had arrived. They came under the influence of members of another mission society, and turned eyes of criticism on him and his methods. Brought up in the orthodoxy of their day, they could only read heresy into Richard's statements and actions and sent a long letter to the Baptist Missionary Society, censuring Richard in regard both to his theological views and his methods. That was indeed a staggering blow both to Richard and his wife. Richard knew that to remain would induce permanent strife, which would be fatal to missionary work. Therefore, he and his wife decided to depart from Shanxi and from the center of the Baptist mission which he had founded. They left Shanxi to go into the wilderness, not knowing what their future would hold. Feeling misunderstood, they withdrew, but, as one of the missionaries afterward said, "Wherever the missionaries went in Shanxi people asked affectionately after 'Li Ti-mo-tai,'" and to Richard, the missionary added, "you've left a trail of light behind you."[19]

ENLIGHTENING EDUCATED MINDS OF CHINA

After departing from Shanxi, in the following four years, Richard and his wife lived like exiles, moving from one place to another continually. Now it became necessary for him to earn a living for himself and his family, and yet at the same time to maintain what he considered to be his divine vocation. It was easy for a man of his gifts, knowledge of the language, and personal magnetism to obtain ample rewards for his service. He was, however, first and foremost a Christian missionary, pledged to do his utmost to establish the Kingdom of God on earth, a Kingdom never to him a material one, but eminently spiritual. During that period of time, Richard wrote a pamphlet, *Modern Education*, and a book, *Historical Evidences of the Benefits of Christianity*, a book on the benefits Christianity had brought to every continent. He also took part in famine relief again in Shandong. During the second General Missionary Conference held in Shanghai in 1890, Richard presented a paper entitled "The Relation of Christian Missions to the Chinese Government." In Tianjin, he was invited by Viceroy Li Hongzhang

---

19. Ibid., 159. Readers will be aware that this narrative comes entirely from Richard's point of view, and is meant to give an idea of his reaction to these sad events. Others saw things differently, of course. [Ed.]

and several personal friends to become the editor of a daily paper, *Shi Pao* ("*Times*") which was circulated in the open ports of China. At that time, there were only six other daily papers in the Empire. Those dailies reprinted half of Richard's articles, and thus Richard was able to spread his ideas in all coastal provinces from Beijing to Guangzhou and from Shanghai to Hankou. This was the beginning of the systematic, daily dissemination of the leading concepts of Christendom among the Chinese people at large.[20]

It was in 1891 that the special call came which settled the future of Richard's work for the remainder of his life. Dr. Williamson, the founder of the Society for the Diffusion of Christian and General Knowledge among the Chinese, died in Shanghai in May of that year. The Committee of that Society saw in Richard a man with the right vision for their organization, and accordingly invited him to succeed Dr. Williamson. Having experienced the widespread influence of a local newspaper, Richard was convinced that he could reach a national public from Shanghai better than from Tianjin. Richard was deeply impressed by the invitation and the aim of the Society, which was to bring works of general, as well as religious, enlightenment, written by Christian men, within the reach of educated Chinese.[21]

In October 1891, Richard and his wife moved to Shanghai, where he took up the position of Secretary to the Society, later renamed the Christian Literature Society, (CLS). At that time, Richard was the only member entirely set apart for literary work, though it had enlisted a few able authors and editors, including Young J. Allen, Ernst Faber, and William Muirhead. They all desired the Society to influence the key group of the country, the educated intellectuals.

In 1892, Richard wrote to a number of leading missionaries in China, asking them to suggest such subjects for translation as they thought most important for Chinese. In this way, he hoped to increase interest in the CLS. A list of about seventy subjects was suggested, and over twenty friends, chiefly educational missionaries, promised to write on some of these subjects. The Society published several important magazines. The most influential, *Wan Kuo Kung Pao*, commonly known as *the Review of the Times*, under the editorship of Young J. Allen, was a valuable source for the mandarins and scholars, opening their eyes to the outside world during the late Qing Dynasty. Another magazine, *The Christian Church Review,* was designed to guide Christian leaders and missionaries in their evangelistic efforts. Richard translated Mackenzie's *History of the Nineteenth Century*, a book on the history of the progress of the nineteenth century in Christendom, which

---

20. Richard, *Conversion by the Millions in China*, 93.
21. Richard, *Forty-Five Years in China*, 217.

became widely read and which influenced the minds of many Chinese in favor of reform.

It must be remembered that at that time, China was asleep. Richard and the CLS had great difficulty distributing their publications. Chinese bookstores would not touch them since the Chinese were not ready to buy foreign books which upset age-old doctrines and systems. These publications had to be distributed through missionaries. His own book *Historical Evidences of the Benefits of Christianity* was given to the candidates at the triennial examinations in Beijing in 1892, thus reaching elite students who would become the influencers of China. In the year of 1893, over sixty thousand publications were distributed among candidates of the official examination in several of the provincial capitals. That year, depots for CLS publications were established in Beijing and several other major cities in China. Richard republished a collection of his articles under the title *Essays for the Times*; prefaces on *"The Importation of Western Learning"* by Viceroy Li Hongzhang and Marquis Tseng (Zheng) were published by the Society.

In 1893, Richard's wife and other women missionaries in Shanghai decided to print a specially designed and decorated New Testament as a present to the Empress Dowager, whose sixtieth birthday was coming. CLS helped to prepare the Bible, bound in solid silver covers, and presented with a beautiful address written by Mrs. Richard and translated into suitable Chinese by Richard with the help of an able Chinese writer. One result of this presentation was that the Guang Xu Emperor himself became interested and sent a eunuch to the Bible Society depot in Peking to procure the whole Bible, along with other Christian books published by CLS.

For centuries, women in China had suffered the cruelty of foot binding. This custom was very painful and resulted in lifelong disabilities. When Richard learned about the Christian women's anti-foot-binding movement, he consented not only to use his magazine to advocate the movement, but also to help produce and publish the literature necessary for arousing public opinion against the practice. Finally, the Empress Dowager issued an edict to exhort her subjects to abandon the custom.[22]

Richard published the work of Chinese writers on various subjects related to the enlightenment of the nation and encouraged them to form societies for the advancement of learning. Within a few years, many high officials were enlightened by these publications and started to appreciate the work done by the CLS. Zhang Zhidong, Viceroy of Central China, sent a donation of a thousand taels. About ten years later, Zhang Zhidong played

---

22. Ibid., 224–28.

a decisive role in helping the Qing Empire to abolish the old educational system and start a new one.

In 1894–95 came the great humiliation of the Qing Dynasty of suffering defeat by the Japanese. Japan had been long despised by the Chinese, but now it had became a threat after adopting Western education and science. The war was a clear indication of the failure of the Qing Dynasty's attempts to modernize its military and fend off threats to its sovereignty. More and more Chinese believed that their country must learn from the West or suffer even greater disaster. They also saw the need for reorganization of the government. A memorial signed by twelve hundred scholars was presented to the Throne, begging for reform on the lines suggested in publications by Richard and the Christian Literature Society. Many officials supported the idea of reformation. The most prominent leader of the reformation movement, Kang Youwei, said that most of his ideas of reformation were formed through reading books and articles written by Richard and Young J. Allen. In their first meeting, Kang Youwei, told Richard that he believed in the fatherhood of God and in the brotherhood of nations taught in the CLS publications.[23]

Richard had close relationships with leaders of the reform and once was asked to revise the rules they wrote for their Reform Society. In February 1898, the Reform Society published a *New Collection of Tracts for the Times*. Forty-four essays were by Liang Qichao, thirty-eight by Kang Youwei, and thirty-one by Richard, a clear indication of the remarkable value of his work. Liang Qichao, another important leader of the reformation movement, once served as Richard's Chinese secretary. Richard also provided many suggestions to those in high positions in the government or close to the Emperor. The Emperor himself read books published by the CLS. Once, the Emperor's tutor told Richard that he had been reading Richard's translation of Mackenzie's *Nineteenth Century* every day for two months with the Emperor.[24]

The reform movement spread rapidly to the country. The Reformers recognized that the ancient system was inadequate for coping with the modern world, and struggled for the adoption of Western learning. They also recognized that hatred of foreigners was neither justifiable nor healthy. Now they requested the government to set up an office to translate Western books into Chinese. They hoped China would build railroads and develop industries. Some even went so far as to advocate the adoption of Christianity

---

23. We see here an adumbration of the idea of the "Fatherhood of God and brotherhood of man" developed by later liberal theologians. [Ed.]

24. Richard, *Forty-Five Years in China*, 253–68.

as the national religion. In 1898, Richard was appointed to serve as one of the Emperor's advisers. Not all people in high positions desired to see China changed however. The Empress Dowager suppressed the reform movement; the Emperor was made a lifelong prisoner and six influential reformers were executed. Richard's wise counsel, writing, and CLS publications continued to be influential, nevertheless, especially after the political turmoil caused by the Boxer Rebellion.

By the end of the nineteenth century, "Li-Ti-Mo-Tai" (Timothy Richard's Chinese name) had become a household word in China. He was respected by all as a promoter of understanding and goodwill, as a life-long advocate of reforms in the spheres of politics, society, and education, and as an authority among Christian missionaries in China. Richard used his contacts with Chinese officials to seek religious liberty for Protestant missionaries and Chinese Christians. Early in 1890, while attending the missionary conference in Shanghai, Richard had pointed out that some the highest officials were the masterminds behind anti-Christian and anti-missionary literature. In 1895, Richard took the leading role in preparing and presenting a memorial from Protestant missionaries to the foreign office of the Qing government asking for an imperial edict assuring Protestant religious liberty. Richard had nine interviews with the highest officials in the government from September 1895 to February 1896. Though the decree was not issued, some of the most prominent officials acknowledged that the unjust attitude toward Protestant missionaries and Chinese Christians should be corrected.[25]

As a missionary statesman recognized among mission societies in Britain and America, in the spring of 1900, Richard was invited to attend the World Missionary Conference in New York. At that time, he was strongly convinced of the danger threatening missionaries and all foreigners in China because of the imminent Boxer uprising and the spread of anti-foreign feeling among officials. Richard pleaded with mission boards and with the leading officials of the United States to take steps to prevent the Boxer uprising from going to extremes. However, the mission board leaders believed that they should not interfere in politics and he was told that the American Government would not act on mere opinion, however strong. That was the final blow to his hopes of inducing America to avert the Boxer catastrophe.

On his way returning to China, the massacre had taken place. He wired the British government urging a concrete measure for the protection of foreign missionaries and Chinese Christians. When arriving in Shanghai, it was

25. Ibid., 242–52.

an overwhelming shock to Richard to hear of the terrible tragedy in Shanxi province. Less than twenty years earlier, Richard and other missionaries had been saving the lives of thousands of starving people in that province. Now, 189 Protestants—men, women and children—forty-seven Catholic priests and nuns, and more than thirty thousand Chinese Catholics, Protestants, and Orthodox Christians were done to death by the brutality of the Boxers and anti-foreign, anti-Christian officials. That was one of the darkest days in China's history and is believed by some to be "the greatest single tragedy in the history of Christian evangelicalism."[26]

After the Boxer uprising was suppressed, in 1901, Richard was invited by the imperial authorities to assist in the settlement of the Shanxi Massacre, as he had lived many years in Shanxi, where he had become well known to the officials and people through distribution of famine relief. Richard replied that the missionary societies would not sell the lives of their missionaries for money, but that, as a great crime had been committed which no government could overlook, he proposed that a fine of half a million taels should be imposed upon the province, to be paid in yearly installments of fifty thousand taels, and that the money should be devoted to the establishment in Taiyuan of a university on Western lines for the education of young men of promise, the aim being to remove the ignorance and superstition that had been the main cause of the massacre of the foreigners. The government accepted all of Richard's proposals about this university and appointed him as the chancellor. This became the third Imperial University of China. Under Richard's direction, Christian missionary professors designed the curriculum and students had an opportunity to choose what they would like to study, including Christian studies.[27]

AMBASSADOR OF GOD

Richard labored in China for over forty-five years. As a pioneer missionary in Shandong and Shanxi, his hard work of seeking the worthy, sowing seeds, and sharing love in famine relief efforts laid a good foundation for Christian communities to be established and grow to maturity. Richard's missionary approach was influenced by his understanding of the gospel. To him, the Kingdom of God embraced the whole of life, now and hereafter, especially now. The Kingdom should come to this world and should be concerned with human bodies as well as human souls. In Shanxi, he developed his idea of enlightening and educating future leaders in order to prevent famine and

26. Brandt, *Massacre in Shansi*, xiii.
27. Richard, *Forty-Five Years in China*, 298–300.

other sufferings. After twenty years of working as an evangelist, he took the opportunity to enlighten educated Chinese through the work of the Christian Literature Society. When he began the literature work in Shanghai, he was the only full-time staff person, and the total value of its property was a mere thousand dollars. Twenty-five years later, CLS had become the most prestigious publisher in China. Richard himself had issued original works or translations numbering over a hundred, and his influence, through literature and personal contact with the most powerful people in the land, had made the name and work of the Christian Literature Society known throughout the country.

Again, his labor was guided by his convictions about the Kingdom of God and seeking the worthy. He carefully studied other Chinese religions and took pains to visit Buddhist temples and consult with their cultured abbots.[28] Richard urged that Buddhism not be judged by the ignorance of the ordinary monk, but by the influence its philosophy has had on great minds in China. It was Richard's belief that Christian faith, much better and brighter that Buddhism, could more powerfully enlighten educated minds in China and the minds of those in high government positions, particularly as evidenced in the reformers.[29] Nor did he neglect evangelism: Five times Richard preached his sermon of the only way of salvation to each member of the Chinese Foreign Office and a sixth time to them collectively.[30]

Those leaders of Reform Movement in 1898 said that they were inspired by the publications of the Christian Literature Society, considered Richard their mentor, and sought his counsel from time to time. He deplored extreme revolution, however. He once answered a Chinese journalist in 1903, "As to reform in China there are two views—one revolutionary and one reformatory. I do not belong to the former as I have seen such terrible disasters arising from violent measures . . . Jesus Christ is conquering the world by spiritual and intellectual rather than by physical force."[31]

Richard's prophetic view deeply reflected his concern for the welfare of Chinese people and for the entirety of mankind. While on his second furlough, Richard appealed to different mission societies for effective production and dissemination of informative literature written from the Christian standpoint. He saw not only the immediate need but also an enormous demand. If the new literature were to be written from the agnostic or anti-Christian standpoint, as was so much the case in Japan, it would result in

28. Burt, "Timothy Richard," 293–300.
29. Soothill, *Timothy Richard of China*, 163.
30. Richard, *Conversion by the Millions in China*, 104.
31. Soothill, *Timothy Richard of China*, 303–4.

the erection of another, more formidable barrier to spreading the Christian faith. He advocated the ministry of the Christian Literature Society and the supreme value of disseminating the best Christian knowledge to a vast body of educated men who might soon otherwise be bombarded with anti-Christian literature.[32]

That Richard sought the conversion and transformation of a great empire is clear. He carried on this mission faithfully and heroically. The headquarters of the Baptist Missionary Society in London displays a global map, which they clearly treasure, because underneath the map in Richard's hand it reads, "The field is the world. Timothy Richard." People either in China or in the West rarely know that Richard was awarded honorary degrees by the University of Georgia and Brown University in the United States, and by the University of Wales, but whenever the name of Timothy Richard is mentioned in China, people remember him as a great Christian missionary. When he was fifteen or sixteen years old, Timothy Richard listened to the sermon, "Obedience is better than sacrifice," and felt that he heard a voice commanding him to go abroad as a Christian missionary. He still remembered that sermon and that calling when he was over seventy years old. Once, two old friends recalled how, when they parted from him to proceed into Shandong, he said, "If you see the Governor, do not look upon yourselves only as the representatives of the Missionary Society; remember that you are ambassadors of God." It is in this way that Richard always thought of himself. China was written upon his heart and he was a faithful ambassador of God to China.

---

32. Ibid., 290.

9

Jonathan Goforth
Tireless Evangelist and Revivalist

G. Wright Doyle

OF ALL THE MISSIONARIES whose stories are told in this book, perhaps none witnessed more dramatic works of God's Spirit than the subject of this chapter. At a time when some missionaries and Chinese Christians were calling for a "modern message" to adapt to "modern times," Jonathan Goforth continued to draw his sermons from the Bible. Higher education and social reform had displaced evangelism and preaching as the highest priorities for many foreign missionaries, especially those in "mainline" denominations, but Jonathan Goforth, a Canadian Presbyterian, bucked the trend despite harsh criticism and devoted all of his energy to the oral proclamation of the New Testament gospel of "Jesus Christ, and Him crucified."[1] Even when fellow evangelicals ["fundamentalists"] could not accept the emotional manifestations of repentance and joy that accompanied revivals, Goforth, while never encouraging such phenomena, refused to quench what he saw as the work of the Holy Spirit. Faithfully assisted by his remarkable wife Rosalind, and despite physical weaknesses and outward obstacles of every kind, he traversed much of China in constant iterant preaching journeys, and was instrumental in turning thousands of Chinese to Christ.

---

1. 1 Cor 2:2.

EARLY LIFE AND EDUCATION

Jonathan Goforth was born on February 10, 1859, the seventh child in a family of nine brothers and one sister. His parents were immigrants from Yorkshire, England, living on a farm outside Thorndale, Canada. From an early age, he was known for his intense religious zeal, as well as quickness of mind. For example, at the age of five he could read all of Psalm 78 aloud to his mother, though he had not yet started school; he had acquired this ability by listening to his older brothers read. His father was too busy working two farms to attend to any sort of religion, but his mother's simple piety impacted Goforth deeply. Reading Psalms to her and going to church on Sunday were the only religious activities of his early years.

When he started school, the slow pace of his classmates frustrated him, but the large map of the world on the wall beside the chalkboard captured his attention at once, and he would spend hours just gazing at it and wondering about the lives of the people who lived in various parts of the world. Later, in high school, he was influenced by the Rev. Mr. Lachlan Cameron, who led a Bible study for the students, so he walked the distance to Cameron's church the next Sunday, and every Sunday after that. Eventually, he decided to commit his life to Christ. Soon he was teaching Sunday school. He even conducted evening devotions for his family when they visited his uncle's home, where he was staying.

Under the sway of their atheistic teacher, his classmates despised and mocked Goforth for his new-found faith and religious zeal. At night, he would study his Bible, searching for answers to the hostile questions they hurled at him. Little by little, his faith grew stronger, so that eventually he was able to persuade both teacher and students to trust in Christ also. Encouraged by this experience, he decided to become a Presbyterian minister, and came under the personal tutelage of Mr. Cameron, who taught him Latin and Greek in preparation for theological studies at Knox College, in Toronto.

Before leaving for college, Goforth was moved by the eloquence and zeal of George Leslie Mackay, who was home on furlough from his work in Taiwan, when he issued a challenge for some young man to catch the vision and become a missionary among the Chinese. Isaiah 6:8 came to Goforth's mind: "Whom shall I send?" Immediately, he sensed that he was meant not for a pastorate in Canada, but to evangelize the far-off Chinese. He was soon reading everything he could about missions in preparation for his future career.

When Goforth first entered Knox College, his fellow students scorned and jeered at him for his unsophisticated country dress and ways, and for his evangelistic passion. Goforth poured his heart into volunteer work at the Toronto City Mission; he distributed tracts in brothels, evangelized gambling dens, and prayed for street children. Though first rejected by prisoners in the city jail, he soon won their trust, and many believed the message he preached. For four years, he sought to visit every home in the Ward, a slum district, going to places that policemen feared to enter. Gradually, his classmates apologized for the cruel hazing to which they had subjected him, and came to respect and admire him, keenly moved by his dedication to evangelism among the poor.

Following his commitment to China, he began purchasing books and tracts about mission work among the Chinese and sending them to pastors and others all over Canada. His favorite title was Hudson Taylor's *China's Spiritual Needs and Claims*. So many responded with letters of gratitude and requests for more books that the work of packaging and sending them became too much for Goforth. By that time, his classmates had caught his passion for God's work among the Chinese, so they organized a team to help him distribute literature. Soon, many people knew of his plans to go to China as a missionary.

Meanwhile, Goforth dedicated himself to the weekend home mission work to which Knox College had assigned him. As he had done in the slums of Toronto, he visited almost every home in the district, personally inviting people to attend services at one of the churches where he would be preaching. The result exceeded his expectations, as overflow congregations gathered to hear this young and zealous preacher of the Word of God. His joy in preaching and the positive response he met further confirmed his sense of leading to go to China as a missionary.

During his third year at Knox College, Goforth met Rosalind Bell-Smith, a talented young artist from a well-to-do and prominent family. After working weekly with her at the Toronto Mission Union, he realized that he wanted to marry her, but feared that the class gap between their families would hinder his prospects. He was surprised when she accepted his proposal, and even more surprised when she agreed to become engaged without his giving her a ring, since he had dedicated his limited funds to the China mission literature project. When she heard the news, Rosalind's widowed mother expressed strong opposition, for she had promised her dying husband to send their daughter to England for further training in art. She told the girl she must choose between submission to her parents or expulsion from the home. Displaying the radical devotion to Goforth that would mark the rest of her life with him, Rosalind chose to remain in Canada, whereupon she moved into her brother's house. Her mother finally softened and received her back into their home.

Upon graduation from Knox College, Goforth wanted to become a Presbyterian missionary, but thought that impossible, since the Presbyterians had no work in China at the time. He had just applied to the China Inland Mission when his classmates surprised him with the promise that they would, as a class, undertake to support him as a Presbyterian missionary themselves. They had been affected by an unprecedented surge of commitment to foreign missions among students in Canada and the United States that had begun at Dwight L. Moody's East Northfield Conference in 1886. Goforth had spoken at a similar conference, Niagara on the Lake, the previous year, with great effect. One listener said that "he had the face of an angel ... and the tongue of an arch-angel."[2] What equally moved people, however, were the charts that Goforth had hung on either side of the pulpit, graphically displaying the contrast between the millions in China living apart from Christ and his gospel compared with the relative abundance of Christians and churches in the West.

At that time, the Canadian Presbyterians had no missionaries in China, and no plans to send any; home missions were also considered the most urgent need. The students at Knox College had to overcome resistance to Goforth's going to China first from the alumni of the college and then from the denomination, but their zeal and persistence, along with Goforth's burning eloquence and fiery passion, melted all opposition. "The real foundation of the China missions [in Canada] did not happen until early 1888, when Jonathan Goforth, influenced by Hudson Taylor, left Toronto eight months before the Taylor contingent's departure from the same Knox Church."[3] Although the new missionaries had been scheduled to leave later, news of the great famine in China prompted them to dispatch Goforth earlier with funds collected for famine relief. He and his bride were sent off at the Toronto train station by a throng of students and others who promised to support them with prayer and finance.

---

2. Rosalind Goforth, *Jonathan Goforth*, 32.

3. Austin, *Saving China*, 27. Alvyn Austin quotes Goforth's friend C. W. Gordon, who described him as "a queer chap—a good fellow—pious—an earnest Christian, but simple-minded and *quite peculiar*." Austin continues, "He had personal magnetism despite his shabby exterior, and relied not on stage oratory but on the power of his 'burning words' and 'right condemning forefinger.' He was, in the terminology of the day, 'a God-intoxicated man,' drunk with the spirit, who could be 'counted insane sometimes because of the tremendous of his fire and zeal.'" Earlier in the book, showing his penchant for painting evangelical missionaries in a less-than-favorable light, he had portrayed Robert Morrison and Robert MacKay as extremely unattractive characters, while almost totally downplaying their lasting contribution to the spread of the gospel in China and Taiwan (Formosa).

BEGINNING LIFE IN CHINA

After a miserable journey, during which they were almost continuously seasick, the Goforths landed in Shanghai, where he turned over famine relief money to the joint commission responsible. In an example of "comity," the various mission societies decided that the "North Honan (Henan) field" be assigned to the Canadian Presbyterians, so Jonathan and Rosalind set off for Chefoo (now Yantai) in Shandong, to commence language study. Rosalind's first great shock came when the house in which they lived burned down, destroying wedding presents, precious photographs, and her artwork. Her husband's comment revealed his relative detachment from this world's goods, as well as his limited ability to sympathize with his wife: "My dear, do not grieve so. After all they're *just things*."[4]

On August 12, amidst a cholera epidemic in which missionaries all around them died, Gertrude Goforth was born. In September, Dr. and Mrs. J. F. Smith, new recruits from Canada, arrived. A veteran missionary, Dr. Arthur H. Smith, offered to take them on an exploratory tour of northern Henan, were they were to begin working. The day they were to cross the border, while reading Isaiah 55:10–11 Goforth sensed that God had promised to prosper the preaching of his word. J. Hudson Taylor, whose writings and example had played such a key role in Goforth's commitment to China, wrote him a letter, which contained this exhortation: "Brother, if you would enter that Province, you must go *forward on your knees*."[5] Those words became the slogan of the North Honan Mission.

The Goforths moved to Pangchwang (Pangzhuang), a village closer to Henan. Not long thereafter, Goforth's best friend while at Knox College, now Dr. Donald McGillivray, arrived from Canada. Their happy association would last until McGillivray died more than thirty-five years later. McGillivray was a brilliant and ready student of Chinese, but Goforth had to struggle hard to gain the language. As soon as he could say a few sentences, however, he was sharing the essentials of the Christian message with anyone who would listen. From the beginning, he used the very words of the Bible as much as possible to convey the gospel of "Christ crucified" for sinners, refusing to rely on his own eloquence or on roundabout ways to attract Chinese hearers. And from the beginning, Chinese responded to this simple biblical evangel with confession of sin and professions of faith in Christ. He

---

4. Goforth, *Jonathan Goforth*, 42.
5. Ibid., 45.

was convinced that "the Gospel which saved the down and outs in the slums of Toronto, is the same Gospel which must save Chinese sinners!"[6]

In later years, he would tell younger missionaries that the secret of his winning so many converts to Christ was "because I just give God a chance to speak to souls through His own Word. My only secret in getting to the heart of big sinners is to show them their need and tell them of a Saviour abundantly able to save. Once a sinner is shown that no flesh can be justified in God's sight by the deeds of the law and that he can attain unto the righteousness of God through faith in the Lord Jesus Christ, he readily yields."[7]

In the spring of 1889, they moved to a village on the Wei river, Linching (now Linqing), which was even closer to Henan. As the frightful heat of summer bore down upon them, little Gertrude came down with dysentery, and died within a week. The grief-stricken father wrote home to his friends and family: "None but those who have lost a precious treasure can understand our feelings, but the loss seems to be greater because we are far away in a strange land... 'All things work together for good' [Rom 8:28]. The Lord has a purpose in taking our loved one away. We pray that this loss will fit us more fully to tell these dying millions of Him who has gained the victory over death."[8]

Returning from the burial, Goforth and McGillivray plunged into full-time study of the language. Once more, while his friend advanced quickly, Goforth made slow progress. He was about to give up in despair, but cried out to God to work a miracle of tongues in his life. Almost immediately, he found that words and phrases that had eluded him now came easily. Later, he learned that a special prayer meeting "just for Goforth" had been held at the very time that he was looking to God for a breakthrough. Thenceforth, he found that he could preach with fluency and power and be understood widely across northern China. Nor did Goforth rely on continuous miracles; he studied Chinese diligently each day for many years as a high priority.

After three more married couples arrived from Canada in December, 1889, Goforth, authorized by the General Assembly of the Presbyterian Church in Canada, convened and established the first presbytery in northern Henan. For two years Linqing was their home base, from which Goforth and other missionaries made evangelistic journeys into surrounding towns and villages. More than once they narrowly escaped angry mobs intent on doing them harm, for anti-foreign feeling was rising throughout the region,

6. Ibid., 46.

7. Ibid., 47. Goforth is referring to several passages of the Bible, including Rom 3:22; Gal 2:16, 21; Phil 3:9.

8. Ibid., 48.

inflamed by posters charging foreigners with the vilest crimes. He wrote, "Several times I have got out of such crowds under a shower of clods and bricks."[9]

In December, 1889, a son was born, whom they named Donald after their friend Donald McGillivray. Tragedy struck again six months later, however, when "wee Don" fell off the veranda of the foreign-style house into which they were preparing to move. He died on July 25, and was buried with his sister. They moved to Chuwang (now Chuwangzhen) a village in Henan, where Rosalind bore another son, Paul. He was joined by a girl, Florence Evangeline, on January 3, 1893.

From this new base, Goforth and his Chinese helpers would go "touring." In order to combat a tendency to laziness in them, and to set an example of humility and frugality, he chose to walk rather than ride on a donkey or even in a hired wheelbarrow; the latter he used for books and other supplies. One of his coworkers said, "Dr. Goforth, while not an athlete, was a great walker, and when on tour covered great distances on foot."[10] After a hard day's journey, when they finally reached an inn, his Chinese and missionary companions would get something hot to drink and a bit to eat, but Goforth immediately plunged into preaching to the other guests. His friend wrote, "That is one of my earliest impressions of him, always at it, and first at it."[11]

STARTING WORK IN HENAN

Finally, in 1895, the Goforths were given permission to move to Changte, in Henan. Before they left Chuwang, a flood devastated the area and ruined almost all of their belongings. From the first, their mission compound in Changte was thronged by people eager to hear the gospel, so that both of them were constantly employed in preaching systematically through the Bible to crowds of listeners. Fearing that their strength would give out entirely, they prayed in faith for God to send them a Chinese evangelist. The next day, Wang Fulin, a converted opium addict, showed up looking for a way to serve God. Thrilled at this apparent answer to prayer, they immediately set him to work preaching to the thousands who filled the chapel and all of the other available rooms. For many years a professional storyteller, Wang, sensing that his time was short, "spoke as a dying man to dying men."[12]

9. Ibid., 56.
10. Ibid., 54.
11. Ibid., 55.
12. Rosalind Goforth, *Goforth of China*, 108.

Many were converted through his ministry. When he died three years later, he was remembered as "the Spirit-filled preacher."

The flood of inquirers did not let up in the ensuing months. While Goforth spoke to the men, his wife addressed the women, until she needed some time to rest and he came to preach to the women as well. Meanwhile, Dr. McGillivray would teach a baptism class and preach several times a day in the chapel. This went on all day, and hundreds were converted to Christ. Within five months, no fewer than twenty-five thousand Chinese come to hear the gospel at their mission station. Of this intense period, Goforth wrote, "It has been our privilege to see the manifest signs of Holy Ghost power among them. None but the Holy Spirit could open these hearts to receive the truth, as we see some receiving it every time we speak. I never saw anything approaching it in previous years."[13]

In the fall of 1897, the Goforths moved out of their Chinese dwelling into a new foreign-style house that the Presbytery had ordered constructed for them. Fearing lest this strange building erect a wall between them and the Chinese, the Goforths decided to open their house to guests. In the next few months, countless visitors toured their home, curious to see all of their foreign furnishings, and especially eager to inspect the cellar, where they had been told missionaries hid the eyes and hearts of little children whom they had kidnapped. Finding nothing out of the ordinary, they changed suspicion into trust and appreciation for their foreign friends. Naturally, the Goforths used these visits as opportunities for sharing the gospel with people who might never come to the chapel.

Their faith was tested again in 1898 when their daughter Gracie died of complications resulting from malaria. Her brother Paul came down with measles shortly afterward, and then both parents, exhausted from constant nursing of their children, succumbed to illness and nearly died, while hundreds of Chinese Christians gathered outside their home and offered fervent prayers for their recovery. In June of 1900 their daughter Florence was taken by meningitis.

Later that summer, the Boxer madness engulfed the entire region. Warned to flee, the Goforths and a few other missionaries made a harrowing journey through Boxer-infested territory towards a river where they could get a boat to safety. Angry mobs surrounded their caravan of carts, while shouts of "Kill! Kill!" rose up from thousands of men intent on murder. They lost all their belongings, and suffered wounds, but finally escaped, thanks to the courageous efforts of officials who had come under the influence of Christianity. Goforth himself nearly died from sword blows

---

13. Ibid., 110–11.

and merciless beating when he boldly rushed toward a mob urging them to "Take all you want, but do not kill." Only God's providence could account for their miraculous deliverance when so many others fell before the enraged rebels. Afterward, Goforth ascribed the rebellion to a very understandable reaction to the rapacious actions of foreign nations that had vied with each other to carve up China into "spheres of influence," as well as to indignation toward the odious opium trade.

The Goforths were sent home to Canada for a much-needed rest, but soon he was receiving invitations to speak on missions and what God was doing in China. He discovered that not only was the spiritual tone among Christians tepid and worldliness rampant, but that German Higher Criticism had influenced the churches, bringing skepticism towards the Scriptures and sapping missions motivation. He longed to be back in China, where he could participate in the great works of the Holy Spirit. Thus, when he learned of preparations being made for missionaries to return, he left his wife and family and headed off to the mission field. Shortly thereafter, however, Rosalind received a message that her husband was ill and she must return quickly, which she did. Goforth had contracted typhoid, so that when they were reunited in Tianjin he was a shadow of his former self, but still buoyant and cheerful.

Indeed, he was filled with joy at the prospect of carrying out a new plan for evangelizing the northeast part of Henan, which had just been assigned to him. The only problem, from his wife's standpoint, was that he envisioned a peripatetic lifestyle: They would live somewhere for a month, until a group of new believers had been gathered, and then they would move on to another location to spread the gospel there. Rosalind was terrified at the thought of taking her little children away from their comfortable home in Changte and exposing them to the danger of disease in rural China. Goforth tried in vain to persuade her to entrust her little ones to God. When they returned to Changte, however, one child came down with dysentery, which almost proved fatal, and their baby daughter Constance then took sick and died. Submitting to her husband and, she thought, to God, she consented to take her remaining children with them as she followed Goforth out into "regions beyond."

This crucial incident highlights Goforth's personality. On the one hand, when he thought that God had guided him to a certain course of action, which usually involved pioneer evangelism, he would persist in his opinion until his wife and his fellow missionaries agreed to let him follow his sense of leading. In that sense, it was hard to live with him and work with him. On the other hand, his wife, who should know, testified to his kindness, gentleness, good humor, and willingness to sacrifice for the sake of others, including his family. When he took them into places of difficulty or danger, he spared no effort to protect and provide for them, always trusting in God to preserve them.

His daily habits reflected his single-minded devotion to God and to the kingdom. He rose early, did a few exercises, then spent almost an hour poring over the Scriptures, taking notes on each passage. Breakfast at 7:00 was followed by a Bible study with his Chinese coworkers, then evangelism and teaching with them, either in the courtyard and chapel or out in surrounding villages. After supper in the evening, Goforth and his evangelists would preach to the crowds who constantly came to hear about God, while Rosalind played the organ as hymns were taught by their Chinese coworkers. After leaving Changte, they lived extremely simply, in rented premises with little furniture and even fewer of the comforts of foreign life. While "on tour," Goforth ate whatever was available with his Chinese companions, sitting like them on the side of the road.

SEEKING AND FINDING REVIVAL

Returning to China in the fall of 1901, he says, "I began to experience a growing dissatisfaction with the results of my work."[14] He felt that he had seen so little harvesting after thirteen years of sowing. What about Jesus' promise that his followers would do "greater works" than he had done, by the power of the Spirit? Despite "success" that would have satisfied most missionaries, Goforth longed to experience more of the work of God in his life and in the lives of the Chinese around him. In 1905, someone in England began sending him pamphlets on the Welsh Revival that was in progress, and then an old friend, now in India, mailed them a little booklet called "A Great Awakening," which contained some passages from Charles Finney's *Lectures on Revival*. Goforth decided that he would seek to fulfill the "conditions" for revival described by Finney, and set his heart to seek the Lord for greater fruitfulness.

He began to study the Bible on spiritual power and to read books on revival, so much that his wife feared his mind was coming unhinged. At a meeting at a fair in 1906, as he was preaching on the death of Christ for sinners, he saw the Spirit work on the hearts of his hearers, who all cried out to know Jesus. He and the Chinese evangelists concluded that "He for Whom we have prayed so long was here in very deed tonight."[15]

---

14. Jonathan Goforth, *By My Spirit*, 19.
15. Ibid., 21.

In the autumn of 1906, he was depressed about the lack of fruit in their outstations, and was about to go on a tour to see what could be done. First, however, he was convicted by God to go and seek reconciliation with a fellow missionary. He refused, believing that the fault lay with the other man, but he kept hearing God telling him to "go and straighten this thing out, so that I may go with you" on the tour.[16] Finally, he told God that he would go to this brother as soon as he could. Immediately, the prayer meeting that he was leading changed, as all the Chinese present seemed to melt in sincere contrition and repentance. "For almost twenty years we missionaries had been working among the Honanese [Henanese], and had longed in vain to see a tear of penitence roll down a Chinese cheek."[17] The results of that meeting and those in the outstations were dramatic, as conversions and baptisms doubled from the previous year.

A few months later, he witnessed the revival in Korea, and learned that missionaries there had prayed together for months for God to do a new and mighty work. After attending one of those prayer meetings, Goforth wrote, "Never have I been so conscious of the Divine Presence as I was that evening. Those missionaries seemed to carry us right up to the very Throne of God. One had the feeling that they were indeed communing with God, face to face."[18] He realized that he and his fellow missionaries in Henan were not at that spiritual level. He noted that the revived Korean Christians filled the church buildings; gave liberally; eagerly shared the gospel with others; zealously sought to understand the Bible; and had a "marvelous spirit of prayer."[19]

On the way back through Manchuria, wherever he told the story of the Korean revival, he was asked to return and hold special meetings. At a gathering in Peitaho, he spoke to a large body of missionaries, who were deeply moved. For the next several days, they discarded the program of addresses and devoted themselves entirely to prayer, with many of them breaking down in tears and openly confessing their sins to each other. At the conclusion, they resolved to pray daily at 4:00 PM for revival until it came. As events turned out, though Goforth was described as "an unprepossessing Canadian Presbyterian," he became "the first missionary to be extensively involved in revivalism."[20]

16. Ibid., 21.
17. Ibid., 22.
18. Ibid., 23.
19. Ibid., 24.
20. Bays, *New History*, 104.

He went to Manchuria in February, 1908, to begin a series of meetings issuing from the invitations the previous year. In the first place, the resident missionary was dubious of the value of a revival meeting, claiming that he had moved on in his theology to more liberal views; his wife showed even less interest. The night before the first meeting, an elder came and confessed that he had pilfered church monies. As Goforth preached, pointing out God's abhorrence for specific transgressions, such as "idolatry, superstition, . . . hatred, jealousy, sexual uncleanness, falsehood and dishonesty, pride, hypocrisy, worldliness and avarice," the congregation came under conviction of sin, and one after another cried out, or came up to confess wrongdoing, starting with that elder, who resigned his position as being unworthy of it; then all the elders, who all likewise resigned. The deacons followed suit, confessing their sinfulness and stepping down.[21] Finally, the pastor rose and tearfully admitted that if he had been a better shepherd, his flock would not have descended to such a deplorable condition. The entire congregation, profoundly moved by these humble confessions, began to cry out, "You are worthy. We appoint you as our pastor, elders, deacons. We are unworthy!" A doctor revealed that, rather than administering healing medicine to a man whom he hated, he had poisoned his trusting patient.

The revival fire spread rapidly to other towns and villages. In one place, the notoriously bad son of a Christian repented, confessed his misdeeds, and came out strongly for Christ. A gambler who had set out on his donkey to wring money out of his debtors was forced to go in another direction by his animal, which finally stopped in front of a church. The gambler, hearing beautiful singing, entered the building. As he listened to Christians confessing their sins with tears, he was overcome with contrition and humbled himself before them all.

After preaching and leading meetings in Mukden and Liaoning, Goforth headed to Kwangning, where the Irish Presbyterian missionaries warned him frankly not to expect such results as he had seen elsewhere. They were astounded, therefore, when the people responded to Goforth's preaching with the same intensity he had met with before. The church leaders, however, were silent during times of prayer, prompting Goforth to say to the missionaries that some sin was hindering them. At the next meeting, after his address was over about half of the congregation suddenly sunk to their knees in prayer, remarkable for Presbyterians, who were accustomed to standing while praying.

The next night, an elder stood to apologize to a fellow elder for having such a bad temper; the other man replied, "It is just as much my fault as

---

21. Goforth, *Goforth of China*, 187.

yours," and begged forgiveness. Then the flood gates burst, and the entire assembly cried out for mercy. As the meetings progressed, outsiders came to see what was going on. Many of them, struck by the humility and sincerity of the Christians' repentance, were themselves pierced to the heart and surrendered themselves to God. Bands of revived Christians fanned out to neighboring villages, calling on people to repent and trust in Christ, with similar effect. A hardened bandit was coaxed to a meeting. Although even torture had not availed to make him reveal information about his gang, God broke his resolve and effected profound conversion. He begged to join one of the revival bands, and was instrumental in bringing many others to humble themselves before God and become Christians.

And so it went, in one location after another. Missionaries were astounded as their congregations, often beginning with the leaders, responded to Goforth's preaching with loud cries and vehement tears of sorrow and hatred for sin, and fervent requests for God to deal with them graciously. Though a Presbyterian, Goforth allowed, as he said, the Holy Spirit to control the meetings. After concluding his message, he would invite the people to pray aloud as they were led by the Spirit. He also permitted, even encouraged, women to express themselves to God. In almost every service, individual prayers would be turned into one loud corporate cry for mercy, as the entire body joined with one voice, as it were, to express their penitent hearts and a newfound trust in God's forgiveness.

One missionary, who had been skeptical about the revival and almost disgusted by the reports of what he considered mass hysteria, later wrote, "Words of mine will fail to describe the awe and terror and pity of these confessions. It was not so much the enormity of the sins disclosed, or the depths of iniquity sounded, that shocked one. . . It was the agony of the penitent, his groans and cries, and voice shaken with sobs; it was the sight of men forced to their feet, and, in spite of their struggles, impelled, as it seemed, to lay bare their hearts that moved one and brought the smarting tears to one's own eyes. Never have I experienced anything more heart-breaking, more nerve-racking than the spectacle of those souls stripped naked before their fellows."[22]

Another, the Rev. James Webster, who accompanied Goforth, wrote: "The Cross burns like a living fire in the heart of every address. What oppresses the thought of the penitent is not any thought of future punishment, but their minds are full of the thoughts of their unfaithfulness, of ingratitude to the Lord who has redeemed them, of the heinous sins of trampling on His love. . . This it is which has pierced them to the heart, moved them

---

22. Goforth, *By My Spirit*, 42.

to the very depths of their moral being, and caused multitudes, being no longer able to contain themselves, to break out into a lamentable cry, 'God be merciful to me a sinner.'"[23]

A WIDER WORK—A GREAT COST

After Goforth returned to Changte, with great reluctance, his presbytery allowed him to give himself to full-time itinerant revival work outside his assigned field for a while. Though the Chinese Christians begged Rosalind to stay behind and take charge of the field in her husband's absence, the Presbytery declined, believing that a woman should not be given that responsibility, and she was told she must take the children back to Canada. Rosalind begged her husband not to allow such a separation, but he reminded her that she had long ago promised always to "let me put the Lord and His work first." As always, she submitted, and took their surviving five children home with her while Goforth went off to preach all over northern China.[24]

In one extraordinary series of services, young people whose parents had been brutally tortured and murdered by the Boxers a few years previously testified to their hatred and intent to wreak vengeance, and begged for forgiveness. This prompted a deacon, who had hitherto been unmoved, to renounce his own plan to kill those who had massacred his family. The list of guilty Boxers whose lives these Christians were fully planning to terminate was taken outside, torn to shreds, and trampled underfoot in the dust.

Missionaries and Chinese Christians alike had told Goforth that the believers in Newchwang (now Yinkou) would never humble themselves, so special prayer was offered as Goforth traveled to speak to the church there. Much to his surprise, even before he began to preach, he saw that virtually every person in the room seemed to be under a sense of God's awful judgment. Without his saying a word, revival broke out there, too. In Shanxi, where the Boxer Rebellion had taken the lives of more than one hundred missionaries and many more Chinese Christians, Goforth found churches that had fallen into spiritual laxity and even serious degeneration. As in Manchuria, so there also the Holy Spirit used his sermons and the prayers of believers to provoke widespread confession of sin and renewed zeal for God.

In each place where revival meetings took place, spiritual fervor among believers returned, sins were confessed and renounced, relationships were

---

23. Goforth, *Goforth of China*, 187.
24. Ibid., 191.

restored, and multitudes of non-Christians were brought into the church through repentance, faith, and baptism. In the course of the next few years, observers asked, "Will this be only a flash in the pan, or will it last?" In response, Goforth told stories of lasting transformation in the lives of lapsed Christians and egregious sinners in the communities where revival took place.

He also records instances of demon possession and exorcism in the name of Jesus. To Presbyterians, these phenomena were quite strange, for many of them were (and are) "cessationists," believing that supernatural gifts of the Holy Spirit and possession by evil spirits were things that ceased after the apostolic era. To most Chinese Christians and the missionaries who worked (and work) among them, however, demon possession and exorcism, as well as divine healing through prayer, are taken for granted. Goforth's narrative shows how he encountered the direct activity of Satan among both Christians and non-believers, and how God demonstrated his power to those who exercised faith.[25]

Frequently, people would attend the meetings with hardened hearts, openly declaring that they would never, ever, repent of their sins, much less confess them openly, as everyone else was doing. As Goforth spoke from the Scriptures about God's view of sin, both mature church leaders and rebellious teenagers would come under conviction wrought by the Holy Spirit and break down in contrite weeping. Sometimes, the Spirit would wait until they had reached home before falling upon them, so that, Goforth believed, the credit would all go to God and not to the preacher or his eloquence.

Perhaps most remarkable of all was the effect of Goforth's preaching, along with united prayer for revival, upon the missionaries themselves. One of Goforth's colleagues at Changte described the scenes when the entire congregation would pray simultaneously: "We remember that the Chinese are not so readily distracted by noise around them as we are, and prayer under such conditions is not so difficult as we might suppose. But how explain the missionaries praying; some in Chinese some in English, men and women, strictly Presbyterian, ordinarily restrained, with Scotch reserve sticking out at all points, raising their voices with the multitude; and all because their hearts were being lifted up as were the Chinese... The missionaries... took part with their Chinese brethren in making acknowledgment of faults and shortcomings, not for any thought of example to the Chinese, but simply

---

25. See especially Goforth, *By My Spirit*, "Evil Spirits Defeated and Cast Out in Honan," 74–82.

because God was moving their hearts and they were led to see themselves under God's searchlight."[26]

Writing later about these revivals, Goforth gave his own evaluation and the lessons he had learned. "My conviction is that the Divine power, so manifest in the church at Pentecost, was nothing more nor less than what should be in evidence in the Church today. Normal Christianity, as planned by our Lord, was not supposed to begin in the Spirit and continue in the flesh. In the building of His temple it never was by might nor by power, but always by His Spirit."[27] "We are convinced that the majority of Christian people are living on a plane far below what our master planned for them."[28] "[A]ny hindrance in the Church is due to sin. . . It is sin in individual Church members, whether at home or on the foreign field, which grieves and quenches the Holy Spirit."[29]

He believed that Christians should first confess their open sins openly; then unbelievers among them would be moved. Usually, secret confession was enough to bring release from secret sins, but sometimes public confession was necessary, especially for church leaders. He taught that sins against individuals should be privately confessed to them, and amendment made. He defended an emphasis on sin this way: "Calvary is His [God's] emphasis upon sin." An over-emphasis on sin "is in the nature of things impossible."[30]

As for demon possession, John Nevius' book had already been out for thirty years.[31] Goforth believed that such bondage still occurred. When fellow Presbyterians expressed distaste and distrust towards the outward display of strong emotions, he replied that when Chinese overcame tradition and culture to confess their sins publicly, the Presbyterian missionaries had to acknowledge the work of the Holy Spirit. Soon, the initiative in revivalism spread from the Presbyterians and members of the China Inland Mission to independent Chinese preachers such as Ding Limei, Wang Mingdao, Ni Tuosheng, and Song Shangjie (John Song).[32]

---

26. Goforth, *Goforth of China*, 199, 201.
27. Goforth, *By My Spirit*, 11
28. Ibid., 13.
29. Ibid., 13.
30. Ibid., 16

31. John Livingston Nevius (1829–93) was a missionary with the American Presbyterian church in China. The first edition of his book on Demon Possession greatly influenced Goforth and other missionaries. He is now famous mostly for his "principles" of missionary work, which stressed the need for local Christians to support their own churches and church workers, and to remain in their occupations after their conversion.

32. See Bays, *A New History*, 104–5.

FURLOUGH AND BEYOND

In 1909, Goforth joined his family in Canada for furlough. When he spoke to the General Assembly of the Holy Spirit's work in China, some received his message with open hearts, leading to open doors to preach in their churches. Most, however, considered him a fanatic, and refused him their pulpits, to his great sadness. Conditions at home were worse than he had thought. When the Goforths went to the British Isles to attend the World Missionary Conference in Edinburgh, the same would have happened, except that Walter Sloan, a widely respected leader of the China Inland Mission, guaranteed him and obtained invitations for him to speak at several large gatherings, including the Keswick convention. The leaders of Keswick even invited him to remain in Britain for a full year, at their expense, to hold more meetings, but he was ordered back to China by the mission board.

Returning to China, Goforth discovered that the inroads of German Higher Criticism that he had witnessed in Canada were now also evident among some of the younger missionaries being sent to China. On the one hand, he continued his criticism of "modernism" among fellow missionaries, though he has been called one of the "mild" fundamentalists, along with Walter Moule, (Anglican), Dixon Hoste (CIM), and Watson Hayes (Northern Presbyterian).[33] When the Laymen's Report on foreign missions was issued in 1932, along with the one-volume summary, *Rethinking Missions*, its strong liberal orientation came under ferocious attack from "fundamentalists" like Nelson Bell and Jonathan Goforth. Goforth said, "Nothing could be clearer than that the Appraisal Committee [which prepared the report] is the enemy of the cross of Christ."[34] The Report's opposition to evangelistic preaching in favor of social service, and its advocacy of collaboration with other religions, evoked sharp rejoinders. Goforth wrote that the last act of Jesus "on earth was to issue his Great Commission. That Commission was in fullest accord with all Scripture. . . That urgency of mission motive at the beginning must hold the same paramount place today."[35] Goforth was one of the "old generation of conservative missionaries like D. E. Hoste, W. S. Moule, J. W. Lowrie" who were a "leading force within the fundamentalist camp" in China. Their main goal was to maintain an orthodox foundation for the whole missionary enterprise.[36]

---

33. Tiedemann, *Handbook*, 540.

34. Yao, *Fundamentalist Movement*, 247, quoting "Jonathan Goforth on the Laymen's Report," *The Sunday School Times* 75 (February 25, 1933) 134.

35. Ibid., 254.

36. Yao, *Fundamentalist Movement*, 285.

At the same time, he redoubled his efforts to focus on the Cross of Christ in his evangelistic preaching. He was also told that he would need to find his own funding for any new work that he began outside of Changte; the Presbytery would not fund such "extra-curricular" activities. Turning to God in prayer, Goforth discovered that God would supply all the financial needs involved in opening new stations and hiring more evangelists through other means. Rosalind wrote later, "Mr. Goforth's faith never seemed to waver, even when, as a family, times of severe testing came. He would never borrow, nor ever go in debt, and God always honored His servant's trust in Him."[37]

Goforth's ministry extended to southern China when the China Inland Mission invited him to speak to their missionaries and Chinese in the Yangzi region. Finally, the strain of constant travel and preaching took its inevitable toll, and in 1916 he was ordered home by physicians who insisted that he give himself a period of complete rest. There, he learned of many Christians who had been burdened by God to pray for him and his ministry. Returning to China in 1917, Goforth refused to compromise with liberals ("modernists") in the Presbytery. He was allowed to remain a member of the North Honan Mission, but was told that he must leave his current home and move elsewhere. The Goforths then built a new home at Kikungshan, several hundred miles south of Changte.

Then commenced a period of extremely demanding itinerant preaching for the Goforths, with his wife accompanying him on almost every trip. They changed locations about every five days. Several other mission societies asked Goforth to address special meetings, and the "Christian" General Feng Yuxiang, asked him to speak to his officers. Later, he spent a full year ministering to the soldiers in that army, with dramatic results. In every place, the response matched what they had seen before. Thousands repented, believed in Christ, and received baptism; they threw out their idols and ancestor tablets, renounced their old ways, and shared the Good News with others. During the terrible famine of 1920, Mrs. Goforth handled funds that were sent to relieve the awful suffering in northern Henan. The next year, they were invited to hold special revival meetings in the areas that were hit hardest, in order to bring hope and new life to those ravaged by the disaster. Once again, people responded with repentance, faith, and requests for baptism. Goforth, known to be a very strict examiner of candidates for baptism, admitted fifteen hundred at one place.

Both at the time and since then, the lasting value of these professions of faith has been questioned. Twentieth-century historian of missions in

37. Goforth, *Goforth of China*, 220.

China Kenneth Scott Latourette concluded his investigation with these words: "Permanent moral and spiritual transformations were recorded and many accessions to the Church. Some converts, however, slipped back into their old ways and in later years the results were believed to have been most lasting in individuals whose excitement had not been so extreme."[38] In a note, he adds, "In 1914 a committee investigated the results of the movement in Manchuria after the lapse of six years and recorded a permanent deepening in the religious life of the church."[39]

The "Christian General" Feng, however, does seem to have lapsed permanently from his earlier apparently zealous Christianity. Latourette's discerning analysis could apply to many other Chinese, both before and after Goforth's time: "The clue to many of his actions seems to lie in his intense nationalism. . . . His patriotism undoubtedly colored his attitude toward Christianity. He probably looked upon the gospel in part as a means of rescuing china from her ills; it may, indeed, have been that feature of Mott's appeal which finally won him. . . . It may have been the failure of Christianity to achieve what he expected of it—constant victory for himself and the early unification of the country—which cooled his ardor."[40] Still, he records: "Some of his officers, however, continued to be very pronounced Christians . . . Compared with the religion of the T'ai P'ings, his faith and that of his soldiers much more nearly approximated to the standards of the New Testament."[41]

After another furlough in 1924, Goforth, nearing seventy, was nevertheless allowed by the mission board to return to China, find a new field, and commence his work afresh. Rosalind's health had broken down, and he did not want to leave her, but she said she would accompany him, which she did. Despite the worst hardship and sickness they had ever experienced, she endured, and eventually regained her health. Receiving invitations to Manchuria, they and three others set out in the dead of winter for Changchun, while hundreds of missionaries were being told by their consuls to evacuate areas south of the border because of the violent Anti-Christian Movement then raging across the nation. Settling in Szepingkai, at the terminus of the South Manchurian Railway, they soon discovered that the millions of immigrants who had flooded into Manchuria after the fall of the Qing Qynasty in 1911 were as hungry for the gospel of Christ as any they had seen in China

---

38. Latourette, *History of Missions in China*, 574–75.
39. Ibid., citing the *China Mission Year Book*, 1915, 45.
40. Ibid., 778.
41. Ibid,. 778–79.

proper. They were overwhelmed by the need, and wrote to the Canadian Presbyterian Church for more recruits and funds.

To their immense disappointment, their plea fell on deaf ears. After a time of intense prayer with his little band, Goforth "rose from his knees, ... drew himself up and with passionate earnestness exclaimed: 'Our home Church has failed us, but the God of Hudson Taylor is ours. He will not fail us if we look to Him. *This field must be evangelized.* If we cannot get Canadians as channels for the Gospel message, we must get Chinese.'"[42] He appealed to Dr. John Hayes, founder and principal of a Bible training school in Shandong, for students to come and help, and received the reply that the civil war in his region had closed all churches, so that the students had nowhere to serve! Several of them arrived soon after, and unsolicited funds for them came in from all directions, confirming Goforth's faith. Three years later, thirty evangelists were working with them, completely supported by unsolicited gifts.

Again, constant travel and work wore him out, and in 1929 Goforth was laid aside by illness for several months. During that time, he dictated to his son Fred the stories of the great revivals, published later as *By My Spirit*. The next year, his eye required repeated surgeries, so he once again had to rest. This time, he recounted stories of Chinese whose lives had been transformed to Miss Margaret Gay, a nurse who devoted herself to caring for him at night; these were issued under the title, *Miracle Lives of China*. These, along with Rosalind's books, are still in print. In 1933, Goforth's other eye failed, and more painful surgeries could not keep him from going completely blind. Nor were these the only obstacles to their ministry. Japanese military officers "visited" them frequently to keep a close watch on them; funds from home dried up as the Great Depression wore on; civil war and banditry disrupted communications and threatened everyone's life at one point or another; and the plague ravaged the region more than once. In all this, Goforth remained cheerful and uncomplaining.

Unable now to speak publicly, Goforth could still draw upon his immense knowledge of Scripture to answer questions and counsel the steady stream of visitors who came to him. Eventually, he recovered enough to resume giving sermons, drawing upon the Scriptures that he had stored away in his heart through repeated readings of the Chinese Bible. His strength was ebbing away, however, and he succumbed to pneumonia and was forced to rest for several months at a seaside resort.

Finally, several prominent ministers in Canada wrote him separately urging him to return and help rekindle the missionary fervor of churches

---

42. Goforth, *Jonathan Goforth*, 127.

there. When his wife's health completely collapsed in 1934, he accepted this as God's leading, and they went back for the last time. Immediately, he was deluged with invitations to speak in churches, first in Vancouver as soon as they landed, then in the rest of Canada. At seventy-six, he found the grueling itinerary that had been arranged for him exhausting, but the old fire kept burning within him and spurred him on. On October 7, 1936, after another strenuous day of speaking, he fell asleep and never woke up.

At his funeral, the Rev. Dr. John G. Inkster, pastor of Knox Presbyterian Church, whence they had been sent out as missionaries many years before, said of Goforth: "He was a God-intoxicated man—fully surrendered and consecrated. Above all, he was humble... He was filled with the Spirit because he was emptied of self—therefore he had power which prevailed with God and man."[43] Perhaps the greatest tribute came from the Rev. James MacKay, who said of the Manchurian Christians, "They loved him ... because he first loved them, and showed his love by giving them his all. He greatly loved and he was greatly loved."[44]

A MAN FULL OF THE SPIRIT

Goforth's wife writes that he lived "an exceedingly strenuous, highstrung life." How did he find any relaxation? She continues, "That which seemed to soothe and rest him more than anything else was when, supper ended, the lights were turned low and he would rest on the sofa for a brief spell before going to the street chapel or other ministry, while I sang and played softly his favorite hymns. Sometimes he would rise and join in singing."[45]

His indomitable spirit and profound trust in God shone clearest in the midst of hardship. His wife recounts that during one long winter "of physically hard labor . . . never once was Mr. Goforth heard to complain." When enduring cold, hard brick beds, or swarms of fleas, "he remained calm and unperturbed. He made light of what he described as 'minor matters,' choosing rather to regard the winter's [preaching] tour as 'a glorious "victory"' for his Lord."[46] According to Rosalind, Goforth had "that 'saving grace of humor, . . . saving the situation for us numerous times."[47] She spoke also of "the evident spiritual power that had come into my husband's life. I, his wife,

---

43. Goforth, *Goforth of China*, 349.
44. Ibid., 349.
45. Rosalind Goforth, *Climbing*, 27.
46. Goforth, *Goforth of China*, 243–44.
47. Goforth, *Climbing*, 31.

could not but see that he was indeed filled with the Spirit of God."[48] Towards the end of his life, she described her husband as "my companion, friend, husband, and hero of almost fifty years."[49]

Goforth's daughter, Mary Goforth Moynan, wrote of him many years later: "Opening a new work at Taonanfu [in Manchuria] was very strenuous. This incident reveals the character of Jonathan Goforth, the pioneer. Father was sitting in an old, broken easy chair in front of the stove. A look of absolute happiness (at 70!) came over his face as he said, 'Oh, is it not grand to be out here to open up such a place to the Gospel! Why, I'd rather be just here than in Windsor Castle!'"[50] Commenting on his parents' habit of sacrificially giving, she recorded some of Goforth's most frequent sayings: "You cannot outgive God!" "Sow sparingly and you will reap sparingly." "Go all out for God and he will go all out for you!"[51] From the time of his youth, Jonathan Goforth went "all out for God," and was rewarded by manifestations of God's favor, in the form of countless converts and revived Christians. May those who follow be imitators of his faith,[52] to the glory of God and of his Son, Jesus Christ.

48. Ibid., 89.
49. Ibid., 190.
50. Ibid., epilogue.
51. Ibid.
52. Heb 6:12.

Bibliography

Aikman, David. *One Nation Without God? The Battle for Christianity in an Age of Unbelief.* Grand Rapids: Baker, 2012.

Allen, Catherine B. "Charlotte (Lottie) Moon (1840–1912) Demonstrating 'No Greater Love.'" In *Mission Legacies: Biographical Studies of Leaders of the Modern Missionary Movement*, edited by Gerald H. Anderson, et al., 205–15. Maryknoll, NY: Orbis, 1994.

Anderson, Gerald H. et al., eds. *Mission Legacies: Biographical Studies of Leaders of the Modern Missionary Movement.* Maryknoll, NY: Orbis, 1994.

Annual Report. National Bible Society of Scotland, 1885.

Austin, Alvyn. *China's Millions: The China Inland Mission and Late Qing Society, 1832–1905.* Grand Rapids: Eerdmans, 2007.

Austin, Alvyn. *Saving China: Canadian Missionaries in the Middle Kingdom, 1888–1959.* Toronto: University of Toronto Press, 1986.

Baldwin, C. C. "To What Extent Ought We as Missionaries Appeal to the Secular Arm in Behalf of Chinese Christians." *The Chinese Recorder and Missionary Journal* 22 (1891) 99–105.

Barnett, Suzanne, and John K. Fairbank, eds. *Christianity in China: Early Protestant Missionary Writings.* Cambridge, MA: Harvard University Press, 1985.

Barr, Pat. *To China with Love: The Lives and Times of Protestant Missionaries in China, 1860–1900.* London: Secker & Warburg, 1972.

Barrett, Tim. *Singular Listlessness: A Short History of Chinese Books and British Scholars.* London: Wellsweep, 1988.

Barwick, John S. "The Protestant Quest for Modernity in Republican China." PhD diss., University of Alberta, 2011.

Bays, Daniel H., ed. *Christianity in China: From the Eighteenth Century to the Present.* Stanford, CA: Stanford University Press, 1996.

———. *A New History of Christianity in China.* Chichester, UK: Wiley-Blackwell, 2012.

———, and Ellen Widmer. *China's Christian Colleges: Cross-Cultural Connections, 1900–1950.* Stanford, CA: Stanford University Press, 2009.

Bebbington, David W. *The Dominance of Evangelicalism: The Age of Spurgeon and Moody.* Downers Grove, IL: InterVarsity, 2005.

Bickers, Robert. *The Scramble for China: Foreign Devils in the Qing Empire, 1832–1914.* New York: Penguin Global, 2011.

Bitton, Nelson. *The Story of Griffith John, the Apostle of Central China.* London: Sunday School Union, 1913.

Blake, Andrew. "Foreign Devils and Moral Panics: Britain, Asia, and the Opium Trade." In *The Expansion of England: Race, Ethnicity and Cultural History*, edited by Bill Schwartz, 232–54. New York: Routledge, 1996.

Bohr, P. Richard. "Jesus, Christianity and Rebellion in China: The Evangelical Roots of the Taiping Heavenly Kingdom." In *The Chinese Face of Jesus Christ*, vol. 2, edited by Roman Malek, 613–62. Monumenta Serica Monograph Series 50. Sankt Augustin: Institut Monumenta Serica and China-Zentrum, 2002.

———. "Liang Fa's Quest for Moral Power." In *Christianity in China: Early Protestant Missionary Writings*, edited by Suzanne Wilson Barnett and John King Fairbank, 35–46. Cambridge, MA: Harvard University Press, 1985.

———. "The Theologian as Revolutionary: Hung Hsiu-ch'üan's Religious Vision of the Taiping Heavenly Kingdom." In *Tradition and Metamorphosis in Modern Chinese History: Essays in Honor of Professor Kwang-Ching Liu's Seventy-Fifth Birthday*, vol. 2, edited by Yen-p'ing Hao and Hsiu-mei Wei, 912–21. Taipei: Institute of Modern History, Academia Sinica, 1998.

Bosch, David J. *Transforming Mission: Paradigm Shifts in Theology of Mission*. Maryknoll, NY: Orbis, 2005.

———. *Witness to the World: The Christian Mission in Theological Perspective*. Eugene, OR: Wipf and Stock, 2006.

Brandt, Nat. *Massacre in Shansi*. Syracuse, NY: Syracuse University Press, 1994.

Bridgman, Eliza, ed. *The Pioneer of American Missions in China: The Life and Labors of Elijah Coleman Bridgman*. New York: Anson Randolph, 1864.

Broomhall, A.J. *Hudson Taylor and China's Open Century*. 7 vols: *Barbarians at the Gates* (1981); *Over the Treaty Wall* (1982); *If I Had a Thousand Lives* (1982); *Survivors' Pact* (1984); *Refiner's Fire* (1985); *Assault on the Nine* (1988); and *It Is Not Death to Die* (1989). London: Hodder and Stoughton and the Overseas Missionary Fellowship.

———. *The Shaping of Modern China: Hudson Taylor's Life and Legacy*. 2 vols. Carlisle, UK: Piquant Editions, 2005. Originally published as *Hudson Taylor and China's Open Century*. 7 vols. London: Hodder and Stoughton and the Overseas Missionary Fellowship, 1981–89.

Broomhall, Q. Marshall. *Robert Morrison: A Master-Builder*. London: Student Christian Movement, 1927.

Bryant, Evan. "Dr. John Forty Years Ago." *The Chronicle of the London Missionary Society* 69 (1905) 113.

Burt, E. W. "Timothy Richard: His Contribution to Modern China." *International Review of Missions* 34, no. 3 (1945) 293–300.

Cai Shaoqing. "On the Origins of the Gelaohui." *Modern China* 10, no. 4 (October 1984) 481–508.

Chang, Irene, et al., eds. *Christ Alone: A Pictorial Presentation of Hudson Taylor's Life and Legacy*. Hong Kong: OMF International, 2005.

Chang, Lit-sen (Zhang Lisheng). "Critique of Indigenous Theology." In *Wise Man from the East: Lit-sen Chang (Zhang Lisheng) Critique of Indigenous Theology; Critique of Humanism*, edited by G. Wright Doyle, translated by G. Wright Doyle and Samuel Ling, 3–174. Studies in Chinese Christianity. Eugene, OR: Pickwick, 2013.

———. *Strategy of Missions in the Orient: Christian Impact on the Pagan World*. Hong Kong: World Outreach, 1968.

Charbonnier, Jean-Pierre. *Christians in China: A.D. 600 to 2000*. Translated by Archbishop M. N. L. Couve de Murville. San Francisco: Ignatius, 2007.

Chesneaux, Jean. *China from the Opium Wars to the Revolution of 1911*. Translated by Anne Dulanay. Harvester, 1977.

Cheung, David (Chen Yiqiang). *Christianity in Modern China: The Making of the First Native Protestant Church*. Boston: Brill, 2004.

China Group. "Taylor, James Hudson." In *A Dictionary of Asian Christianity*, edited by Scott W. Sunquist. Grand Rapids: Eerdmans, 2001.

Collie, David, trans. *The Chinese Classical Work Commonly Called the Four Books*. Malacca: Mission, 1828.

Covell, Ralph. *W. A. P. Martin: Pioneer of Progress in China*. Washington, DC: Christian University Press, 1978.

Creegan, Charles Cole, and Josephine A. B. Goodnow. *Great Missionaries of the Church*. New York: T. Y. Crowell, 1895.

Daily, Christopher A. *Robert Morrison and the Protestant Plan for China*. Hong Kong: Hong Kong University Press, 2013.

The Diamond Jubilee Report 1876–1938, of The Religious Tract Society in China. History and Statistics. Head Office Press: Hankow.

Douglas, R. K. (rev. Robert Bickers). "Morrison, Robert." In *Oxford Dictionary of National Biography*, edited by H. C. G. Matthew and Brian Harrison, 39:353–54. Oxford: Oxford University Press, 2004.

Doyle, G. Wright. "Problems in Translating the Bible into Chinese: The Name(s) for God." No pages. Online: http://www.chinainst.org/en/articles/christianity-in-china/problems-in-translating-the-bible-into-chinese-the-names-for-god.php.

———. Review of Alvyn Austin, *China's Millions: The China Inland Mission and late Qing Society, 1832–1905*. No pages. Online: http://www.globalchinacenter.org/analysis/christianity-in-china/chinas-millions.php.

———, ed. *Wise Man from the East: Lit-sen Chang (Zhang Lisheng) Critique of Indigenous Theology; Critique of Humanism*. Translated by G. Wright Doyle and Samuel Ling. Studies in Chinese Christianity. Eugene, OR: Pickwick, 2013.

Dunch, Ryan. "Science, Religion and the Classics in Christian Higher Education to 1920." In *China's Christian Colleges: Cross-Cultural connections, 1900–1950*, written by Daniel H. Bays and Ellen Widmer, 57–82. Stanford, CA: Stanford University Press, 2009.

Duus, Peter. "Science and Salvation in China: The Life and Work of W. A. P. Martin." In *American Missionaries in China: Papers from Harvard Seminars*, edited and with an introduction by Kwang-Ching Liu, 11–41. Cambridge, MA: Harvard University Press, 1966.

Editorial Correspondence, no. 25, 30, December 1889. Bible Society Archives. Cambridge, UK.

Fairbank, John King. *The Great Chinese Revolution, 1800–1985*. New York: Perennial Library, 1987.

———, ed. *The Missionary Enterprise in China and America*. Vol. 6 of *Harvard Studies in American-East Asian Relations*. Cambridge, MA: Harvard University Press, 1974.

Fitch, G. F. "Further on the Translation of Scripture." *Chinese Recorder and Missionary Journal* 16 (1885) 457–60.

———. "On a New Version of the Scriptures in Wen-li." *Chinese Recorder and Missionary Journal* 16 (1885) 298.

Foster, Arnold. "The Chinese New Testament." *Chinese Recorder and Missionary Journal* 17 (1886) 192–97.

———. "The Opium Commission Report." *Chinese Recorder and Missionary Journal* 27 (1896) 25–26.

Flynt, Wayne, and Gerald W. Berkley. *Taking Christianity to China: Alabama Missionaries in the Middle Kingdom, 1850–1950*. Tuscaloosa, AL: University of Alabama Press, 1997.

Franz, Michael, and Chung-Li Chang. *The Taiping Rebellion: History and Documents*, vol. 1. Washington: University of Washington, 1972.

George, Timothy. "Evangelical Revival and the Missionary Awakening." In *The Great Commission Evangelicals and the History of World Missions*, edited by Martin I. Klauber and Scott M. Manetch, 44–64. Nashville: B&H, 2008.

Gernet, Jacques. *China and the Christian Impact*. Translated by Janet Lloyd. Cambridge: Cambridge University Press, 1985.

Gibbard, Noel. *Griffith John: Apostle to Central China*. Bridgend: Bryntirion, 1998.

Gillison, Thomas. "Report of the Hospital at Hankow." *The Chinese Recorder and Missionary Journal* 16 (1885) 399.

Girardot, Norman J. *The Victorian Translation of China: James Legge's Oriental Pilgrimage*. Berkeley: University of California Press, 2002.

Glover, Archibald E. *A Thousand Miles of Miracle in China*. Glasgow: Pickering & Inglis, 1931.

Goforth, Jonathan. *By My Spirit*. Nappanee, IN: Evangel, 1983.

Goforth, Rosalind. *Climbing: Memories of a Missionary's Wife*. First edition, Toronto: Tyndale University College and Seminary, 1940; second edition, 1996; re-issue, Nappanee, IN: Evangel, 1996; third edition, Nappanee, IN: Evangel, 2008.

———. *Goforth of China*. Grand Rapids: Zondervan, 1937. Reprint, Eugene, OR: Wipf & Stock, 2014.

———. *Jonathan Goforth*. Minneapolis: Bethany House, 1986.

Hamberg, Theodore. *The Chinese Rebel Chief, Hung-Siu-Tsuen; and the Origin of the Insurrection in China*. London: Walton and Maberly, 1855.

Hamrin, Carol Lee, and Stacey Bieler, eds. *Salt and Light: Lives of Faith that Shaped Modern China*, 3 vols. Studies in Chinese Christianity. Eugene, OR: Pickwick, 2009–11.

Hancock, Christopher D. "*A Parting Memorial*: Morrison and Missionary Motivation." In *Ching Feng*, New Series 8, no. 1–2 (2007) 45–72.

———. *Robert Morrison and the Birth of Chinese Protestantism*. New York: T. & T. Clark, 2008.

Harrison, Brian. *Waiting for China: The Anglo-Chinese College at Malacca, 1818–1843, and Early Nineteenth Century Missions*. Hong Kong: Hong Kong University Press, 1979.

Ho, Tsun-sheen, and James Legge. *Huafan hehe tongshu: riyue kedu*. Sino-Anglo Almanac. Hong Kong: Anglo-Chinese College Press, 1844.

Hsieh, Fang-Lan. *A History of Chinese Christian Hymnody: From Its Missionary Origins to Contemporary Indigenous Productions*. Lewiston: Edwin Mellen, 2009.

Hudson, Anne Rosemary Hickling. "The Response of Protestant Missionaries to the Anti-missionary Disturbances in China, 1891–1907." Master's thesis, University of Hong Kong, 1968.

Hunt, Everett N., Jr. "John Livingston Nevius (1829–1893) Pioneer of Three-Self Principles in Asia." In *Mission Legacies: Biographical Studies of Leaders of the Modern Missionary Movement*, edited by Gerald H. Anderson et al., 190–96. Maryknoll, NY: Orbis, 1994.

Hunter, James Davison. *Evangelicalism: The Coming Generation*. Chicago: The University of Chicago Press, 1987.

Hutchison, William R. "Modernism and Missions: The Liberal Search for an Exportable Christianity, 1875–1935." In *The Missionary Enterprise in China and America*, edited by John K. Fairbank, 110–31. Cambridge, MA: Harvard University Press, 1974.

Hyatt, Irwin T., Jr. *Our Ordered Lives Confess: Three Nineteenth-Century American Missionaries in East Shantung*. Vol. 8 of *Harvard Studies in American-East Asian Relations*. Cambridge, MA: Harvard University Press, 1976.

John, Griffith. *China; Her Claims and Call*. London: Hodder and Stoughton, 1882.

———. "Discussion." *Shanghai Conference, 1877*.

———. "The Easy Wen Li New Testament." *The Chinese Recorder and Missionary Journal* 17 (1886) 381–96.

———. "Griffith John in Hunan." *The Chinese Recorder and Missionary Journal* 23 (1891) 361–70.

———. Griffith John Papers. National Library of Wales, Aberystwyth.

———. *Hope for China*. London: Hodder and Stoughton, 1872.

———. "How to Deal with Persecution." *The Chinese Recorder and Missionary Journal* 29 (1898) 538–39.

———. "In Memorium." *The Chinese Recorder and Missionary Journal* 32 (1901) 1–2.

———. "Journal." Unpublished. Griffith John Papers, National Library of Wales, Aberystwyth.

———. "Leading Rules for Translation." *The Chinese Recorder and Missionary Journal* 16 (1886) 145–48.

———. Letters. Griffith John Papers, National Library of Wales, Aberystwyth.

———. Letters. Council for World Mission, Central China, School of Oriental and African Studies, London.

———. "Opium." *Shanghai Conference, 1877*.

———. "Present Aspect of Missionary Work." In "Missionary Conference Held at Kuling, Central China, August 22nd to 25th, 1898." *The Chinese Recorder and Missionary Journal* 29 (1890) 493–500.

———. *The Reason Why*. Hankou: 1903.

———. *Y Rheswm Paham (The Reason Why)*. Translated by John Bodvan Anwyl. London: London Missionary Society, 1915.

———. "The Rev. Griffith John on Opium in China." *The Chinese Recorder and Missionary Journal* 25 (1893) 194–200.

———. *Sowing and Reaping: Letters from the Rev. Griffith John*. London: London Missionary Society, 1897.

———. *Spiritual Power for Missionary Work*. London: Morgan and Scott, 1882.

———. *The Supreme Motive in Foreign Missions*. London: London Missionary Society, 1882.

———. *Then and Now in China*. London: London Missionary Society, 1907.

———. *A Voice from China*. London: James Clarke, 1907.

Johnson, Eunice V., with Carol Lee Hamrin, ed. *Timothy Richard's Vision: Education and Reform in China, 1880–1910*. Eugene, OR: Pickwick, 2014.

Jones, Ieuan Gwynedd. "The Making of an Industrial Community." In *Swansea: An Illustrated History*, edited by Glanmor Williams, 115–144. Swansea: Christopher Davies, 1990.

Jones, Robert Tudur. *Congregationalism in England*. London: Independent Press, 1962.

Julian, John D. "Chinese." In *A Dictionary of Hymnology: Setting Forth the Origin and History of Christian Hymns and Hymnwriters of All Ages and Nations*, 4:743–45. Revised edition. London: John Murray, 1907. Originally published as *A Dictionary of Hymnology: Setting Forth the Origin and History of Christian Hymns of All Ages and Nations*. New York: Charles Scribner's Sons, 1892.

Kane, J. Herbert. "J. Hudson Taylor, 1832–1905: Founder of the China Inland Mission." In *Mission Legacies: Biographical Studies of Leaders of the Modern Missionary Movement*, edited by Gerald Anderson et al., 197–204. Maryknoll, NY: Orbis, 1994.

Kwok, Pui-Lan, *Chinese Women and Christianity, 1860–1927*. Atlanta: Scholars, 1992.

Lai, John T. P. "Institutional Patronage: The Religious Tract Society and the Translation of Christian Tracts in Nineteenth-Century China." In *The Translator* 13:1 (2007) 39–61.

———. *Negotiating Religious Gaps: The Enterprise of Translating Christian Tracts by Protestant Missionaries in Nineteenth-Century China*. Sankt Augustin: Institut Monumenta Serica, 2012.

Lai, Whalen W. "The First Chinese Christian Gospel: Liang A-fa's 'Good Words to Admonish the World.'" *Ching Feng* 38:2 (May 1995) 83–105.

Latourette, Kenneth S. *A History of Christian Missions in China*. New York: Macmillan, 1929.

Legge, James. *An Argument for Shang-Te as the Proper Rendering for the Words Elohim and Theos in the Chinese Language*. Hongkong [sic]: Hongkong Register Office, 1850.

———, trans. and comp. *The Chinese Classics*. 5 vols. Hongkong [sic]: Anglo Chinese College Press, 1861–72. Second partially revised version: Oxford: Clarendon Press, 1893–95. Most recent republication with a general essay in Chinese (written by Zhang Xiping and Lauren F. Pfister) and introductory essays in Chinese written by Lauren F. Pfister (vols. 1, 2, and 4) and Liu Jiahe with Shao Dongfang and Lauren Pfister (vols. 3 and 5) Shanghai: East China Normal University Press, 2010.

———. "Christianity and Confucianism Compared in their Teaching of the Whole Duty of Man." In *Non-Christian Religions of the World*, edited by William Muir, 3–36. New York: F. H. Revell, 1890.

———. "The Colony of Hong Kong. From a Lecture by the Rev. James Legge, D.D., LL.D. On Reminiscences of a Long Resident in the East, Delivered in City Hall, November 5, 1872." *China Review* 1 (1872) 163–76.

———. *Confucianism in Relation to Christianity. A Paper Read Before the Missionary Conference in Shanghai, on May 11th, 1877*. Shanghai: Kelly and Walsh; London: Trübner, 1877.

———. "Journal of a Missionary Tour along the 'East River' of Canton Province." Supplement to *The China Mail*, no. 853 (20 June 1861) 1–4.

———. *The Land of Sinim: A Sermon Preached in the Tabernacle, Moorfields, at the Sixty-fifth Anniversary of the London Missionary Society*. London: John Snow, 1859.

———. *A Lexilogus of the English, Malay, and Chinese Languages: Comprehending the Vernacular Idioms of the Last in the Hok-keen and Canton Dialects*. Malacca: Anglo-Chinese College Press, 1841.

———. *The Notions of the Chinese concerning God and Spirits: with an Examination of the Defense of an Essay on the Proper Rendering of the Words Elohim and Theos into the Chinese Language by William J. Boone*. Hongkong [sic]: Hongkong Register Office, 1852.

———. *The Ordinance of the Sabbath: Three Sermons on the Institution of the Sabbath, the Christian Sabbath, the Sabbath in the Colonies*. Hongkong [sic]: China Mail Office, 1850.

———. *Prolegomena*. In *The Sacred Books of China*, written by James Legge. 6 vols. Oxford: Clarendon, 1879–91.

———. *The Religions of China: Confucianism and Tâoism Described and Compared with Christianity*. London: Hodder and Stoughton, 1880.

———, trans. and comp. *The Sacred Books of China*. 6 vols. Oxford: Clarendon, 1879–91. Constituting vols. 3 (1879), 16 (1882), 27–28 (1885) and 39–40 (1891) of *The Sacred Books of the East*, edited by F. Max Müller.

———. *Shenghui zhunsheng (Standards for the Sacred Community)*. Hong Kong: Anglo-Chinese College Press, 1867.

———. *Wang Jinshan yaojue (Important Advice for Those Going to the Gold Mountains)*. Hong Kong: Anglo-Chinese College Press, 1858.

———. *Yabolaihan jilüe (The Faith Creed of Jesus' Disciples)*. Hong Kong: Anglo-Chinese College Press, 1857.

———. *Yesu mentu xinjing (The Faith Creed of Jesus' Disciples)*. Hong Kong: Anglo-Chinese College Press, 1854.

———. *Yuese jilüe (A Brief History of [the Life of] Joseph)*. Hong Kong: Anglo-Chinese College Press, 1853.

———, and John Legge, eds. *[George Legge's] Lectures on Theology, Science and Revelation: with a Memoir by James Legge*. London: Jackson, Walford and Hodder, 1863.

———, et al. *Journal of a Missionary Tour Along the East River of Canton Province*. Hongkong [sic]: A. Shortrede, 1861.

———, et al. *Three Weeks on the West River of Canton. Compiled from the Journals of Rev. Dr. Legge, Dr. Palmer, and Mr. Tsang Kwei-Hwan*. Hongkong [sic]: De Souza, 1866.

Liang, A-fa. *Good News to Admonish the Ages (Quan shi liang yan)*. Taibei Shi: Taiwan xue sheng shu ju, 1965.

Liu, Kwang-Ching, ed. *American Missionaries in China: Papers from the Harvard Seminars*. Cambridge, MA: East Asian Research Center, Harvard University, 1966.

Liu, Lydia He. *The Clash of Empires: The Invention of China in Modern World Making*. Cambridge, MA: Harvard University Press, 2004.

Lodwick, Kathleen L. *Crusaders Against Opium: Protestant Missionaries in China, 1874–1917*. Lexington: University Press of Kentucky, 2007.

———. "Good Works." In *Handbook of Christianity in China, Volume Two: 1800-present*, edited by R. G. Tiedemann and Nicolas Standaert, 428–35. Leiden: Brill, 2010.

———. "Missionaries and Opium." In *Handbook of Christianity in China, Volume Two: 1800-present*, edited by R. G. Tiedemann and Nicolas Standaert, 354–60. Leiden: Brill, 2010.

London Missionary Society. "Register of Missionaries" Entry 108. SOAS Morrison Collection (Archive of the Council for World Mission).

Lovell, Julia. *The Opium War: Drugs, Dreams and the Making of China*. New York: MacMillan, 2011.

Luo, Weihong. *Christianity in China*. Translated by Zhu Chengming. Beijing: China Intercontinental Press, 2004.

Lutz, Jessie Gregory. "China and Protestantism: Historical Perspectives, 1807–1949." In *China and Christianity: Burdened Past, Hopeful Future*, edited by Stephen Uhalley Jr. and Xiaoxin Wu, 179–93. Armonk, NY: M.E. Sharpe, 2001.

———. *Opening China: Karl F. A. Gützlaff and Sino-Western Relations, 1827–1852*. Grand Rapids: Eerdmans, 2008.

MacGillivray, Donald. *Encyclopedia: List of Chinese Hymn Books*. No. 27 (1911).

Martin, W. A. P. *Cycle of Cathay, or China, South and North, with Personal Reminiscences*, 2nd ed. Edinburgh: Oliphant Anderson and Ferrier, 1897.

———. Letter to Board 1863. In *W. A. P. Martin: Pioneer of Progress in China*, 146. Washington, DC: Christian University Press, 1978.

———. *The Lore of Cathay, or The Intellect of China*. New York: F. H. Revell, 1912.

———. "The Native Tract Literature of China." *The Chinese Recorder and Missionary Journal* 18 (1887) 330.

Mateer, C. A. "Easy Wen Li New Testament." *The Chinese Recorder and Missionary Journal* 17 (1886) 51–53.

———. "Mr. John's New Testament." *The Chinese Recorder and Missionary Journal* 16 (1885) 53.

Mathews, Robert Henry, Minyuan Wang, and Yuen Ren Chao. *Mathews' Chinese-English Dictionary: A Chinese English Dictionary Compiled for the China Inland Mission*. Rev. American ed. Cambridge, MA: Harvard University Press, 1931; reprint, 1996.

McGavran, Donald Anderson. *Understanding Church Growth*. Grand Rapids: Eerdmans, 1970.

McNeur, George Hunter. *China's First Preacher: Liang A-fa, 1789–1855*. Shanghai: Kwang Hsueh Publishing House; Shanghai: Oxford University Press, China Agency, 1934. An earlier version was published in Chinese: George Hunter McNeur, Hu Canyun, trans. *Zhonghua zui zao de budaozhe Liang Fa*. Shanghai: Guangxue Hui Chu Ban, 1931. Edited and annotated by Jonathan Seitz. Pickwick, 2014.

Meadows, Thomas Taylor. *The Chinese and their Rebellions, Viewed in Connection with Their National Philosophy, Ethics, Legislation, and Administration. To which is Added, an Essay on Civilization and Its Present State in the East and West*. London: Smith, Elder, 1856.

Medhurst, Walter H. *China: Its State and Prospects, with Especial Reference to the Spread of the Gospel: Containing Allusions to the Antiquity, Extent, Population, Civilization, Literature, and Religion of the Chinese*. London: John Snow, 1838.

Milne, William. *A Retrospect of the First Ten Years of the Protestant Mission to China, (Now, in Connection with the Malay, Denominated, the Ultra-Ganges Missions) Accompanied with Miscellaneous Remarks on the Literature, History, and Mythology of China, &c.* Malacca: Anglo-Chinese Press, 1820.

Moffett, Samuel Hugh. *A History of Christianity in Asia, Volume II: 1500–1900.* Maryknoll, NY: Orbis, 1998.

Moreau, A. Scott, Gary R. Corwin, and Gary B. McGee. *Introducing World Missions: A Biblical, Historical, and Practical Survey.* Grand Rapids: Baker Academic, 2004.

Morris, William, ed. *American Heritage Dictionary of the English Language.* "Harmonium." Boston: Houghton Mifflin, 1969.

Morrison, Eliza, comp., and Robert Morrison. *Memoirs of the Life and Labours of Robert Morrison, D.D.* 2 vols. London: Longman, 1839.

Morrison, Robert. *China: A Dialogue, for the Use of Schools: Being Ten Conversations Between a Father and His Children Concerning the History and Present State of that Country.* London: James Nisbet, 1824.

———. *Chinese Miscellany; Consisting of Original Extracts from Chinese Authors, in the Native Character; with Translations and Philological Remarks.* London: London Missionary Society, 1825.

———. *Dialogues and Detached Sentences in the Chinese Language; with a Free and Verbal Translation in English.* Macao: East India Company Press, 1816.

———. *A Grammar of the Chinese language.* Serampore: Mission-press, 1815.

———. *A Narrative of the Affair of the English Frigate Topaze, 1821–22.* Malacca: Mission Press, 1823.

———. *Narrative of the Fire at Canton.* In *Memoirs of the Life and Labours of Robert Morrison, D.D.*, vol. 2, written by Robert Morrison and compiled by Eliza Morrison, Appendix, 33ff. London: Longman, 1839.

———. *A Parting Memorial: Consisting of Miscellaneous Discourses, Written and Preached in China; at Singapore; on Board Ship at Sea in the Indian Ocean; at the Cape of Good Hope; and in England. With Remarks on Missions, &c. &c.* London: W. Simpkin and R. Marshall, 1826.

———. *Proposal for Bettering the Morals and Conditions of Sailors in China*, dated September 25, 1822. In *Memoirs of the Life and Labours of Robert Morrison, D.D.*, vol. 2, written by Robert Morrison and compiled by Eliza Morrison, Appendix, 43–45. London: Longman, 1839.

———. *Remarks on Homicides Committed by Europeans on the Persons of Natives at Canton.* Appended to his *Narrative of the Affair of the English Frigate Topaze, 1821–22.* Malacca: Mission, 1823.

———. *Review of the First Fifteen Years of the Mission.* In *Memoirs of the Life and Labours of Robert Morrison, D.D.*, vol. 2, written by Robert Morrison and compiled by Eliza Morrison, 180ff. London: Longman, 1839.

———. *A View of China for Philological Purposes; Containing a Sketch of Chinese Chronology, Geography, Government, Religion & Customs.* Macao: East India Company Press, 1817.

Moseley, William W. *A Memoir on the Importance and Practicability of Translating and Printing the Holy Scriptures in the Chinese Language; and of Circulating Them in That Vast Empire.* London: Simkin and Marshall, 1842.

———. *The Origin of the First Protestant Mission to China.* London: Simkin and Marshall, 1842.

Moule, Arthur Evans. *Half a Century in China, Recollections and Observations*. London: Hodder and Stoughton, 1911.
Muirhead, William. *China and the Gospel*. London: James Nisbet, 1870.
Neill, Stephen. *A History of Christian Missions*. New York: Penguin, 1986.
Nevius, John L. "Methods of Mission Work." *The Chinese Recorder and Missionary Journal* 17 (1886) 55–64.
Newman, R. K. "Opium Smoking in Late Imperial China." *Modern Asian Studies* 29 (1995) 765–94.
Ng, Peter Tze Ming. *Chinese Christianity: An Interplay between Global and Local Perspectives*. Boston: Brill, 2012.
―――. "Timothy Richard: Christian Attitudes Towards Other Religions and Cultures." *Studies in World Christianity* 14:1 (2008) 73–92.
Paley, William. *Natural Theology: or, Evidences of the Existence and Attributes of the Deity, Collected from the Appearances of Nature*, 6th ed. London: R. Faulder, 1803. [1802].
Pfister, Lauren F. "Attitudes Towards Chinese Culture(s), 1860–1900." In *Handbook of Christianity in China. Volume Two: 1800–present*, edited by R. G. Tiedemann, 405–16. Leiden: Brill, 2010.
―――. "Bible Translations and the Protestant 'Term Question.'" In *Handbook of Christianity in China. Volume Two: 1800–present*, edited by R. G. Tiedemann, 361–70. Leiden: Brill, 2010.
―――. "China's Missionary-Scholars." In *Handbook of Christianity in China. Volume Two: 1800–present*, edited by R. G. Tiedemann, 742–65. Leiden: Brill, 2010.
―――. "Classics or Sacred Books? Grammatological and Interpretive Problems of Ruist and Daoist Scriptures in the Translation Corpora of James Legge (1815–1897) and Richard Wilhelm (1873–1930)." In *Kanonisierung und Kanonbildung in der asiatischen Religionsgeschichte*, edited by Max Deeg et al., 421–63. Vienna: Austrian Academy of Sciences Press, 2011.
―――. "Discovering Monotheistic Metaphysics: The Exegetical Reflections of James Legge (1815–1897) and Lo Chung-fan (d. circa 1850)." In *Imagining Boundaries: Changing Confucian Doctrines, Texts, and Hermeneutics*, edited by On-cho Ng, et. al., 213–54. Albany: State University of New York Press, 1999.
―――. "Evaluating James Legge's (1812–1897) Assessment of Master Meng's Theory of the Goodness of Human Nature: Comparative Philosophical and Cultural Explorations." *Universitas: Monthly Review of Philosophy and Culture* 40:3 (March 2013) 107–30.
―――. "From Derision to Respect: The Hermeneutic Passage within James Legge's (1815–1897) Ameliorated Evaluation of Master Kong ('Confucius')." *Bochumer Jahrbuch zur Ostasienforschung* 26 (2002) 53–88.
―――. "In the Eye of a Tornado: Lessons Learned from Critiques of Christian Missionaries." *Ching Feng* 8:1–2 (2007) 91–116.
―――. "James Legge." In *An Encyclopedia of Translation: Chinese-English, English-Chinese Translation*, edited by Chan Sin-wai and David E. Pollard, 401–22. Hong Kong: Chinese University Press, 1995.
―――. "Mediating Word, Sentence, and Scope without Violence: James Legge's Understanding of 'Classical Confucian' Hermeneutics." In *Classics and Interpretations: The Hermeneutic Traditions in Chinese Culture*, edited by Ching-I Tu, 371–82. New Brunswick, NJ: Transaction, 2000.

———. "The Mengzian Matrix for Accommodationist Missionary Apologetics: Identifying the Cross-cultural Linkage in Evangelical Protestant Discourse Within the Chinese Writings of James Legge (1815–1897), He Jinshan (1817–1871), and Ernst Faber (1839–1899)." *Monumenta Serica* 50 (2002) 391–416.

———. "Nineteenth Century Ruist Metaphysical Terminology and the Sino-Scottish Connection in James Legge's *Chinese Classics*." In *Mapping Meanings: The Field of New Learning in Late Qing China*, edited by Michael Lackner and Natascha Vittinghoff, 615–38. Leiden: Brill, 2004.

———. "The Proto-martyr of Chinese Protestants: Reconstructing the Story of Chëa Kam-kwong." *Journal of the Hong Kong Branch of the Royal Asiatic Society*, 42 (2002–3) 187–244.

———. "Resetting 'Our' Cosmic and Historical Time-pieces: The Coining of the First Sino-Christian Almanac as a Protestant Evangelistic Strategy." *Journal of the History of Christianity in Modern China* 9 (2012) 34–48.

———. "The Response of Wang Tao and James Legge to the Modern Ruist Melancholy." *History and Culture* 2 (2001) 1–20.

———. "Rethinking Missions in China: James Hudson Taylor and Timothy Richard." In *The Imperial Horizons of British Protestant Missions, 1880–1914*, edited by Andrew Porter, 183–212. Grand Rapids: Eerdmans, 2003.

———. *Striving for the "Whole Duty of Man": James Legge (1815–1897) and the Scottish Protestant Encounter with China*. 2 vols. Frankfurt am Main: Peter Lang, 2004.

———. "A Transmitter but not a Creator: The Creative Transmission of Protestant Biblical Traditions by Ho Tsun-Sheen (1817–1871)." In *Bible in Modern China: The Literary and Intellectual Impact*, edited by Irene Eber, et. al., 165–97. Nettetal: Steyler, 1999.

Pollock, John. *The Cambridge Seven: The True Story of Ordinary Men Used in No Ordinary Way*. Fearne, Scotland: Christian Focus Publications, 2006.

Porter, Andrew, ed., *The Imperial Horizons of British Protestant Missions, 1880–1914*. Grand Rapids: Eerdmans, 2003

Rees, Thomas, and John Thomas. *Hanes Eglwysi Annibynol Cymru (History of the Independent Churches in Wales)*, vol. 2. Liverpool: Tyst Cymreig (Welsh Witness), 1872.

Ricci, Matteo. *A True disputation about God*, published as *The True Meaning of the Lord of Heaven*. Translated with Chinese text by D. Lancashire and P Hu Kuo-chen. St Louis: Institute of Jesuit Sources, 1985.

Richard, Timothy. *Conversion by the Million in China*. Shanghai: Christian Literature Crusade, 1907.

———. *Forty-five Years in China: Reminiscences by Timothy Richard, D.D, Litt.D.* London: T. Fisher Unwin, 1916.

———. *The Man Who Could Not Be Denied*. London: Carey Press, 1945.

———. *The New Testament of Higher Buddhism*. Edinburgh: T. & T. Clark, 1910.

Robert, Dana. *Christian Mission: How Christianity Became a World Religion*. Malden, MA: Wiley-Blackwell, 2009.

Roberts, J. A. G. *China Through Western Eyes: The Nineteenth Century*. Gloucestershire, UK: Alan Sutton, 1991.

Robson, William. *Griffith John: Founder of the Hankow Mission, Central China*. London: S. W. Partridge, 1888.

Sanneh, Lamin. *Disciples of All Nations: Pillars of World Christianity*. New York: Oxford University Press, 2008.

Shen, Dingping and Weifang Zhu. "Western Missionary Influence on the People's Republic of China: A Survey of Chinese Scholarly Opinion between 1980 and 1990." *International Bulletin of Missionary Research* 22 (October 1998) 154–58.

Sng, Bobby Ewe Kong. *I Must Sow the Seed: Liang Afa: China's First Preacher*. Singapore: Trinity Theological College, 1998.

Soothill, William Edward. "Chinese Music and Its Relation to Our Native Services." *The Chinese Recorder and Missionary Journal* 21 (1890) 221–28.

———. *Timothy Richard of China: Seer, Statesman, Missionary and the Most Disinterested Adviser the Chinese Ever Had*. London: Seeley Service, 1926.

Sparham, C. G. "Griffith John and His Work." *The Chronicle of the London Missionary Society* (1905) 103–8.

Spence, Jonathan D. *The Search for Modern China*. New York: W. W. Norton, 1990.

Steer, Roger. *J. Hudson Taylor: A Man in Christ*. Singapore: OMF Books, 1990.

Sunquist, Scott W. *Understanding Christian Mission: Participation in Suffering and Glory*. Grand Rapids: Baker Academic, 2013.

Taylor, Dr. and Mrs. Howard. *Hudson Taylor's Spiritual Secret*. Chicago: Moody, 1989.

Taylor, Geraldine. *Pastor Hsi: A Struggle for Chinese Christianity*. Fearn, Scotland: Christian Focus Publications, 1997.

Taylor, J. Hudson. Letter, "Appeals for Redress." *The Chinese Recorder and Missionary Journal* 26 (1895) 575–78.

———. *Retrospect*. Sevenoaks, UK: Overseas Missionary Fellowship, 1974. Published as *To China . . . with Love*, Bethany Fellowship, 1972; and as *Looking Back*, Singapore: OMF Books, 2007, with modernized English.

Thompson, R. Wardlaw. *Griffith John: The Story of Fifty Years in China*. London: The Religious Tract society, 1906., 9.

Tiedemann, R. G., and Nicolas Standaert, eds. *Handbook of Christianity in China. Volume Two: 1800–present*. Leiden: Brill, 2010.

Thompson, R. Wardlaw. *Griffith John: The Story of Fifty Years in China*. London: Religious Tract Society, 1906.

Tsou, Mingteh. "Christian Missionary as Confucian Intellectual: Gilbert Reid (1857–1927) and the Reform Movement in the late Qing." In *Christianity in China: From the Eighteenth Century to the Present*, edited by Daniel H. Bays, 73–90. Stanford, CA: Stanford University Press, 1996.

Uhalley, Stephen Jr., and Xiaoxin Wu, eds. *China and Christianity: Burdened Past, Hopeful Future*. Armonk, NY: M.E. Sharpe, 2001.

Walls, Andrew F. *The Cross-Cultural Process in Christian History: Studies in the Transmission and Appropriation of Faith*. Maryknoll, NY: Orbis, 2002.

Wang, Mary, and Gwen and Edward England. *The Chinese Church That Will Not Die*. Carol Stream, IL: Tyndale House, 1972.

Wason, Charles William. "Descriptive and classified missionary centenary catalogue of current Christian literature 1907, continuing to 1901." In the Charles William Wason Collection, "China and the Chinese", Cornell University. http://www.archive.org/details/cu31924024003 85.

Welch, Ian. "The 'Vegetarians': A Secret Society in Fujian Province, 1896: A Paper Prepared for the Biennial Conference of the Asian Studies Association of Australia, University of Wollongong, New South Wales, 26–29 June 2006."

Wigram, Christopher E. M. *The Bible and Mission in Faith Perspective: J. Hudson Taylor and the Early China Inland Mission.* Zoetermeer: Uitgeverij Boekencentrum, 2007.

Wilson, J. Wallace. "Memories of a Colleague." *The Chronicle of the London Missionary Society* (1931) 277–78.

Wolffe, John. *The Expansion of Evangelicalism: The Age of Wilberforce, More, Chalmers and Finney.* Downers Grove, IL: InterVarsity, 2007.

Wong Man-Kong. "Christian Missions, Chinese Culture, and Colonial Administration: A Study of the Activities of James Legge and Ernest John Eitel in Nineteenth Century Hong Kong (United Kingdom)." PhD diss., Chinese University of Hong Kong, 1997.

Wylie, Alexander. "China." *Monthly Reporter of the British and Foreign Bible Society* (1869) 49–51, 66–70.

———. *Memorials of Protestant Missionaries to the Chinese.* Shanghai: American Presbyterian Mission Press, 1867.

"Y Maes Cenadol" ("The Mission Field"). Report of Griffith John's Address at Exeter Hall, London, 11 May 1871. *Y Dysgedydd* (*The Instructor*) (1871).

Yao, Kevin Xiyi. *The Fundamentalist Movement Among Protestant Missionaries in China, 1920–1937.* Lanham, MD: University Press of America, 2003.

Zetzsche, Jost Oliver. *The Bible in China: The History of the Union Version, or, the Culmination of Protestant Missionary Bible Translation in China.* Netettal: Steyler, 1999.

Index of Subjects

Bolded page numbers indicate that the listing is found only in the footnotes of that page.

aggression, aggressor(s), aggressive, 4, 14–15, 33, 123, 135
American
  Presbyterian, 124, **180, 206**
  Southern Baptist, 10, 60
ancestor(s), 13, 16, 51, 120, 124, 128, 130, 132–33, 145–46, 148, 154–56, 174, 208
Anglican, 36–37, **38**, 69, 72, 84, 105, 207
Anglo, 33, 52, 55, 68, 75, 77, 80, **134**
Anglo-Chinese, 33, 52, 55, 68, 75, 77, 80, **134**
Anglophone, 71, 74
Asia, 70, **115**, 123
Australia, 12, 114, 121

Baptist(s), 10, **22**, **55**, 60, 72, 174–77, 181–83, 190
bishop(s), 5, 9, 38, 105, 163, 165
Buddhism, Buddhist(s), 3, 13, **22**, 51, 56–57, 107, 112, 127–28, 130–32, 146, 150, 178, 189

Calvinism, Calvinist(s), Calvinistic, 36–37
Canada, Canadian(s), 14, 114, 191–96, 199, 201, 204, 207, 210–11
  Presbyterian(s), 14, 191, 194–95, 201, 210

chapel, 13, 17–18, **25**, 61, 70, 79, 82, 86–87, 91, 93, 100, 111–12, 126, 136, 138, 158, 173, 176–77, 197–98, 200, 211
Chinese
  Catholicism, Catholic(s), 38, 188
  Christianity, Christian(s), 7, 8, 10, 12, 15–16, **21**, 23–24, **25**, 26–27, 49–50, **54**, 57–58, 60, 63–64, 66–67, **68**, 72–73, **75**, 76–77, 79, 82, 93, 111, 114–15, 120, **121**, 143, 157, 187, 191, 198, 204–5
  classics, 11, 18, 65, **66**, 68, 70–71, 79, 81, 89, 120, 127, 129, 137, 162, 178
  Empire, 3, 68, 70–71, 74–79, 81–82, 132, 174, 182, 184, 186
  Protestantism, Protestant(s), Protestant Church, 64, 66–68, 70–71, 75, 77–78, 80–82, 121, 188
christendom, 33, 180, 184
church(es), 1–2, 4, 9, 11–12, 16–20, 23, 26–28, 36–38, 46, 49–50, 53, 55–56, 60, 62–64, 66–68, 71–72, 74–76, 78, 80–87, 89, 96, 100, 105, 107–9, 111, 113–15, 118–20, **121**, 123–26, 132, 136, 144–45, 155, 157, 159, 163, 166–67, 174–75, 177, 179, 181–82, 184, 192–94, 196, 199, 201–2, 204–7, 209–11

227

228 Index of Subjects

college(s), 18, 21, 23–24, 30, **52**, 55, 66–69, 77, 80, 84, 87, 91, 100, 104, 117, 120, 136, 139, 175, 182, 192–95
commerce, commercial; trade, trader(s), tradesmen, 3–4, 9, 14–15, 20, 31, 33, 34, 36, 41, 51, 58, 85–86, 91, 98, 123, **134**, 136, 141–42, 151, 174, 176, 199
Communism, Communist(s), 1, 24–25, 148
Confucianism, Confucian(s), Confucianist(s), 3, 5, 12, 66, 68, 77, 96, 107, 120, 127–31, 139, 143, 145–46, 150, 152, 178
Congregationalism, Congregationalist(s), Congregational, 63, 67, 69, 70, 72, 76–78, 86
conservative (theology), 16, 18, 20–23, 26–27, 96, 147, 207
consulate, consul(s), consular, 16, 91–93, 102, 105, 110, 119, **137**, 209
conversion, 20–21, 31, 49–50, 52–54, 56, 58, 60–61, 64, 95, 102, 123, 125–26, 137, 139, 146, 161, 190, 201, 203, **206**
culture
  Chinese, 11–13, 18–20, 24, 26, 32, 40, 78, 81, 104, 109, 117, 120, 130, 146, 148, 206
  Western, 28, 40, 102, 141, 146, 148

Daoism, Dao, Daoist(s), 132, 150, 178
democracy, democratic, 19, 24–25, 28
denomination(s), denominational, nondenominational, interdenominational, 15, 23, 25, 72, 76–77, 80, 86, 102, 108–9, 114, 182, 191, 194
dissenter(s), dissenting, 37, 69
Dominicans, 16

East, Eastern, Far East, 32, **125**, 126
education, educator(s), educational, educate(d), 5–6, 9, 11, 12–14, 17–25, 27, 30, 39, 40, 47, 51, 69–70, **71**, 75, 77, 80–81, 102, 109, 112, 114, 120, 123–24, 126–27, 130, 138–140, 142, 145, 147–48, **163**, 174–75, 180–84, 186–92
elite, 3, 6, 17–20, 22, 24, 32, 112, 126, 185
emperor(s), 3, 6, 25, 50, 129, 133, 138–40, 143, **144**, 146, 150, 174, 180, 185–87
England, English, Englishman, 11, 32–34, 37, 40, 46, 51, 56–58, 67–68, 77, **79**, 84, 87, 94, 100–102, 105, 108–13, **134**, 135, 151, 180, 182, 192–93, 200
English (language), 12, 18, 25, 31–33, 39, 41, 52, 56, 63, **66**, 68, 71–72, 80, 82, 89, 117, 138–39, 141, 159, 205
Episcopal, 9, 38
Europe, European(s), 1–3, 7, 12, 40, 73–74, 114, 121, **134**, 139, 141, 159, 175
Evangelicalism, evangelical(s), 2, 7–**8**, 12, 14, 20, 22, 27–28, 30, 32, 35, 37–40, 47, 51, 65, 70, 84, **97**, 109, 120, 123, 147, 188, 191, **194**
  revival, 30
evangelism, evangelization, evangelist(s), evangelistic, evangelize(d), evangelizing, 7–9, 11–12, 14, 17–20, 22–23, 26, 39, 45, 49–50, 56, 59–63, 66, 75–76, 79, 81, 83, 85, 87–88, 90–91, 95, 98, 101–2, 104–6, 109, 111–13, 118, 120, 123, 128, 136, 140, 146–47, 155–56, 173, 176–77, 179, 182, 184, 189, 191–93, 196–97, 199–200, 207–8, 210

famine(s), 17, 113, 151, 174, 179–81, 183, 188, 194–95, 208
Feng shui, 6
France, French, 4, 6, 38, 117, 134–35, 182
Franciscans, 16
French Catholic, 38
Fujian, Fujianese, **66**, 68, 106

fundamentalism, fundamentalist(s), 2, 22, 191, 207

Geordie, 30
Germany, German, 22, 104, 114, 117, **125**, 199, 207
  higher criticism, 22, 199, 207
Great Awakening, 7, 200
Great Britain, Britain, British Isles, British, 2–4, 6–7, 9, 11, 15–16, 33–34, 40, 45, 58, 65–66, 69–71, 73–75, 77, 79, 81, 85, 90, 92–94, 98, 105, 110, 114–15, 119, 123, 125, 134–35, **137**, 143, 176, 180, 187, 207
Greece, Greek, 15, 30, 40, 67, 69, 117, 192

High-Church Anglican, 72
hospital(s), clinic(s), 50, 58, 61–62, 64, 83, 86–87, 91, 100, 108, 111–12

imperialism, imperialist(s), imperialistic, 2–7, 9, 14, 28, 33, 41, 100
India, 3, 34, 200
Irish Presbyterian, 202

journal(s), 1, 38, 50, 52, 73, 76, 84–86, **89**, 141

Keswick, Keswick movement, 7, 8, 95, 207
Kingdom of God, 20–21, 97, 139, 174, 177, 181–83, 188–89

Latin, 30, 67, 69, 117, 192
learning, Western, 13, 18, 185–86
liberalism
  education, 18
  eolitics, 123
  theology, 2, 10, 14, 18, 21–23, 25–27, 96–97, **186**, 202, 207–8
literature, 2, 11–12, 17–18, 20, **39**, 40, 55, 58, 66, 68, 78, 88, 92, 98, 105, 111, 125, 127, 136, 145, 174, 178, 184–87, 189–90, 193

magazine(s), 13, 116, 141, 184–85
Manchuria, Manchurian, 14, 180, 201–2, 204, 209, 211–12
Manifest Destiny, 123
Marxist, 1, 80
medicine(s), medical, 9, 12, 17–18, 23, 43, 61, 91, 98, 102–4, 106, 108, 111–12, 117, 119, 136, 153, 156–58, 165, 167, 170, 177, 202
Methodist, 102
millennialism
  pre-millennialism, 21
  post-millennialism, 21, 69–70, 81
mission society, 12, 41, 104, 114, 183
modern, modernizer(s), modernizing, **3**, 6, **11**, 12–14, 18–19, 21, 23–25, 27–29, 40, 48, 57, 120, 138, 140, 149, 174, 180, 183, 186, 191
modernism, modernist(s) (theological), 14, 22, 207–8
Muslims, 3

nationalism, nationalist(s), 18, 24, 148, 209
Nationalist Government, 18
negotiation(s), negotiator(s), negotiate, 4, 13–14, 33–34, 58, 64, 135, 137
Netherlands, Dutch, 3, 11, 122
Non-Anglican, 37–38
noncomformist(s), 36, 47, 51, 84
North America(n), 7, 23, 87, 114, 121
Northern Ireland, 175
Northern Presbyterian, 207
Norway, 175
nun(s), 5, 188

opium, 3–5, 9, 12, 14–15, 33, 42, 58–59, 61, 79, 86, 98, 123, **125**, 128, **134**, 144, 149, 151, 153–58, 165, 167, 169–70, 176, 197, 199
  trade, traders, 9, 14–15, 33, 98, 134, 199
Orient, Oriental, 57, 71, 139, 143
Orientalist, 80
Orthodox, 174, 188

Palestine, 123
politics, politician(s), political(ly), 2, 5, 7, 12–13, 21, 24–28, 32–33, 35–36, 42, 51, 76–77, 81, 85, 92, 94, 98, 135, 138–39, 144, 147, 187
Portugal, Portuguese, 3, 11, 37–38
   Catholics, 37
preacher(s), preach(ing), 9, 11–14, 17–19, 22–23, 26, 55, 57, 60, 62–64, 68, 72, 74, 78, 84, 86, 88–91, 96, 100, 105, 107–8, 111, 115, 118–20, 125–26, 136, 139–40, 143, 147, 149, 151, 154, 157, 160–62, 172–73, 176–77, 189, 191, 193, 195–98, 200, 202–8, 211
Presbyterian(s), 14, 30, 36, 105, 123–24, 126, 136, 138, 140, **180**, 181, 191–92, 194–96, 201–3, 205–7, 210–11
priest(s), 3, 5, 38, 129, 133, 188
progress(ion), progressive(ness), progressed, 2, 6, 12, 22, 32, 69, 77, 97, 109, 122–23, 133, 141, 143–45, 148, 184
Protestantism, Protestant(s), 1–2, 4–5, 7–10, 20, 22–24, 28, 30, 32, 36–37, 42, **45**, 47, 49, **56**, **61**, 64, 66–73, 75–82, **92–93**, 96, 102, 105, 113–14, 121, **125**, **127**, 140, 146, 174, 181, 187–88
publisher(s), publish(ing), 23, **33**, **34**, 50, **51**, 57, 61, 65–66, 68, 70, 74, 81, 98, 126–27, 141, 144, 159, 173, 184–86, 189, 210

reform, reformer(s), reformed, 2, 5–7, 12–13, 17, 19, 21–22, 24–27, 44, 55, 75, 112, 139–41, 143–45, 147, 181, 185–87, 189, 191
revival, revivalist, 7–8, 14, 30, 87, 95, 175, 191, 200–6, 208, 210
revolution, revolt, revolutionary, revolutionaries, 1–3, 5, 58, 60, 82, 128, 133, 144, 189
riot(s), 5, 16, 93, 109, 135, 181

rite(s) (Confucian, ancestor), 3, 13, 16, 68, 120, 128, 133, 139, 145
(Roman) Catholicism, (Roman) Catholic(s), 1, 5, 11, 37–38, 72–73, 86, 88, 104, 140, 146, 174, 177, 188
Roman, Romanized, 8, 125, 128
Rome, 40
Ruism, Ruist, Ruified, 66, 68, 71, 74, 77–80, 82
   (Confucian) Scriptures, 68
Russian, 174
Russian Orthodox, 174

Sabbatarianism, 37
Sabbath, 53, 63, 69, 73–75, 81
   culture (*anxiri wenhua*), 69, 73, 75, 81
Scandinavia, 114
scholarship, scholar(s), scholarly, 1, 4, 6, 12, 20, 28, 31–33, 37, 40–42, 44, 47, 57, 65–67, **68**, 69–71, 74, 78, 80–82, 88–89, 92, 117, 122, 137–38, 144, 147, 150, 155, 174, 180–81, 184, 186
school(s), schooling, schoolrooms, 6, 12–13, 17–18, 25, 50–52, 57–58, 60, 63–64, **68**, 69, 77, 83, 86–87, 91, 104, 107, 111, 114, 117, 120, **121**, 123–24, 126, 130, 132, 136–41, 143, 150, 175, 181, 192, 210
science, scientific, 2, 5, 12–13, 18–19, 24–25, 28, 84, 98, 123–24, 128, 136–37, 139–142, 145–46, 148, 174, 180–82, 186
Scotland, Scottish, Scot(s), Scotch, 30, 37, 40, 65–67, 69, 71–75, 77–78, 105, 114, 123, 136, 175, 177, 181, 205
   Calvinists, 37
   Commonsense (Common Sense) philosophy, 69, 123
   Congregationalism, Congregationalists, 77–78
   Realism, 69
Seminary, seminaries, 2, 23, 67, 69, 77, 80, 124

Index of Subjects   231

sinology, sinologist(s), sinologue, sinalogue, sinological, 11–13, 15, 32, 39, 44, 66, **69**, 71, 85, 104, 142
South Africa, 123
Stoics, 131
Sweden, 175

Taoism, 107
teacher(s), teaching(s), teach(able), taught, 4, 7–8, 11–13, 16–19, 21, 22, 25–26, 28, 38, 40, 55–56, 58, 60–61, 64, 68–69, 72, 77–78, 85, 88, 91, 94–95, 97–98, 104, 107, 109, 112–13, 123–26, 129–30, 132, 137–39, 143–44, 146–47, 151–55, 160, 162–64, 167, 170, 175, 177–78, 186, 192, 198, 200, 206
terms for God:
  Elohim, 15, 78, 129
  Ho theos, 78
  Shang Di, Shangdi, Shang-ti, Shang-ti, 15, 78, 127, 129–30, 132
  Shen (lesser deities), 15, 78, 127
  Supreme Being, 15
  Supreme Lord, 129
  Supreme Power, 129
  Theos, 15, 129
  Tien, T'ien-chu, 127, 129
theology, theologian(s), theological(ly), 2, 14, 18, 22–23, 25–27, 36–39, 55, 70–71, 77–78, 80, 87, 91, 95–97, 108, **113**, 117, 124, 127, 133–34, 136, 147, 182–83, **186**, 192, 202
Tibet, 3
Tibetan Buddhism, 3
tract(s), 5, 11, 50, 56–61, 66, **68**, 88, 97–98, 100, 102, 105, 154, 177–79, 181, 186, 193
translation, translator(s), translate, 9–13, 15, 17, 30–33, 41, 43–45, **51**, 52, **55**, 56–57, **58–59**, 62, 64, **66**, 72–73, 78, 80, 83, 86, 97, 99, 120, 126, 128–29, 137, 139, 141, 159, 184–86, 189
treaty, treaties, 4–5, 13–16, 58, **59**, 76, 79, 93–94, 105–6, 109, 118, 134–35, 176
trinitarian, 95

UK, 30, **40**, 43
United States, (United States of) America, American, US, 2, 9, 11, 13, 15, 33, 36, 40, 44, 51, **56**, 60–61, 65, **67**, 101, 114, **120**, 122–26, 129, 134–36, 138–40, 142–43, 148, 151, 175, **180**, 187, 190, 194, **206**
university, universities, 12, 23, 31, 51, 57, 65, **66**, 67, 69, 108, 123, 139, 140, 174, 188, 190

viceroy, 58, 180, 183, 185
Victorian, 27, 97

Wales, Welshman, Welsh, 8, 14, 83, 86–87, 89, 94–95, 175, 180, 190, 200
  revival(s), 8, 14, 95, 200
war(s), warfare, wartime, 2, 4, 23, 26–27, 42, 58–59, 61, 92, 96, 101, 123, 125, 134–35, 145, 154, 176, 186, 210
Wesleyan, 63, **180**
West, Westerner(s), Westernization, Western, 1, 4–8, 12–15, 18–19, 22, 24–25, 27–28, 31–32, 39, 48, 92, 100, 102, 104–5, 111–14, 117–18, 120, 123, 127–28, 135, 137, 139, 141, 142–46, 148, 151, 173–74, 176, 180–81, 185–86, 188, 190, 194
Western Europe, 1
woman, women, 2, 5, 8–10, 20, 25, 28, **55**, 61–62, 89, 92, 112–13, 117–19, 125, 130, 136, 149–50, 154, 161, 163, 169, 173, 185, 188, 198, 203–5

Index of Names
(including Scripture Index)

Bolded page numbers indicate that the listing is found only in the footnotes of that page.

1 Corinthians, **19**, 191
1 Peter, 94
1949 Revolution, 58

Abeel, David, 9
Aberdeen University, 31, **67**
Aberdeen, 31, 67, 69
Abraham, Abrahamic, 45
A-chim, 55
Acts (Bible), 39, 96, 108
Africa, African, 57, 71, 176
Aikman, David, *One Nation Without God?*, 120
Aldersey, Mary Ann, 10, 107
Alexander, William, 123
Allen, Catherine B., "Charlotte (Lottie) Moon", **10**
Allen, Young J., 141, 184, 186
American Board of Commissioners for Foreign Missions, 40, 56
American Protestant Episcopal Church in China, 9
Amoy (Xiamen), 3, 176
Analects, **68**
Anglo-Chinese College (Ying Hua shuyuan), **52**, 55, 68, 77, 80
Anglo-Chinese press, 75
Annual Report, National Bible Society of Scotland (NBSS), **99**

Anti-Christian Movement, 25, 209
Apostles, 177
Apostles' Creed, 37
Appraisal Committee, 207
Archive of World Christian Missions, 71
Arrow War, 134
Athens, 19, 96
Atlantic Ocean, 12
Austin, Alvyn, 28, 115, 150, 152–53, 157–58, 194
  China's Millions, 28, 115, 150, 152–53, 157
  Saving China, 194
Autumn Gold, 63

Bagnall, Benjamin, 165
Baldwin, C. C., "Missionaries appeal to secular arm", **94**
Baptist Mission, 174
Baptist Missionary Society, 175–77, 182–83, 190
Barnes, "Revelation", **84**
Barnett and Fairbank, eds., *Christianity in China*, **32**
Barnett, Suzanne, **32**
Barnsley, Yorkshire, 102
Barr, Pat, *To China with Love,* 4–5, 13, 21, 28

233

Index of Names

Barrett, Tim, *Singular Listlessness*, 67, 69
Barwick, John S., "The Protestant Quest for Modernity in Republican China", 24
Bays, Daniel H., 7, 18, 21, 23, 25, 201, 206
  A New History of Christianity in China, 7, 23, 201, 206
  and Widmer, *China's Christian Colleges*, 18, 21, 25
Bebbington, David W., *The Dominance of Evangelicalism*, 7–8
Bedford Academy, 84
Beech, W. R., 63
Beer, Robert, 96
Beijing Court, 92
Beijing Foreign Studies University, 66
Beijing, 6, 66, 92, 93, 134, 135–36, 138, 140, 143–44, 176, 184–85
Bell, Nelson, 207
Berkley, Gerald W., 10
Berlin, 182
Bible Society, Peking, 185
Bible Society, 41
Bible Union, 23
Bickers, Robert, *The Scramble for China*, 94
Bieler, Stacey, 27
Biographical Dictionary of Chinese Christianity, 7
Biron (Byron), Lord, 40
Bitton, Nelson, 99
  The Story of Griffith John, 99
Blackpool, 69
Blake, Andrew, "Foreign Devils", 86
Blatchley, Emily, 110–11
  ed., *Occasional Paper*, 111
Blodget, Henry, 137
Bloomington, 123
Bogue, David, 11, 30
Bohr, P. Richard, 50, 54
  "Jesus, Christianity and Rebellion in China", 50
  "Liang Fa's Quest for Moral Power", 50, 54
  "The Theologian as Revolutionary", 50

Book of Common Prayer, 11, 37
Boone, William, 9
Bosch, David J., 7, 97
  Transforming Mission, 7
  Witness to the World, 97
Boston, 115, 122
Boxer Rebellion, Boxer(s), 5–6, 93–94, 115, 140, 143, 187–88, 198, 204
Brandram, A., 41
Brandt, Nat, *Massacre in Shansi*, 188
Brecon Independent College, 84
Bridgman, Elijah C., 9, 56, 135
Bridgman, Eliza, ed., *The Pioneer of American Missions in China*, 56
Brighton Beach, 108
British and Foreign Bible Society, 85, 90
British East India Company, 3
Broomhall, A. J., 3–4, 7–10, 14, 16, 20, 26, 27, 41, 86, 109–10, 117, 119, 121, 146, 155, 160
  Hudson Taylor and China's Open Century, 7 vols: *Barbarians at the Gates; Over the Treaty Wall; If I Had a Thousand Lives; Survivors' Pact; Refiner's Fire; Assault on the Nine; and It Is Not Death to Die*, 3–4, 7–10, 14, 16, 20, 26–27, 41, 86, 109–10, 117, 119, 121, 146, 155, 160
  The Shaping of Modern China, 27
Broomhall, Q. Marshall, 32, 44, 47
Brown University, 190
Brown, William, 177
Bryant, Evan, 87, 95
  "Dr. John Forty Years Ago", 95
Buddha, 76
Buddhist Diamond Classic, 178
Burdon, John S., 105, 137, 141
Burns, William C., 9, 20, 73, 105–6, 111, 136
Burt, E. W., "Timothy Richard", 189

Cai Shaoqing, "On the Origins of the Gelaohui", 92
Calcutta, 38
Calvary, 206

Index of Names

Calvin, John, 47
Cambridge Seven, 109, 114, **163**, 165
Cameron, Lachlan, 192
Campbell, R. J., 97
Canton (aka Guangzhou), 3, 11,
    31–34, 36–38, 40, 44, 46–48, 51,
    55, 57, **58**, 59, 61, 124, 176
Cantonese, 68, 72–73, 76, 82
Carey, William, 51, 97
Cassels, William Wharton, 161
Catholic Apostolic Church, 177
Centenary Missionary Conference,
    22, 144
Central Kingdom, 3
Chëa Kam Kwong (Che Jinguang), 76,
    79–80
Ch'ing, 179
Chalmers, John, 73
Chang, Irene, ed., *Christ Alone*,
    110–12, 117
Chang, Lit-sen (Zhang Lisheng),
    26–27
    "Critique of Indigenous Theology",
        26–27
    Strategy of Missions in the Orient,
        26–27
Changsha, 91, 115
Changte, 197, 199, 200, 204–5, 208
Charbonnier, Jean-Pierre, *Christians in China*, 7
Chau, 62
Che Jingguang, 9
Chefoo School, 114
Chesneaux, Jean, "Taiping", 85
Cheung, David (Chen Yiqiang),
    Christianity in Modern China, 9
China East Outgoing, 94
China Inland Mission (CIM), 4, 12,
    14, 16, 20, 23, 26, **28**, 57, 97, 102,
    106–16, 119–20, **121**, 151, 153,
    155, 157, 159–60, **161**, **163**, 165,
    166–67, **180**, 182, 194, 206–8
China Institute of Overseas Sinology,
    66
China Mission Year Book, **209**
Chinese Central Television (CCTV),
    66
Chinese Christian Union, 75

Chinese Evangelization Society (CES),
    102, 104–7, 109
Chinese Foreign Office, 189
Chinese Maritime Customs, 63
Chou Han, 92
Christian Church Review, The, 184
Christian Literature Society (CLS),
    174, 184–87, 189–90
Christmas, 74
Chuck, J. Lewis, 9
Chung-hsi wen-chian-lu (Peking magazine), 13, 141
Church Missionary Society, 105
Church of England, 37
Church of Scotland, 37
Chuwang (Chuwangzhen), 197
Clunie, John, 40
Collie, David, 69
Commissariat Department, 46
Confucius, 16, 128–31, 133, 139, 143
    The Book of Odes, 129
Cooper, William, 115
Corinthian, 125
Corpus Christi College, 66, 68
Corwin, Gary R., 7
Council for World Mission, 84, 94
Cousins, **92**
Covell, Ralph, **122–23**, **126–29**, **134–35**, 136, **137–44**, 146, **147–48**
    W. A. P. Martin: Pioneer of Progress in China, **122–23**, **126–29**,
        134–44, **146–48**
Cox, J., 63
Crawford, Tarleton Perry, 10
Creegan, Charles Cole, 83
    and Goodnow, *Great Missionaries of the Church*, 83
Crickney, **180**
Cultural Revolution, 1–2

Dai Desheng, 121
Dai Wenguang, 9
Daily, Christopher A., *Robert Morrison and the Protestant Plan for China*, 11, 30, 51–52
Daoguang, Emperor, 150
Darwin, Charles, *Origin of Species*, 96
Davies, David, 84

Index of Names

Davies, Thomas, 84
Davos, Switzerland, 115
Delegates Version, 98
Deng Xiaoping, 2
Deveron Arts, 65
Dikotter, "Patient Zero", 98
Ding Limei, 206
Divinity College, 87
Dixon, 44
Doctrine of the Mean (The State of Equilibrium and Harmony), 68
Douglas, R. K., "Morrison, Robert", 42
Doyle, G. Wright, 15, 28, 101–172
  "Review of *China's Millions*", 28
  Hudson Taylor's Attitude towards Chinese Culture, 121
  "Problems in Translating the Bible into Chinese", 15, 129
Drake, S. B., 155
Dunch, Ryan, "Science, Religion, and the Classics", 24
Duus, Peter, "Science and Salvation in China", 126, 131, 139, 146
Dyer, Maria Tarn, 10
Dyer, Samuel, 9, 61, 107

East India Company (EIC), 3, 14–15, 31–33, 35–36, 40, 45–47
East Northfield Conference, 194
East River, 79
Easter, 74
Easton College, 136
Ebenezer Independent Church, 84
Ecumenical Missionary Conference, 115
Edinburgh, 66, 67, 207
Editorial Correspondence, 99
Edkins, Joseph, 85, 105, 141
EIC's Select Committee, 36
Elisha, 100
Empress Dowager, 6, 134, 140, 143, 185, 187
England, Gwen and Edward, 26
Essence of the Lotus Scripture, The, 22

Faber, Ernst, 184
Fairbank, John King, 1, 2–3, 21, 24, 25, 32
  The Great Chinese Revolution, 3
  ed., *The Missionary Enterprise in China and America*, 2, 21, 24–25
Famine Relief Committee, 179
Fan (Elder), 157, 164–67
Fellowship of the Royal Society, 31
Feng Yuxiang ("Christian General" Feng), 208–9
Finney, Charles, 7, 200
  Lectures on Revival, 200
First Red Button Grade of the Mandarin, 174
Fitch, F. G., 99
  "On a New Version of the Scriptures in Wen-li", 99
Five Classics, The, 68
Flynt, Wayne, 10
  and Berkley, *Taking Christianity to China*, 10
Foochow (Fuzhou), 176
Forbidden City, 3, 6
Formosa (Taiwan), 3, 24–25, 148, 192, 194
Foshan (Buddha Mountain), 76, 79–80, 82
Foster, Arnold, 87, 94, 99
  "New Testament", 99
Four Books, The, 68–69
Fraser, Sir William, 36
Free Trade port of Canton, 31
French, Francesca, 159
Frost, Henry, 28, 114, 157

Galatians (Bible), 196
Gardner, Christopher, 92
"Gatekeeper" Sung, 152
Gay, Margaret, 210
General Assembly of the Presbyterian Church in Canada, 196, 207
General Missionary Conference, 145, 183
George (recipient of Griffith John's letters), 96–97
George IV, 31
George, Timothy, "Evangelical Revival and the Missionary Awakening", 97
Gibbard, Noel, 83–100

Index of Names   237

Griffith John, 84–88, 90–95, 99
Gilbert, "The Atonement", 84
Gillison, Thomas, "Report of the Hospital at Hankow", 91
Girardot, Norman J., *The Victorian Translation of China,* 11, 28, 69, 80
Goforth, Constance, 199
Goforth, Donald, 197
Goforth, Florence Evangeline, 197–98
Goforth, Fred, 210
Goforth, Gertrude, 195–96
Goforth, Gracie, 198
Goforth, Jonathan, 7–8, 14, 18–20, 22–23, 26–27, 191–212
   By My Spirit, 200, 203, 205–6, 210
   Miracle Lives of China, 210
Goforth, Paul, 197–98
Goforth, Rosalind (Bell-Smith), 10, 14, 26, 29, 191, 193, 194, 195, 197, 199–200, 202, 204, 206, 208–11
   Climbing: Memories of a Missionary's Wife, 10, 211
   Goforth of China, 26, 29, 197, 202, 204, 206, 208, 211
   Jonathan Goforth, 194–95, 210
Golden Pill (*Jindan*) sect, 150
Goodnow, Josephine A. B., 83
Gordon, C. W., 194
Gospel (books of the Bible), 22, 137, 152
Gosport Academy, 11, 30, 51
Gough, Frederick F., 108
Grand Canal, 85
Grant, Charles, 45
Great Century of Christian expansion, 2
Great Commission, 18, 56, 108, 118, 207
Great Depression, 210
Great Learning, 68
Green, Newington, 115
Griffith John Memorial Building, 98
Griffiths, David, 84
Guang Xu emperor, 185
Guangdong, 60, 72, 79

Guangzhou, 3–4, 51, 55, 58, 134, 176, 184
Guanyin, 51
Gui-Zi-Da-Ren ("Your Excellency the Devil"), 180
Gutzlaff, Charles (Karl Friedrich August Gützlaff), 9, 59, 75, 79, 104, 125

Hainan Island, 143
Hakka, 51
Hamberg, Theodore, *The Chinese Rebel Chief,* 59
Hampshire, 30
Hamrin, Carol Lee, 27
   and Bieler, eds., *Salt and Light,* 27
Han, 51
Hancock, Christopher D., 30–48
   "*A Parting Memorial*: Morrison and Missionary Motivation", 39
   Robert Morrison and the Birth of Chinese Protestantism, 31, 35, 40, 43
Hangzhou (Hangchow), 90, 94, 109
Hankou, 13, 86–87, 90, 92, 94, 100, 184
Hankow Tract Society (Central China Tract Society), 97, 100
Harrison, Brian, *Waiting for China,* 68
Hart, Sir Robert, 137
Haverfordwest, 175
Hayes, John, 210
Hayes, Watson, 207
Hayes, 44
He Jinshan, 9, 72
Heart Sutra, 54
Hebrew(s), 15, 67, 69, 117, 129
Hebrews (Bible), 10, 71, 212
Henan, 14, 172, 195–201, 208
Highbury College, 67, 69
Hill, David, 151–54, 180
Ho Tsun-sheen (He Jinshan) (Ho Fuk-tong), 72–76, 78–80, 82
Hobson family, 35
Hobson, Benjamin, 61–63
Hobsons (Mary's parents), 36
Honanese (Henanese), 201

Index of Names

Hong Kong, 55, 66, 68, 70–82, 105, 122, 125, 176
Hong Rengan, 75, 81
Hong Xiuquan (Hung Hsiu-Ch'uan), 59, 60, 104, 133
Hong-t'ung Conference, "Testimony of Mr. Hsi", 153
Hop Yat Church, 72
Horace, 40
Horne, 180
Hoste, Dixon E., 29, 115, 117, **149**, 160, 165–66, 168, 172, 207
Hoxton Academy, 30, 40, 42, 51
Hsieh, *Chinese Christian Hymnody*, 72–73
Hsieh, Fang-Lan, 72, 73
Hubei (Hupeh), 90, 93
Hudson, Anne Rosemary Hickling, "Response of Protestant Missionaries", 92–93, **96**
Hull, 103–4
Hunan, 90–93, 100
Hunt, Everett N., Jr., "John Livingston Nevius", 10
Hunter, James Davison, *Evangelicalism: The Coming Generation*, 120
Huntly, Scotland, 65, 67, 69
Hutchison, William R., "Modernism and Missions", 25
Hyatt, Irwin T., Jr., *Our Ordered Lives Confess*, 10

Imperial Maritime Customs Service, 137
Imperial Palace, 13
Imperial University, 139, 188
Indiana University, 123
Industrial Revolution, 2
Inkster, John G., 211
International Reform Bureau, 144
International Settlement, 101
Irving, Edward, 177
Isaiah (Bible), 84, 192, 195

Jacob, Elijah, 84
James, Mr. and Mrs., 180
Japan, Japanese, 5–6, 22, 92, 139, 186, 189, 210

Jesuits, 16, 178
Jews, 19, 123, 137
Jezebel of Samaria, 140
John (Bible), 22, 108, 111, 128, 137
John of Hankow (Griffith John), 13
John the Baptist, 177
John, Griffith, 7–8, 13, 18–20, 22, 26–27, 83–100, 116, 147–48
   "Against Opium", 98
   "Child's Catechism", 98
   China: Her Claims and Call, 88, 92
   Conference Shanghai, 86, 88
   "Discussion", 95
   "How to Deal with Persecution", 93
   "In Memorium", 85
   "Journal," Griffith John Papers, 84–86
   "Leading Rules for Translation", 99
   "Leading the Family in the Right Way", 98
   Letters, Council for World Mission (CWM), 87, 89, 92–94, **96**
   Letters, National Library of Wales (NLW), 96–97
   "The Moral Teaching of Christianity", 98
   "Opium in China", 98
   "Present Aspect of Missionary Work", 86
   "Religious Toleration", 98
   "Response to Directors", **94**
   "The Truth Stated in Eight Chapters", 98
   A Voice From China, 90–92, 95–97
John, Jeannette, 91
John, Margaret (Griffiths), 84, 91
"Jonathan Goforth on the Laymen's Report," *The Sunday School Times*, 207
Jones, Alfred, 179
Jones, Ieuan Gwynedd, "The Making of an Industrial Community", 83
Jones, John, 106
Jones, Mary, 106
Jones, Robert Tudur, *Congregationalism in England*, 97
Julian, John D., "Chinese," *A Dictionary of Hymnology*, 87

Index of Names 239

Kang Hsi (Kuang-hsi), 140, 143
Kang Youwei, 6, **141**, 186
Kew A-Gong, 57, 61
Kidd, Samuel, 67, **69**
Kikungshan, 208
King's College, Aberdeen, 67, 69
Knox College, 192–95
Knox Presbyterian Church, 211
Korea(n), 10, 14, **111**, 201
Kowloon, 72, **134**
Koxinga (Zheng Chenggong), 3
Kwangning, 202
Kwok, Pui-Lan, *Chinese Women and Christianity*, 55

Lai (surname of Liang Fa's wife), 55
Lai, John T. P., "Institutional Patronage", **98**
Lai, Whalen W., "The First Chinese Christian Gospel", **54**, 58
Lam (Lin), 56
Lammermuir, 109
Lantao, 122
Laozi, 96
   Dao De Jing, 96, 132
Latourette, Kenneth Scott, 2, 7, 31, 174, 209
   A History of Christian Missions in China, 7, 31, **174**, **209**
Laughton, R. F., **176**
Laymen's Report, 207
Leang-kung-fah, 53
Lechler, Rudolph, 73
Lee, Joseph, 60
Legge, George, 69–70
Legge, James, 11, 15–16, 27, 65–82, 117, 120, 129, 133
   An Argument for Shang-Te, 78
   trans. and comp., *The Chinese Classics*, 65, **66**, 68, 70–71, 79, 81
   "Christianity and Confucianism Compared", **79–80**
   "The Colony of Hong Kong", 68, 80
   Confucianism in Relation to Christianity, 79
   Journal of a Missionary Tour Along the East River of Canton Province, 73, 76

The Land of Sinim, 70, 79
A Lexilogus of the English, Malay, and Chinese Languages, 68
The Notions of the Chinese concerning God and Spirits, 78
The Ordinance of the Sabbath, 74
Record of the Rites (Liji), 68
The Religions of China, 78, 80
The Sacred Books of China, 67–68, 80
Sacred Odes to Nourish the Heart-Mind (Yang xin Shen Shi), 72
Shenghui zhunshen (Standards for the Sacred Community), 66, 72
Wang Jinshan yaojue (Important Advice for Those Going to the Gold Mountains), 66
Yabolaihan jilüe (The Faith Creed of Jesus' Disciples), 66
Yesu mentu xinjing (The Faith Creed of Jesus' Disciples), 66
Yueshe jilüe (A Brief History of [the Life of] Joseph), 66
   and John Legge, eds., *[George Legge's] Lectures on Theology, Science and Revelation*, 69–70
Legge, Mary Isabella (Morison), 70
Legge, William, 55
Li Hongzhang, 180, 183, 185
   and Marquis Tseng (Zheng), *The Importation of Western Learning*, 185
Li San, 57
Li T'i-mo-t'ai (Timothy Richard), 174, 183, 187
Li Yuan-hung, 144
Liang Fa (Liang A-fa), 8–9, 11–12, 49–64, 73
   Good News to Admonish the Ages, 50, 52, 54–55, 57, 59
   and Ira Tracy, "Address of the Singapore Agricultural and Horticultural Society to the Chinese Agriculturists" (Xinjiapo zaizhonghui gaosu zhongguo zuochan zhi ren), 61

Liang Fa (Liang A-fa) (*continued*)
and Ira Tracy, "Incentives to Abandon Opium" (Yapian su gai wen), 61
Liang Jinde (Liang Chin-The, A-teh, or Ade), 55–56, 63
Liang Qichao, 186
Liaoning, 202
Linching (Linqing), 196
Liu, Lydia He, *The Clash of Empires*, **59**
Livonia, Indiana, 123
Lockhart, William, 85, 104, 108
Lodwick, Kathleen, 21, 25, 98, 157
  Crusaders Against Opium, **98**
  "Good Works", 21, 25
  "Missionaries and Opium", 157
Lohtsun (Gulao Cun), 50
London Missionary Society (LMS), 11, 31–33, 35, 37–38, 42, 45, 49–55, 59–61, 63, 66–68, 70, 72, 75, 81, 83–87, 90, 93, 100, 104–5
London Missionary Society, "Register of Missionaries", 31
London University, 57
London, 11, 30–31, 40, 49–51, 57, 60, 66–67, 69, 71, 81, 83–87, 90, 93, 98, 100, 104–5, 111, 115, 180, 190
Lord's Supper, 56
Lottie Moon, 10
Lovell, Julia, *The Opium War*, **93**
Lowrie, J. W., 207
Luke (Bible), 108
Luo Zhongfan, 74
Luo, Weihong, *Christianity in China*, 14, 17
Luther, Martin, 47, 162
Lutz, Jessie, 7, 9
  "China and Protestantism", 7
  Opening China, **9**

Macao, 3, 11, 30, 37, 40, 46–48, 52, 58
Macau, 58
MacGillivray, Donald, *Encyclopedia: List of Chinese Hymn Books*, 87
Mackay, George Leslie, 192
MacKay, James, 211
MacKay, Robert, **194**
Mackenzie, 184, 186
  History of the Nineteenth Century, 184
Madagascar, 84
Malacca, 40, 51–52, 55, 59, 61, 67, **68**, 69, 73, 77
Malay Peninsula, 107
Malay, 73, 107
Manchu, Manchu dynasty, 3, 6, 85, 134, 143,
Mandarin (language), 68, 99, 104, 107, 117, 125–26, 137, 141
Mansion House Relief Fund, 180
Manual of Devotion, 37
Mao, 1–2
Mark (Bible), 108
Marquis Tseng (Zheng), 185
Mars Hill, 19
Martin, Claude, 136
Martin, Newell A., 136
Martin, Pascal, 136
Martin, Samuel, 123–25, 147
Martin, William Alexander Parsons, 5–6, 10, 13–16, 18–20, 22, 25, 27, **97–98**, 120–48
  The Awakening of China, 143
  Chinese Legends and Other Poems, later *Chinese Legends and Lyrics*, 144
  Christian Evidences / T'ien-tao su-yuan (Evidences of Christianity), 124, 126
  Cycle of Cathay, or *China, North and South*, 13, **98**, 122–23, 125–26, 128–29, 131, 134–36, 138, 140–41, 142, 145, 147
  A History of the Revolution, 144
  Letter to Board, 137
  The Lore of Cathay, or *The Intellect of China*, 13, **122**, 130–31, 142
  "The Native Tract Literature of China", 97
  Siege in Peking, 143
  "The Uses of the Physical Sciences as an Equipment of the Missionary", 124
Martin, William, 123

Martin, Winfred Robert, 136
Mateer, C. A., "Easy Wen Li New Testament", 99
Mateer, Calvin W., 10, 98–99
Mathews, Robert Henry, 57
　Wang, and Chao, *Mathews' Chinese-English Dictionary*, 57
Matthew (Bible), 19, 27, 57, 62, 97, 108, 128, 177
McCartee, Divie B., 124, 126, **135**, 136
McCarthy, John, 109
McGavran, Donald Anderson, *Understanding Church Growth*, 26
McGee, Gary B., 7
McGillivray, Donald, 195–98
McNeur, George Hunter, 49–52, 55, 56–57, 59, **61**, 62–63
　China's First Preacher, 49–51, 55, 57, **61**–63
Meadows, Thomas Taylor, *The Chinese and their Rebellions*, 60
Medhurst, Walter H., Sr., 9, 85, 103–5
　China: Its State and Prospects, 103
Melchizedek, 133
Mencius, 78, 152
Mencius, The, 68
Michael, Franz, and Chung-Li Chang, *The Taiping Rebellion*, 60
Middle Eden, 170–71
Mildmay Conferences, 8
Milne, William, 9–11, 33, 35, 37, **38**, 51–56, 63, 67, **68**
　A Retrospect of the First Ten Years, 9, 33, **38**, **51**, 53
　Treatise of the Life of Christ, 52
Ming, 3, 44
Minister of Education, Berlin, 182
Missionary Convention of 1890, 121
Moffett, Samuel Hugh, *A History of Christianity in Asia*, 7
Mohammed, 96
Moody, Dwight L., 7–8, 87, 114, 194
Moreau, A. Scott, 7
　Corwin, and McGee, *Introducing World Missions*, 7
Morison, John, 70

Morris, William, ed., "Harmonium," *American Heritage Dictionary*, 116
Morrison, Eliza (Armstrong), 10, 32–33, 35, 42–44
　comp., and Robert Morrison, *Memoirs of the Life and Labours of Robert Morrison*, 30, 32, 33, **34**, 35, 37–**40**, 42, 43, **44**, **46**, 56
Morrison, John Robert, 31, 43–44, 56, 58
Morrison, Mary (Morton), 10, 31, 35–36
Morrison, Mary Rebecca, 43–44
Morrison, Robert, 2, 4, 10–11, 14–15, 27, 30–48, 51–52, 54–59, 61, 63, 67, **68**, 69, 176, **194**
　China: A Dialogue for the Use of Schools, 31
　Chinese-English Dictionary, 31, 33
　Chinese Miscellany, 31, 38
　Dialogues and Detached Sentences in the Chinese Language, 31
　A Grammar of the Chinese Language, 31
　A Narrative of the Affair of the English Frigate Topaze 1821-22, 34
　Narrative of the Fire at Canton, 38
　A Parting Memorial, **35**, 39, 41, **45**, **47**
　Proposal for Bettering the Morals and Conditions of Sailors in China, 39
　Remarks on Homicides Committed by Europeans on the Persons of Natives at Canton, 34
　Review of the First Fifteen Years of the Mission, 39
　A View of China for Philological Purposes, 31
　and Milne, *Hymns in Chinese*, 37
　and Milne, *Morning and Evening Prayer*, 37
　and Milne, *Psalter*, 37
Mosaic Decalogue, 73
Moses, Mosaic, 73, 130, 164, 177

Moseley, William W., 45
  A Memoir on the Importance and Practicability of Translating and Printing the Holy Scriptures in the Chinese Language, 45
  The Origin of the First Protestant Mission to China, 45
Moule, Archdeacon, 99
Moule, Arthur Evans, 96, 98
  Half a Century in China, 96
Moule, G. E., "Mr. John's New Testament", 99
Moule, Walter S., 207
Moynan, Mary (Goforth), 212
Muirhead, William, 85, 96, 99, 184
  China and the Gospel, 96
Mukden, 202
Nanhai District, 72
Nanjing Decade, 24
Nanjing, 24, 106
Napier, Lord, 34, 58, 64
National Bible Society of Scotland, 99
National Christian Council, 23
Neill, Stephen, *A History of Christian Missions*, 94
Nevius, John Livingston, 10, 88, 111, 206
  Demon Possession, 206
  "Methods of Mission Work", 88
New Albany Theological Seminary, 124
New Testament, 12, 31, 33, 52, 69, 71, 78, 91, 98–99, 108, 117, 128, 141, 152, 177, 185, 191, 209
New York Times, 138–39
New York, 67, 115, 143, 187
New Zealand, 177
Newcastle-upon-Tyne, 30
Newchwang (Yinkou), 204
Newman, R. K., *Opium Smoking in Late Imperial China*, 98

Ng, Peter Tze Ming, 12, 21, 25, 26, 120
  Chinese Christianity, 21, 25–26, 120
  "Timothy Richard: Christian Attitudes Towards Other Religions and Cultures", 12

Ni Tuosheng, 206
Niagara on the Lake, 194
Nicodemus, 19
Ningbo (Ningpo), 3, 10, 106–8, 117, 124–26, 128, 136, 147, 176
North American Council, 114
North Honan (Henan), 14, 195–97, 199, 201, 208
North Honan Mission, 195, 208
North Temperate Zone, 175
Northern China, 179

Old Testament, 33
Olyphant, D. W. C., 36
OMF International, 107, 112, 115, 165
Opening and Reform campaign, 2
"Opium," *Shanghai Conference*, 98
Opium War, First, 4, 61, 123
Opium War, Second, 134
Opium Wars, 4, 42, 58–59, 61, 123, 125, 134, 176
Order of the Double Dragon, 174
Overcomer of Demons, Overcomer of Evil (Xi Shengmo), 12, 149, 154
Oxford University, 12, 66, 68, 79

Paley, William, 124, 126, 127
  Natural Theology, 124, 127
Pangchwang (Pangzhuang), 195
Paris, 182
Parker, Peter, 9, 61, 135
Parker, William, 105–6
Parsons, Levi, 123
Paul, 19, 32, 96, 100, 133
Payne, "Original Sin", 84
Pearl River, 31, 46
Peitaho, 201
Peking (also see Beijing), 13, 135, 138–141, 143, 176, 185
Peking Oriental Society, 139
Peking Presbytery, 140
Peng, 91
Pentecost, 95, 206
Peter, 19
Pfister, Lauren F., 21, 65–82, 121
  "Attitudes Towards Chinese Cultures", 68

"Bible Translations and the Protestant 'Term Question'", 78
"Discovering Monotheistic Metaphysics", 74
"In the Eye of a Tornado", 80
"The Mengzian Matrix for Accommodationist Missionary Apologetics", 78
"Nineteenth Century Ruist Metaphysical Terminology", 78
"The Proto-Martyr of Chinese Protestants", 76
"Resetting 'Our' Cosmic and Historical Time-pieces", 74
"The Response of Wang Tao and James Legge to Modern Ruist Melancholy", 75
"Rethinking Missions in China", 21, 121
Striving for the "Whole Duty of Man", 67–79, 81
"A Transmitter but not a Creator", 72
Philippians (Bible), 196
Philips Academy, 136
Pickwick Publications, 27
Pingyang, 151, 153, 161
Plato, 133
Poklo, 76, 80, 82
Pollock, John, *The Cambridge Seven*, 109
Polycarp, 47
Presbyterian Foreign Mission Board, Board of Foreign Missions, 124, 129, 137–38, 140
Presbytery (North Henan), 196, 198, 204, 208
Princely Man, 152
Proverbs (Bible), 99, 108
Psalms (Bible), 99, 128, 192
Pure Land, Western Paradise, 132

Qianlong (Emperor), 50
Qing, Qing dynasty, Qing empire, 3–4, 6, 14–16, 50, 58–59, 66–68, 70–71, 74–79, 81–82, **93**, 128, **144**, 173–74, 184, 186–87, 209
Qingzhou, 177–79

Quarterman, John, **135**
"Questionnaire," Council for World Mission, 84

Rabe, Valentin, 23
Reform Society, (100 Days' or Hundred Days') Reform Movement, Reformers, 13, 139, 186, 189
Reform Society, *New Collection of Tracts for the Times*, 186
Reid, Gilbert, 10, 18, **141**, 145–46
Religious Tract Society in London, 98
Republic of China, 24, **25**, 144
Rethinking Missions, 207
Ricci, Matteo, 16, 38, **127**, 136, 145–46, 178
A True Disputation about God, 127
Richard, Mary (Martin), 181, 185
Richard, Timothy, 5–6, 10, 12–17, 19, 21–22, 24–27, 88, **97**, 120, **141**, 145–47, 173–90
Conversion by the Millions in China, 88, **175**, 177, **184**, 189
Essays for the Times, 185
Forty-five Years in China: Reminiscences, 6, 173, **176**, 179–80, **184**, 186, **188**
Historical Evidences of the Benefits of Christianity, 183, 185
Modern Education, 183
The New Testament of Higher Buddhism, 13, **22**
"The Relation of Christian Missions to the Chinese Government", 183
Richenet, 38
Ride, 44
Robert, Dana, 7
Christian Mission, 7
Roberts, Evan, 96
Roberts, Issachar J., 9, 60, 85
Roberts, J. A. G., *China Through Western Eyes*, 85
Robson, William, *Griffith John: Founder of the Hankow Mission, Central China*, 87–88, **99**
Romans (Bible), 28, 106, **196**
Rong Hong (Yung Wing), 9
Royal College of Surgeons, 117

Royal Commission on Opium, 98
Royal Geographic Society, 117

Samchow (Sanzhou), 50, 58
Sandwich Islands, 123
Sankey, Ira, 87
Satan, 154–55, 158, 162, 166, 205
Schaal, 38
Schereschewsky, S. I. J., 137
School of Oriental and African Studies, London University, 57, 71
Scotch United Presbyterian Mission, 181
Second Anglo-Chinese War, 134
Seitz, Jonathan A., 49–64
Shaanxi, 172
Shandong, 114, 173–74, 176–77, 179, 182–83, 188, 190, 195, 210
Shanghai, 20, 65, 80, 85–86, 99, 101–2, 104–6, 109, 115, 120, 136, 143–45, 173, 176, 179–80, 183–85, 187, 189, 195
Shanghainese, 117
Shanxi Massacre, 188
Shanxi, 150–51, 168, 173–74, 179–83, 188, 204
Shen, 87, 98
  "On Atonement", 98
  "Regeneration", 98
Shen, Dingping and Weifang Zhu, "Western Missionary Influence on the People's Republic of China", 24
Shenling, 78
Shi Pao (Times), 184
Shingling, 78
Shrubsole, William, 35
Si (Elder), 170
Sichuan (Szechwan), 90, 92
Singapore, Singaporean, 40, 59, 61, **62**
Sino-Foreign Protestant Establishment (SFPE), 23
Sloan, Walter, 207
Smith, Arthur H., 195
Smith, J. F., 195
Smith, Mrs. J. F., 195
Smith, Stanley, 159–60, 163–65

Sng, Bobby Ewe Kong, *I Must Sow the Seed*, **50**
Society for the Diffusion of Christian and General Knowledge, 184
Society for the Diffusion of Useful Knowledge, 140
Solomon, 129
Song Shangjie (John Song), 206
Soothill, William Edward, 87, **178**, 180, 189
  "Chinese Music and Its Relation to Our Native Services", 87
  Timothy Richard of China, 178, 180, 189
South China, 60
South Manchurian Railway, 209
Sparham, C. G, "Griffith John and His Work", 87
Spence, Jonathan D., *The Search for Modern China*, 3
Spurgeon, 100
Staunton, Sir George, 33
Staunton, Sir William, 36
Stephen, 47
Stevenson, John W., 115, 160–163
Stewart, Dugald, 69
Straits Settlements, Malay Peninsula, 107
Stronachs, 9
Summer Palace, 6, **134**, 137
Sunquist, Scott W., *Understanding Christian Mission*, 7, **8**
Swansea, Wales, 83–84, 100
Swatow (dialect), 117
Swatow (Shantou), 105
Szepingkai, 209

T'ai P'ings, 209
T'ung Wen Kuan ("School of combined Learning"), 138–39
Taiping King, 76
Taiping Rebellion, 59, 64, 81, 104, 133
Taiping(s), 3–4, 57, 59–60, 64, 75–77, 81, 85–86, 90, 104, 133–34
Taiyuan, 113, 180–81, 188
Taonanfu, 212
Tartar, 140
Taylor, Amelia, 102

Taylor, Dr. and Mrs. Howard, *Hudson Taylor's Spiritual Secret*, 104
Taylor, Geraldine, *Pastor Hsi: A Struggle for Chinese Christianity*, 152, 156–57, 159–61, 164, 166, 172
Taylor, Geraldine, 29, 115, **149**
Taylor, Howard, 112, 115
Taylor, James H., III, **112**
Taylor, James Hudson, 3–4, 7–8, **9**, 10, 12, **14**, 15–16, 18–20, 22, 26–29, **41**, 67, 87, 94, **97**, 101–21, 128, 144–45, **146**, 147–48, **155**, 157, 160, 161, 163, **180**, 193–95, 210
"Appeals for Redress", **94**
ed., *China's Millions*, 111, 116
China's Spiritual Need[s] and Claims, 108, 193
Looking Back, **101**, 107
Retrospect, **102**
"The Source of Power for Foreign Missionary Work", 115
Taylor, Jennie Faulding, 10, 111, 113–15, 119, **180**
Taylor, Maria Dyer, 10, 107–10, 113–14, 116, 119
Taylor, Noel, 110
Taylor, Samuel, 110
Temple of Heaven, 133
Temple to Master Kong, 76
Terranova, 33
Thomas, Margaret, 44
Thomas, Millicent, 44
Thompson, R. Wardlaw, *Griffith John: The Story of Fifty Years in China*, 84–85, 88–90, 92, 98
Thomson, J. C., 63
Thorndale, Canada, 192
Three-Self Patriotic Movement, 25
Tian, T'ian (heaven), 130
Tianjin, T'ien-tsin, Tientsin, 13, **134**, 135, 140, **176**, 180, 183–84, 199
Tiechiu, 117
Tiedemann, R. G., and Nicolas Standaert, eds., *Handbook of Christianity in China*, 3, 7, 21, 83, 207
Toronto City Mission, 193

Toronto Mission Union, 193
Toronto, 192–94, 196
Townsend, 44
Tracy, Ira, 61
Treaty of Nanking (Nanjing), 105–6
Treaty of Tientsin (T'ien-tsin), 13, 135, **176**
Trevor Chapel, 70
Trinity, 53, 128
Tsae A-ko, 52
Tsae Low-heen, 52
Tsou, Mingteh, "Christian Missionary as Confucian Intellectual", 10
Tsungli Yamin, 139
Tung, 89
Turner, Joshua, 151, 153, **180**

Unequal Treaties, 4, 14, 58, 76, 79
Union Church, 68, 72, 74–76, 78, 80
Union Version, 99
University College in London, 69
University of Edinburgh, 67
University of Georgia, 190
University of London, 67
University of Wales, 190
US Congress, 61

Vancouver, 211
Van Sant, Jan, 124
Vegetarian Society, Vegetarians, 92–93
Venerable Preacher, Venerable Chief Pastor (Hudson Taylor), 115, 163
Verbiest, 38
Vivian and Sons, 83
Vulgate, 41

Walker, 44
Walls, Andrew F., *The Cross-Cultural Process in Christian History*, 21–22
Wan Kuo Kung Pao (Review of the Times), 184
Wang Fulin, 197
Wang Laedjun, 108–9
Wang Lien-king, 90
Wang Man Kong, "Chinese Culture", 77

Index of Names

Wang Mingdao, 206
Wang Tao, 9, **68**, 75
Wang, Mary, **26**
   and Gwen and Edward England, *The Chinese Church That Will Not Die*, **26**
Wang, Minyuan, 57
Ward (slum district of Toronto), 193
Wartburg, 162
Wason, Charles William, "Descriptive and Classified Missionary Centenary Catalogue", 98
Way, Richard, **135**
Webster, James, 203
Wei river, 196
Wei village, 91
Welch, Ian, "The 'Vegetarians'", 92
Wenli, 68, 98–99
Wenzong Wang, 173–190
Wesley, John, 45
Western Zhang village, 150–51
Wheaton, Henry, *Elements of International Law*, 137
White Lotus rebellions, 60
Whitehouse, 87
Whiting, Albert, **180**
Wigram, Christopher E. M., *The Bible and Mission in Faith Perspective*, **8**, **106**, **113**
Wilberforce, William, 39, 44–45
Willetts, Hannah Mary (Johnston), 70
Williams, Samuel Wells, 9, **135**
Williams, 44
Williamson, 184
Wilson, Daniel, 38
Wilson, J. Wallace, "Memories of a Colleague", **91**
Wilson, Robert, 86
Wilson, Thomas, 35
Windsor Castle, 212
Wolffe, John, *The Expansion of Evangelicalism*, 7
Wong Shing (Huang Sheng), 75
World Missionary Conference, 187, 207
World War I, First World War, 23, 27
Wright-Bruce, Frederick, 81
Wuch'ang University, 140

Wuchow, 63
Wuhan, 100
Wylie, Alexander, 44, 61, 85, 90, **98**, 104, 123
   "China", 90
   Memorials of Protestant Missionaries to the Chinese, **61**, **98**

Xi Liaozhi, 150
Xi Shengmo (Pastor Hsi, Xi Liaozhi), 9, 12, 16, 20, 27–29, 112, 149–72
   "How to Obtain Deliverance from Calamity", 154
   "The Ten Commandments of God", 154
   with Francesca French, trans., *Songs of Pastor Hsi*, 159
Xi, Mrs. (second wife of Xi Shengmo), 150–51, 154–55, 157, 159, 169–70
Xiucai, 150
Xueshanzhe ("Student of the Good"; Liang), 54

"Y Maes Cenadol" ("The Mission Field"), 88
Yading Li, 149–172
Yangtze, 2
Yangzhou, 16, 110
Yangzi, 208
Yantai (Chefoo), 114, 176, 181, 195
Yao, Kevin Xiyi, *The Fundamentalist Movement Among Protestant Missionaries in China*, **22–23**, **207**
Yihetuan (Society of the Righteous Fist), **93**
YMCA, 23
Yorkshire, 102, 192
Yuan Keting, 144
Yuan Shikai, 144
Yueyang (Yo-chow), 91

Zetzsche, Jost Oliver, *The Bible in China*, 78
Zhang Zhidong, 181, 185
Zhengjiang, Jiangsu, 116
Zhili (Hebei), **172**